Ivan Horrocks

Change and Reality: Exploring the Structure-culture-agency Dynamic

Ivan Horrocks

Change and Reality: Exploring the Structure-culture-agency Dynamic

A Critical Realist Analysis of Information Systems Development and Organisational Change in British Local Government

VDM Verlag Dr. Müller

Impressum/Imprint (nur für Deutschland/ only for Germany)
Bibliografische Information der Deutschen Nationalbibliothek: Die Deutsche Nationalbibliothek
verzeichnet diese Publikation in der Deutschen Nationalbibliografie; detaillierte bibliografische
Daten sind im Internet über http://dnb.d-nb.de abrufbar.
Alle in diesem Buch genannten Marken und Produktnamen unterliegen warenzeichen-, marken-
oder patentrechtlichem Schutz bzw. sind Warenzeichen oder eingetragene Warenzeichen der
jeweiligen Inhaber. Die Wiedergabe von Marken, Produktnamen, Gebrauchsnamen,
Handelsnamen, Warenbezeichnungen u.s.w. in diesem Werk berechtigt auch ohne besondere
Kennzeichnung nicht zu der Annahme, dass solche Namen im Sinne der Warenzeichen- und
Markenschutzgesetzgebung als frei zu betrachten wären und daher von jedermann benutzt
werden dürften.

Coverbild: www.purestockx.com

Verlag: VDM Verlag Dr. Müller Aktiengesellschaft & Co. KG
Dudweiler Landstr. 99, 66123 Saarbrücken, Deutschland
Telefon +49 681 9100-698, Telefax +49 681 9100-988, Email: info@vdm-verlag.de
Zugl.: Milton Keynes, The Open University, Diss., 2006

Herstellung in Deutschland:
Schaltungsdienst Lange o.H.G., Berlin
Books on Demand GmbH, Norderstedt
Reha GmbH, Saarbrücken
Amazon Distribution GmbH, Leipzig
ISBN: 978-3-639-09421-3

Imprint (only for USA, GB)
Bibliographic information published by the Deutsche Nationalbibliothek: The Deutsche
Nationalbibliothek lists this publication in the Deutsche Nationalbibliografie; detailed
bibliographic data are available in the Internet at http://dnb.d-nb.de.
Any brand names and product names mentioned in this book are subject to trademark, brand or
patent protection and are trademarks or registered trademarks of their respective holders. The
use of brand names, product names, common names, trade names, product descriptions etc.
even without a particular marking in this works is in no way to be construed to mean that such
names may be regarded as unrestricted in respect of trademark and brand protection legislation
and could thus be used by anyone.

Cover image: www.purestockx.com

Publisher:
VDM Verlag Dr. Müller Aktiengesellschaft & Co. KG
Dudweiler Landstr. 99, 66123 Saarbrücken, Germany
Phone +49 681 9100-698, Fax +49 681 9100-988, Email: info@vdm-publishing.com
Copyright © 2008 VDM Verlag Dr. Müller Aktiengesellschaft & Co. KG and licensors
All rights reserved. Saarbrücken 2008

Printed in the U.S.A.
Printed in the U.K. by (see last page)
ISBN: 978-3-639-09421-3

Table of Contents

Figures

INFORMATION SYSTEMS RESEARCH IN PUBLIC ADMINISTRATION

Introduction

The primary aim of this book is to analyse the complex relationships between agency (i.e. populations, organised groups, individual actors and collectivities), structure (i.e. systems, institutions, roles, positions), and culture (ideas, theories, beliefs and values) in the specific context of cycles of information systems (IS) development and organisational change in English local government. When undertaking such a task a number of theoretical and methodological approaches present themselves, of course. However, in order to avoid treating either agents or structures as largely epiphenomenal to the other the preference here is for the adoption of a non conflationary approach to the analysis of the agency/structure dynamic – specifically the morphogenetic approach devised by Margaret Archer (1988, 1995, 1998b, 1998c, 2002).

Archer's work is widely regarded as the 'methodological complement' (Archer 1995:167) to *critical realism*. It follows, therefore, that critical realism is the philosophical standpoint that underpins this book. Thus, and as with any meta-theory, it provides, in broad terms, recommendations on how to approach substantive subjects: for example, and crucially, that:

> ...the world is not only differentiated but 'stratified'; that some kinds of objects, for example biological phenomena, are 'emergent from' their constituents (chemical and physical processes, in this case)... In other words, from certain conjunctions or interactions of objects, new emergent properties develop which are irreducible to those of the objects on which they depend.
> (Sayer 2004:9)

Importantly, with its commitment to ontological realism (that there is a reality which is differentiated, structured, layered and can often be independent of mind), epistemological relativism (that all beliefs are socially produced and therefore potentially fallible) and judgemental rationality (that it is possible to provide justifiable grounds for preferring one theory over another) (Goatcher 2004), critical realism sits in opposition to '…relativist, idealist and strong social constructivist tendencies in social science.' (Sayer 2004:11), and furthermore, that '…*critical realism is not synonymous with discourses such as naïve realism, positivism, scientism or other associated empiricist paraphernalia: in fact, it is antithetical to these discourses.*' (Fleetwood 2004:31–32. Original emphasis).

A detailed discussion of critical realism and of the morphogenetic approach is reserved for the next chapter. However, it is appropriate to highlight here that a key feature of both that makes them of particular relevance to the subject matter of this book is their focus on providing explanations of what produces change through the identification and examination of the causal processes at work in specific contexts (Archer 1995, 1998b, Sayer 1998). The result is that much more emphasis is placed on the conceptualisation and description of the causal powers that are present and active in any situation than on the regularities between events. From a critical realist perspective, therefore, retroduction ('…the process of identifying which causal powers are active in a given situation…' Sayer 2004:11) and abstraction are as important as generalisation to social research and it is crucial to distinguish between these when analysing social change. Retroduction and abstraction, while not necessarily telling us much about frequency, regularity, or distribution, are essential to explain what produces specific states and changes (Figure 1.1). Generalisation offers the reverse option (Sayer 2004).

2

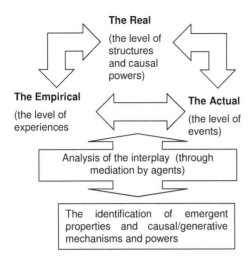

Figure 1.1 The process of retroduction

This is where Archer's morphogenetic approach comes fully into play. First, it provides a framework and methodology for *analysing the relationship between structure, culture and agency* and of the complexity of this relationship. Second, Archer's approach is targeted at *identifying and documenting the conditions for change or stasis* in structure, culture and agency, in delineating the relationships between these within any social system, and exploring how developments in one system act as opportunities or constraints in another. Put simply, the morphogenetic approach is concerned with exploring and explaining cycles of *emergence – interplay – outcome* (Figure 1.2) in any social setting. This book details and discusses the application of the morphogenetic approach to data from a specific 15 month long case study of IS development at one large English local authority. It therefore provides a critical realist perspective on such events and developments.

The present chapter introduces the intent and structure of the book. The aims and analytical approach to be adopted have already been dealt with, above. The next section of the chapter explores the nature of IS in UK government and the public sector (due to the staged nature of the morphogenetic approach a detailed discussion of IS development in English local government specifically, and how this conditioned and shaped the agents and structures of Council X, is held over until Chapter 4). This leads on to an examination of the 'conflationary' approaches to analysing and theorising technology/IS and organisational change that are usually applied in this field of research, before contrasting these with critical realism and the morphogenetic approach specifically. The book's claims to originality are then introduced and the chapter concludes with a brief outline of each of the following chapters.

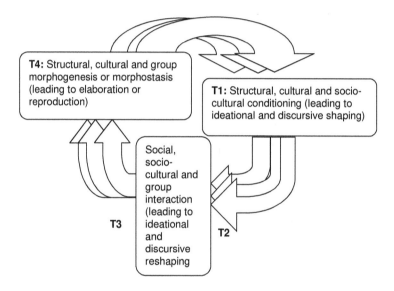

Figure 1.2 A multi dimensional cycle of change

Based on Archer 1995

Information systems, government and the public sector

Discussion of the information age 'revolution' has historically tended to focus on the implications for business and commerce and with some exceptions (e.g. Lyon 1988, Mansell 1993, Winston 1998) is extremely deterministic, upbeat and unquestioning of the possibilities and practicalities (e.g. Naisbitt 1984, Toffler 1990, Gasman 1994,

4

Barnatt 1995). Less interest was shown in the implications and developments within and by governments. Throughout the 1990s, however, governments worldwide, and OECD countries in particular, increasingly strove to place themselves at the forefront of this technological 'revolution' (OECD 1998a, 1998b).

In the United States, government was able to harness a relatively well established belief in the ability of new information and communication technologies (ICTs) to transform social and economic relations (e.g. Bell 1973, Mumford and Sackman 1975, Laudon 1977, Toffler 1980, Dutton, Blumler and Kraemer 1987). For example, the provision of computerised information terminals or kiosks for public use (i.e. electronic public information systems) such as are commonplace nowadays in airports, shopping centres and other public spaces, can be traced back to the early 1970s (Sackman and Boehm 1972, Sackman and Nie 1973). From the mid 1980s, however, almost all levels of government began exploiting the potential of new ICTs (Danziger 1982, King and Kraemer 1986), with state and local governments in particular taking the lead in developing examples of the electronic delivery of services (Dutton et al 1991, US Congress Office of Technology Assessment 1993, Bellamy, Horrocks and Webb 1995).

The US federal government made its commitment to promoting widespread access to the tools and technologies of the information age clear when in 1990 the US Congress Office of Technology Assessment published *Critical Connections for the Future*. This groundbreaking report stated that 'The opportunity for people to participate in economic, political and cultural life depends on their ability to access and use communication and information services. Unequal access to communication resources leads to unequal advantages, and ultimately to inequalities in social and economic opportunities' (1990:8).

The early 1990s also saw lobby and support groups, such as the National Public Telecomputing Network (NPTN), the Alliance for Public Technology (APT) and the

Center for Civic Networking (CCN) begin to heavily promote the idea of '…applying information infrastructure to the broad public good.' (Horrocks and Webb 1994:25). FreeNets and electronic town meetings were two of the most prominent results (Barber 1984, Elgin 1993). Ultimately the metaphor of the "information superhighway", based as it was on the overwhelmingly popular view amongst US citizens of the American Interstate Highway System, became the inspiration and goal of US ICT policy (Kubicek, Dutton and Williams 1997).

At a European level developments inspired by the ideas and rhetoric about the information age had broadened and deepened significantly by the early 1990s from a preoccupation with industrial policy and economic development that had been a hallmark of the 1987 report of the High-Level Group on Europe and the Global Information Society (more often referred to as the Bangemann Report). Subsequent EU (European Union) initiatives laid growing emphasis on the use of ICTs to strengthen democratic values and widen access to public services (Dutton 1996, Bellamy and Taylor 1998, Kinder 2002). For example, by the mid 1990s a range of 'digital city' initiatives had developed across the EU (Tsagarousianou, Tambini and Bryan 1998).

Based on the north American idea of freenets, early examples of digital cities, such as Manchester HOST and Amsterdam Digitale Stad noted above, provided local communities with the means to access local area networks (LANS) and use these as 'on-ramps' to the internet. A crucial aim of these developments was to provide users with access to information resources and opportunities to communicate via bulletin boards and discussion groups. As the popularity and sophistication of digital cities grew through the 1990s (due primarily to technological advances such as the advent of web technology) so the potential for their use was increasingly realised. Consequently, by the latter part of the decade they had begun to stimulate the deployment of new approaches to the provision of citizen (or consumer) orientated

6

(and supposedly more efficient) public services, with more and more of these accessible on line (Bellamy and Taylor 1998, Kinder 2002, www.direct.gov.uk).

The discussion so far clearly illustrates that by the mid 1990s new ICTs were beginning to have a profound impact on many aspects of government and public administration. Within the public administration discipline technological change in an institutional setting was, as noted above, often referred to as informatization and subsequently popularised by scholars associated with EGPA's Permanent Study Group on Informatization (e.g. Frissen and Snellen 1990, Frissen et al 1992, Donk and Tops 1995, Taylor et al 1997, Snellen and Donk 1998).

Informatization was (and still is) almost always a powerful feature of more broad ranging initiatives aimed at organisational change in the public domain (Taylor et al 1997, Bellamy and Taylor 1998), just as it was (and still is) in the commercial sector (Zuboff 1988, Knights and Murray 1994, Castells 1996, Walsham 2000). This is not surprising, of course, given that a core function of public administration is '...information acquisition, storage, handling, diffusion and communication.' (Donk and Snellen 1998:34) and that since the 1960s ICT/IS have become fundamental to the performance of that function. Furthermore, because public administration takes on both service-providing and democracy-enhancing functions, through the relationship between it and the polity, the complexity of public administration is greatly increased. This, and the key role and function of information as artefact, increasingly led to the view that relations within information age public administration could best be conceptualised as an 'information polity' (Taylor and Williams 1991, Bellamy and Taylor 1994) which '...is concerned as much with those networks comprised of information flows and organisational relationships as it is with computer networks in and around government.' (Taylor 1998:31).[1]

---

[1] This is another clear illustration of the strong parallels between informatization and many definitions and conceptualisations of IS.

The relationship between ICT/IS and the 'democracy enhancing' dimension of public administration has consistently attracted the interest of scholars, think tanks and politicians and policy makers since the 1960s. Usually categorised as electronic democracy, teledemocracy, digital democracy and, most recently, cyberdemocracy, early ground breaking studies of this subject all stem from the work of American scholars (e.g. Laudon 1977, Danziger et al 1982, Arterton 1987, Abrahamson, Arterton and Orren 1988, Winner 1992) who, from the late 1970s onwards, were able to draw on data from projects designed to test out the feasibility of electronic democracy (Horrocks and Webb 1994, Percy-Smith 1995). European scholars and other opinion formers came later to the subject (e.g. McLean 1989, Demos 1994a, Demos 1994b, Donk and Tops 1992, Percy-Smith 1995) but by the mid to late 1990s had established a clear European strand to this research (e.g. Donk, Snellen and Tops 1995, Ward and Gibson 1998, Hoff, Horrocks and Tops 2000, Axford and Huggins 2001, Kinder 2002).

A powerful force driving interest in electronic democracy has been the declining turnout of voters at both local and national elections and the so called 'democratic deficit' that appears to be a consistent trend in the US, UK and elsewhere (Budge 1996, Wring and Horrocks 2001). The response of government in the UK was to launch a raft of pilot projects aimed at testing the feasibility of using new ICTs, such as mobile phones and the internet, to allow remote voting (Electoral Commission 2002, Hansard Society 2003–04). This, it is believed, will harness some of the enthusiasm for such methods that has grown from their highly successful use on a range of 'reality' TV shows, such as, *Big Brother, Pop Idol,* and *I'm a Celebrity Get Me Out of Here.* While it remains unclear as to the extent that technology can 'fix' the democratic deficit (Wring and Horrocks 2001, The Electoral Commission 2002), it is obvious that UK policy makers, as elsewhere, are committed to increasing the pace of adoption, and scale, of electronic democracy (e.g. Implementing Electronic Voting in the UK 2003, Headstar 2002–03).

The "fragile" nature of these developments was illustrated at the 2005 general election in the UK, however, when problems arose from the use of an old technology for voting – the post/snail mail. Shortly after the election significant doubts were raised concerning the identity of those who had cast their vote using the massively expanded facility for postal voting. Evidence suggested that in some areas of the country postal votes had not been used by those to whom they had been issued. The Government was subsequently criticised by a range of bodies, including the Electoral Commission, for the over hasty way in which postal voting had been implemented and the lack of safeguards to ensure the system was not open to abuse. This had a knock on effect, bringing into question the security of other forms of remote voting, such as email and text messaging, and appears to have dampened enthusiasm for such developments. Given the continuing low turnout at elections in the UK (only 36% at the local government elections of May 2006) it is likely that this will only be a temporary setback, however.

The application of ICT and IS to the 'service providing' dimension of public administration has traditionally attracted less attention from scholars and researchers than its democracy enhancing cousin (Frissen 1998). The reluctance of government and public service organisations to allow access to case studies no doubt has a bearing on this and is an understandable position, perhaps, given the potential for ever more bad press in the wake of such large scale IT 'disasters' as have befallen the London Ambulance Service, the Passport Office, DSS, Inland Revenue and, more recently, the Criminal Records Agency and Family Tax Credits (to name but a few of the 'known' examples). More recently the advent of public private partnerships (PPPs) and the Public Finance Initiative (PFI) to fund IS developments in the public domain has led those involved to claim 'commercial sensitivity' as a justification for denying access to IS/ICT projects. Nevertheless, the ESRC (Economic and Social Research Council) has supported several major research projects that have a government/public administration focus, under the umbrella of a variety of major research programmes. The PICT (Programme on Information and Communication

Technologies (1986–95) and the Virtual Society programmes (1997–2000) are two past examples. Two of the 'thematic priorities' of the ESRC in the early 2000s continued to fund ICT and public administration/public service projects. However, by the mid 2000s ICT/IS projects remained a minor focus of attention when compared to the funding allocated to mainstream management, business practice and economic development and environmental management.

Since the late 1980s ICTs have increasingly been seen by UK central government policy makers as *the* major drivers of organisational change in public administration, enabling the 'reinvention of government' for the information age (Osbourne and Gaebler 1992, Bellamy and Taylor 1998, Margetts 1998, Pratchett 1999, see also www.direct.gov.uk, www.local.gov.uk and www.idea.gov.uk). From the early to mid 1990s the task of developing and championing this agenda fell to the CCTA (Central Computing and Telecommunications Agency). One of their first reports was an overview of changes and trends in ICT use by central government (CCTA 1990). This was followed in 1994 by a consultation paper on the development of a British information superhighway (CCTA 1994). Further reports in 1995 dealt with online information and public services and the potential of what was at the time a rapidly developing new area of technological development – the internet, and specifically, the development of the World Wide Web (www) and Web related technologies (CCTA 1995a, 1995b).

The prominence of the CCTA was largely eroded following the setting up of the Cabinet Central IT Unit (CITU) in 1995. However, if anything, this only served to speed up the development of a vision of electronic government, with the publication of the *government.direct* Green Paper of 1997 serving to provide the underpinning and inspiration for all subsequent developments. By 2002, and despite some significant set backs, such as some of the disasters noted above, and with the appointment of an e-envoy, it became clear that central government had become entirely committed to ICT driven 'joined up' e-government' (Ling 2002, Chadwick and May 2003), as well as subscribing to its importance for more general social and economic change (for examples see http://www.direct.gov.uk/Homepage).

Although the office of the e-envoy was abolished in 2005 by this time the CITU had morphed into the e-Government Unit (e-GU), the largest unit in the Cabinet Office (see http://www.cabinetoffice.gov.uk/e-government) and responsible for:

- formulating information technology (IT) strategy and policy
- developing common IT components for use across government
- promoting best practice across government
- delivering citizen-centred online services

Under the guidance of the e-GU the Government's increasing belief in, and commitment to, electronic service delivery was confirmed in November 2005 with the publication of *Transformational Government – Enabled by Technology*. The e-Government Unit web site notes that: 'The strategy sets out how effective use of technology to deliver services designed around the needs of citizens and businesses can make a real difference to people's lives.' However, the report makes no bones about its real purpose: '...to seize the opportunity provided by technology to transform the business of government.' (Cabinet Office 2005:2). Much of the strategy is therefore focused on rationalising the number of ICT systems operating across both central and local government, such as web sites and call centres, and using ICTs to achieve major efficiency saving in transactional services. The latter strongly parallels the findings of the Gershon Report, discussed below.

A particularly interesting feature of the implementation plan for *Transformational Government* is that it signals the arrival of the 'Government IT Profession': 'The aim of the Profession is to create a joined up, government-wide IT profession which provides IT professionals with a career of mutual benefit to the individual and the government.' (http://www.cio.gov.uk/itprofession/). The IT Profession is only one of several areas of activity to be 'professionalised', however, for reasons clearly set out on page 14 of the implementation plan (and also set out on the home page of the Chief Information Officer Council):

> Government's ambition for technology enabled change is challenging but achievable provided it is accompanied by a step-change in the professionalism with which it is delivered. This requires: coherent, joined up *leadership and governance; portfolio management* of the technology programmes; development of *IT professionalism and skills*; strengthening of the controls and support to ensure *reliable project delivery*; improvements in *supplier management*; and a systematic focus on *innovation.*
>
> (Cabinet Office 2005:14. Original emphasis)

The explicit recognition that the delivery of e-services, and the broader agenda of technology enabled change, will not happen successfully without changes in organisational culture and work practices clearly echoes the themes of two other Government reports of 2004. The first was the *Independent Review of Public Sector Relocation*, by Sir Michael Lyons, published in July 2004. ICTs underpinned Lyons' recommendations concerning the relocation of civil servants out of London because of his belief that: 'Use of modern communication technology in an inclusive, communicative, organisation culture allows policy makers to have extensive dealings with London while permanently based elsewhere.' (Lyons 2004:84). He does, however, go on to recognise that '…there is a need for Government to showcase and overcome cultural resistance to communication technologies…' (ibid:85). It is no surprise therefore, that 'change agents' – primarily human – also feature prominently in Lyon's report and recommendations, as they do alongside new technology, in the next report of significance.

The *Independent Review of Public Sector Efficiency* carried out by Sir Peter Gershon and published in July 2004 also makes prominent mention of ICTs. Thus, the Review argues that 'Transactional services direct to the public...have the potential for complete transformation through ICT.' (Gershon 2004:38). Crucially, the Review sees this transformation as being created by, and creating, a future public sector that employs fewer, more professional, staff (the genesis of the IT Profession, noted above) and that this transformation is heavily dependant on ICTs. Thus, two of the four areas of development identified as fundamental to deliver these changes will be: i/ the creation of virtual professional communities; and, ii/ the provision of the right ICT infrastructure. Gershon estimated that taken together ICT enabled changes in transactions and work practices would result in savings of £5 billion.

A full discussion of similar developments to those discussed above in English local government is held over to Chapter 4. Suffice to note here that while often not as grandiose as the developments pursued by central government, and therefore less prone to the claims for the transformative powers and potential of ICTs/IS, many local authorities have embraced a similar vision, and for almost as long, as has central government (see for example, FITLOG 1993, 1994, LGMB 1993, Worral 1995). Furthermore, given the increasingly subordinate role of local government to central government from the early 1980s (discussed in detail in Chapter 4) the latter has been able to significantly shape and control the ICT agenda of local government, as well as closely monitoring outcomes. For example, the *Transformational Government* strategy covers *all* levels of government and the public sector, while a brief review of www.local.gov.uk and www.idea.gov.uk, clearly illustrates both the extent of contemporary ICT developments and the relationship between central and local government in this policy domain.

As the concluding chapters of this book demonstrate, although local government based, the application of the morphogenetic approach to the case study of Council X produces a wealth of material that is directly relevant to the claims, beliefs, assumptions, propositions and recommendations concerning ICTs/IS and institutional and social change set out in the reports briefly outlined above. For example, they raise significant questions over Lyons' and Gershon's timetables for implementing the changes they outline; of their belief in the capacity of 'change agents'; of Lyons' apparent ignorance of the aspects of social interaction other than communication that take place when people meet face to face; and that cultural and structural change (i.e. morphogenesis) may well be highly fragmented across an organisation and between different groups and actors, and are as likely to be out of synchronisation with each other as they are in step, while certain combinations of morphogenesis/stasis are more likely to lead to social and agential change than others. All of the points above are of considerable importance when one considers that the Employers' Organisation for Local Government concluded in 2002 that: 'More than 50% of projects to implement new ICT [in local government] fail because of cultural and organisational issues rather than technical problems.' (EOLG 2002:1).

From informatization to information systems research

The origins of this book lie in the author's involvement from 1993 to 1997 with the Programme for the Study of Telematics and Governance (PSTAG) – jointly located within the Department of Economics and Politics at Nottingham Trent University and the School of Management at Glasgow Caledonian University. PSTAG members also played an important role in the European wide network of researchers centred on the European Group for Public Administration's (EGPA) Permanent Study Group on Informatization and the European Commission's COST A14 research programme – Governance and Democracy in the Information Age (GaDIA). Despite the reference to telematics, research focused on informatization: a generic term that was at that time commonly applied to any one or more of the following five dimensions of IS development undertaken in a governmental and/or public sector setting:

- the application of ICT [information and communication technology] in order to (re) shape important parts of information processing and communication facilities;

- the introduction of specialised expertise in the area of information processing (officers, departments, and organisations with explicit tasks and responsibilities);
- the (re) establishment of internal and external information flows and information relations;
- the development of information policies within and between organisations;
- the redesign of internal and external organisation structures and work processes that are related to the introduction of ICT.

    (Donk and Snellen 1998:6)

Reference to informatization throws up an issue that needs to be addressed before progressing this book further. Although not explicitly acknowledged throughout the 1990s within either the informatization or IS domains the two fields of research have many similarities. Thus, all of the aspects of informatization noted above would be covered by Galliers' (1991, 1992) taxonomy of the main approaches to IS research (i.e. stages of growth; organizational; informational; applications; systems; technological). Furthermore, the crossover became ever more pronounced as both the informatization and IS research domains expanded their boundaries to encompass more and more of the "social" alongside the "technological" when defining what is and is not informatization or an information system. Therefore, because of the close similarities between the two fields of research and the fact that the term informatization has largely fallen from favour (as has the term telematics, which was also a product of early studies of the emergent information society (e.g. Bell 1973, Nora and Minc 1980, Zuboff 1988), IS will be used here. There are, however, occasions where the use of both terms is unavoidable.

Researching IS in government and the public sector

The concept of the 'information polity', discussed above, clearly signals recognition of the complexity of events, actions and phenomena that constitutes any example of IS development in government and the public sector. Whether or not it is possible to capture this complexity is a moot point, but is, as outlined at the beginning of this chapter, a challenge this book attempts to overcome. The outcome should further advance both theories of the relationship between technology and public administration specifically, and organisational change generally, as well as illustrating that scholarly *and* practitioner interests very often combine in public administration research (White and Adams 1994, Wamsley 1996, Bannister 2004). This applies to all of the 'levels' of theory development that Donk and Snellen note as marking out the terrain of theories of informatization: concepts as mini theories, statements as prototheories, and empirical generalisations as embryonic theories. In each case the starting point for theorising has most usually been existing theoretical frames of reference from political science and public administration (e.g. institutionalism), or similarly dominant theoretical perspectives for scholars of IS/ICT working within mainstream organisation and management studies (e.g. the work of Zuboff 1988, Scarborough and Corbett 1992, Galliers 1993, Willcocks 1997, Willcocks, Currie and Mason 1997, Walsham 2000). This trend has continued into the 21st century (e.g. Dawson and Gunson 2002, Bannister 2004, Castells 2004) with a small body of work employing an approach similar to my own and utilising the morphogenetic approach/critical realism to analyse the relationship between IS and other organisational entities and activities (e.g. Mutch 1999a, 1999b, 2002, Carlson 2004).

The next section of this chapter is devoted to a brief review of the most commonplace of the theories/approaches of the relationship between technology and organisational change. These are presented chronologically in terms of their emergence as schools of thought, although they all now coexist in one form or another. This section then provides the basis for a return to a fuller discussion of the ontological and epistemological position that underpins this book.

Technology and theories of organisational change

New technologies have long been recognised as fundamental variables in organisational theory. Yet despite many years of research and study there is no consensus amongst scholars on the precise role of technology in organisational affairs

16

(e.g. Orlikowski 1992, Scarborough and Corbett 1992, DeSanctis and Poole 1994, Knights and Murray 1994, Castells 1996, Walsham 2000). And not surprisingly, therefore, there is no shortage of critiques of social research and technology (e.g. Markus and Robey 1988, Orlikowski and Barudi 1991, Orlikowski, Walsham and Jones 1995, Feenberg 1999, Carlsson 2004). Interestingly, one of the most often critiqued (and criticised) theories is also one of the most enduring. This is the widely held and supposedly 'commonsense' view that technological change is the prime cause of social change, and that technological and technical innovations emerge from the working out of intrinsic, disembodied, impersonal logic and not from any social influence. Furthermore, this deterministic view underpins many later theories of technology and often (albeit in a fairly weak form) creeps into the work of scholars and authors who would maintain they are adopting a non deterministic approach (such as some examples of my own work: e.g. Horrocks 1997).

Technological Determinism

Technological determinism holds that human and social factors merely mediate technological developments that are essentially inevitable, although it is recognised that human/social factors may perhaps control the timing of such developments. There is little disagreement that for most of the 20th century this was the most influential theory of the relationship between technology and society (MacKenzie and Wajcman 1985, Winner 1996, Clegg and Hardy 1999), and although a deterministic approach to the study of technological change has dissipated somewhat with the advent of 'social' theories of technology (see below) by the mid 1990s it remained the dominant tradition in certain disciplines. Thus, for example, writing about the 'inherent' democratic character and qualities of ICT and especially the internet, Grossman concludes that '...the question is not whether the transformation to instant public feedback through electronics is good or bad, or politically desirable or undesirable. Like a force of nature, it is simply the way our political system is heading (Grossman 1995:154).

17

One of the main reasons for the enduring nature of technological determinism is that in late modern society divorcing the human from the technological becomes ever more difficult. Thus, one of the leading scholars of the information age, Castells, takes issue with the many scholars who are forthright in their denunciation of technological determinism when he states:

> Of course technology does not determine society. Neither does society script the course of technological change, since many factors, including individual inventiveness and entrepreneurialism, intervene in the process of scientific discovery, technological innovation and social applications, so that the final outcome depends on a complex pattern of interaction. Indeed, the dilemma of technological determinism is probably a false one since technology is society, and society cannot be understood or represented without its technological tools.
> (Castells 1996:5)

Castells rightly draws attention to the view that society is complex in the extreme and that in the developed world at least, technology, in one form or sense, is now implicated in almost everything we do. Accepting this argument does not detract from the fact that in seeking to understand and predict the likely consequences of new technologies a deterministic approach is often an easy option to follow. It is, therefore, not difficult to understand why this type of research has acquired, and to a large extent retains, a pre-eminence in many fields of technology research. For if we are able to claim to be able to predict the consequences of a particular technology then we ought also to be able to act to prevent any negative effects. However, by largely ignoring the basic question of what is shaping technological change in the first place, technological determinism fails to provide a complete picture of technological change, over-eggs the role of technology and thus distorts analysis of its impact on and/or implications for organisations, institutions, markets, industries and, or course, individuals.

The Decision Making School

The decision making school is rooted in the positivist tradition of research and has traditionally dominated the study of organisational change and new technology. Decision theorists promote the view that technology should consist of structures (e.g. data and models) designed to overcome human 'weaknesses'. Once applied therefore, technology will deliver efficiency and productivity and thus benefit and bring satisfaction to organisations and individuals (Bartol and Martin 1998). Of course, there are variants within the decision school. Jarvenpaa (1989) for example, argued for models of technology use based on identifying the best fit between work task and technology. Failure to do so results in the non-achievement of the potential improvements which may have been promised by the technology, or achieved in other (existing) locations. Interestingly, in the early and mid 1990s this viewpoint became a particularly powerful line of argument within a good deal of the literature on organisational reengineering (for example, Jayachandra 1994, Scott Morton 1991) and was a subject dealt with (in a critical way) by several of those involved with the EGPA group on informatization (e.g. Taylor 1995, Pratchett 1997, Taylor et al 1997).

As might be assumed given the positivist stance of decision theorists, there is a strong tendency to an engineering view of organisational change. The result is that failure to achieve the desired level of change in an organisation is taken to indicate a failure in the availability of the appropriate technologies, and/or in technology design and/or implementation. Fairly hard line determinism, or a more moderate contingency approach, provides the grounding for decision theorists' research and data collection, while analysis is typically conducted using quantitative methods to 'measure' the effects of technology on outcomes. In other words, the premise is that organisational, individual and technological variables can be measured and predicted. Human behaviour and other organisational properties are influenced by technology, which operates as an independent variable exerting unidirectional, causal pressures similar to those operating in nature. As noted above, in some of this research it is accepted that the impact of technology can be moderated by contextual variables, thus proposing a contingency model of technology. The result is that while this approach can provide valuable insights into the 'determining aspects of technology' the actions of humans are largely ignored. The result is 'an incomplete account of technology and its interaction with organisations' (Orlikowski 1992).

Socio-technical perspectives

Socio-technical studies based on the premise that ICTs are now a major and perhaps the most important factor for the restructuring of organisations, work processes and practices are particularly powerful within the strategic choice literature on management (Danziger 1991, Hoff 1992, Hughes et al 1994). The basic argument is that if ICT is designed to embody the required features, be they empowering or upskilling, or controlling and deskilling, and if managers are committed to such a strategy, organisations and productive process can be reengineered and better performance will follow (Hammer and Champy 1993). As might be expected, once the gloss of the harder models of reengineering failed to deliver the promised benefits softer models emerged that factored in the human dimensions of organisations and, in particular, organisational culture (Davenport 1993, 1994, Willcocks 1996).

The socio-technical approach has experienced something of a re-emergence in popularity since the beginning of the 21st century. For example, reengineering 'tool-kits', mainly produced by management consultants or those of a related ilk, are again popular. This also confirms that while business process reengineering/process reengineering is still the most common term used to describe this form of organisational change organisational reengineering (OR) is now seen as a more holistic term, with more prominence ostensibly given to the human side of organisations. Thus one consultancy firm that had been working with a large English local authority stated that its approach to OR was aimed at 'moving beyond technology' and that 'Technology is first and foremost about people.' (Northgate 2005). Nevertheless it is evident from the literature, and from reports such as those

20

by Gershon and Lyons cited above, that despite these claims there is a renewed bias towards technology in contemporary agendas for organisational 'transformation.' How seriously these claim should be taken is open to question, however, when David Craig who had been a leading consultant with Capgemini in the mid 1990s, has admitted that 'transformation' '...was only a trick, only a way of selling lots and lots of consulting with lots of IT systems behind it.' (Craig 2006).

In academic circles the situation differed somewhat from that described above. Here, the socio-technical approach began to rely 'to heavily on the capability of human agents' (Orlikowski 1992:401), while taking too little account of such things as the institutional properties of organisations, politics, the external and internal environment and unintended consequences of organisational change. Because of the highly influential nature of the work it is worth noting, as an aside, that Orlikowski cites Zuboff's *In the Age of the Smart Machine* (1988) as an example of the socio-technical approach. Knights and Murray (1994:8), however, are forthright in their claim that Zuboff is guilty of 'continuing in a technological determinist tradition...'.

Clearly Zuboff cannot be 'guilty' of such a degree of technological determinism *and* such a clear supporter of the capabilities of agents at the same time and so one or other view of her work is wrong. My view would be that Zuboff's concentration on discussing the properties of technology (which takes up the majority of her book) gives the impression that she is a highly determinist. However, it is clear from comments she makes throughout (but perhaps not as prominently as she should) that her underlying ontological position is to oppose this view.

The importance of variations in organisational context for the development and application of ICT, and the need to take account of the social and work needs of an organisation's work force in the systems design process, have been a particularly important contribution that researchers working within the socio-technical "school" have made to the ICT literature (e.g Willcocks and Mason 1987, Willcocks, Currie and Mason 1997). Particular importance is often ascribed to powerful human actors and in particular ICT specialists, acting as 'project champions', or the 'change agents' of the Gershon Review and the Government's *Transformational Technology* strategy, discussed above. Despite this acknowledgement of different sources of influence, management is nevertheless seen as rational and benign. Thus, there is a strong tendency to ignore or downplay power relations within organisations and the external environment in which they operate. Where power is recognised a resource dependency theory of power is employed and little account is taken of the weakness of political analysis based on such a theory (Knights and Murray 1994). True to the strictures of scientific management, politics is seen as disruptive unless employed to further managerial goals (Morgan 1997).

Processual and Pluralist Perspectives

These approaches emerged from the criticisms of the socio-technical approach, as did the increasing interest in systems theory. The 'politics of management' is a central focus of the processual perspective (Davenport 1992, Guthrie and Dutton 1992) although, as with the socio-technical perspective, politics per se is often seen as a constraint on and disruption to rational and strategic planning (Knights and Murray 1994). Pettigrew (1973, 1980) was the first and one of the most influential advocates of this approach to technology and organisational change research. In his ground breaking study of ICI from the early 1970s Pettigrew brought together the literatures on sub-unit competition and career and political dynamics to develop a much broader theory of organisational politics than had previously been recognised. Pettigrew saw power as a social relationship and recognised decision-making as a political process. In particular he drew attention to the ability of experts to exercise power through the control of access to and accumulation of specialist knowledge and information. The processual approach became a popular path to follow in British academia during the early and mid 1990s, (e.g. Bloomfield and Coombs 1992, Scarborough and Corbett 1992, Knights and Murray 1994) with particular attention paid to control and power and the role of experts in these relations.

Pluralist theories of technology and organisations emerged in the USA in the 1980s. Mintzberg (1979, 1983) was one of the key advocates of this approach - which set out to question the rationalist view of organisational life. ICT research inspired by pluralist thinking has focused particularly on the place of politics in ICT departments and systems development, hence the coupling of this approach with the discourse of user involvement which was emerging in the late 1970s and early 1980s.

Although raising the awareness of the importance of power and politics was seen as path-breaking in its day, the rather narrow definition of politics which this perspective employs (there is no recognition of the inequalities of resource distribution sanctioned by organisations and society in general [Knights and Murray 1994]), and the close affiliation of scholars to the ICT practitioner community have tended to undermine the analytical credibility of the perspective.

Social Construction and Related Perspectives
Advocates of theories of the social construction of technology, such as Hughes and Pinch (1987) Bijker (1995) and Bijker and Law (1992), and related approaches such as actor-network theory (Callon 1987, Latour 1987, 1992) share with those who support the social shaping paradigm (below) hostility to the technological determinism of some of the historically dominant approaches to technology studies discussed above. They seek instead to explore and understand the 'genesis and crystallisation of new technologies in organisations and the marketplace.' (Knights and Murray 1994:21). In attempting this both approaches accept the union of the 'social' and 'technical' phases of ICT development, arguing that nothing is purely technological (Scarbrough 1995, Hoff 2000). Thus, social constructionist theorists are concerned to study:

...how specific knowledge and technologies are the outcome of a complex set of social processes or moments of translation involving the definition of problems (problematisation), the arousal of social interests (interessement), the enrolment of a variety of agencies and actors, and, finally, the mobilisation of network members when social investment reaches a point where withdrawal would be unlikely.

(Knights and Murray 1994:21).

Both approaches challenge numerous assumptions regarding the relations and boundary between the technological and social. However, one significant difference is that the advocates of the actor network approach dispense with the distinction between inanimate and animate objects – networks are constructed of human and non human 'actors' (Mackay and Gillespie 1992).

The social construction approaches are extremely useful in providing a framework to describe the detail of network formation and thus avoid a voluntaristic approach to understanding technological development (Hirscheim and Klein 1989, Hoff 2000). In so doing both perspectives highlight the role networks of actors play in the development and use of technological innovations. Therefore, power, politics, accidents and unintended consequences are all accepted as integral to these processes. However, although the profoundly social and political nature of technological innovations is recognised these perspectives pay little or no attention to the broader powers and inequalities that are both the condition and the consequence of network formation (Knights and Murray 1994).

Given that the role of networks of actors/agents/artefacts features prominently in this book, as chapters 4–6 will demonstrate, it is unsurprising that actor network theory resonates with my work, as does a weak form of social construction, as the discussion of the genesis of this book later in this chapter explains. It is also worth adding that there are some parallels between actor network theory and the policy networks approach that developed in politics and policy studies during the early 1990s (Jordan 1990, Rhodes and Marsh 1992, Dowding 1995, Rhodes and Marsh 1996). Unlike actor network theory, however, the policy networks approach was not developed with technology specifically in mind. Nevertheless, Pratchett (1994, 1999) successfully applied the approach to the formation of ICT policy in British local government in the 1990s, thereby illustrating the networks and groups active in the technology policy domain and their influence on the 'social' construction of both local government ICT policy and the resulting technological applications and systems. Meanwhile, Huigen (1993) carried out a similar analysis in The Netherlands.

Social Shaping of Technology

Social shaping shares much in common with two schools just noted. Nevertheless, there is a distinction to be drawn: actor-network theorists are more radical in their break with Marxist and humanist traditions in social theory whereas the social shaping perspective draws on Marxian and feminist concerns with class and gender (Galaskiewicz and Wasserman 1993). Thus, in attempting to address one of the major 'weaknesses' of the social-construction paradigm advocates of social shaping see the most important condition in the development and use of technologies as power, and the interests that are its medium and outcome. Like the last two perspectives, social shaping is one of a number of recent approaches that sets out to challenge the technological determinism inherent in many accounts of technology and organisations. Unfortunately, and as with other approaches, it can be argued that it simply substitutes one determinism for another: interests rather than technology (Coombs, Knights and Willmott 1992).

Although it is true to say that social shaping is more wide ranging than processual theory at recognising the cultural and socio-political conditions which apply outside the context of the immediate organisation, or technology, its major focus is clearly on social interests. This leaves the social shaping perspective in a weak position as an instrument for the study of the accidental and unintended consequences of technology use (Knights and Murray 1994). More importantly, perhaps, this approach is also ill suited to exploration of the often contradictory nature of the global context within which particular organisational and technological changes take place.

The social shaping of technology and social construction/actor-networks perspectives are all bound by a common interest in addressing the problems that come with accepting technological innovation as a 'given' – a 'black box', to use an often used term. The aim is, therefore, to allow exploration of what is inside the black box – to explore the social processes that shape the form and content of technical knowledge and technological change. As Edge (a participant in the ESRC PICT programme noted above) points out: '...a basic assumption of this approach is that the relationship between technology and society is genuinely an *interaction*, a *recursive process*: causes and effects stand in a complex relationship.' (Edge 1987:14. Original emphasis).

From neo-institutionalism to critical realism

From knowledge of the EGPA study group on informatization and an ongoing review of informatization literature, it is clear that over the years the trajectory of IS research and theorising in public administration has followed similar paths to that of mainstream IS research in the disciplines of management and organisation studies. By the late 1990s, therefore, most members of the European informatization fraternity had begun to embrace social construction or social shaping to a greater or lesser extent. Nevertheless, socio-technical and processual/pluralist approaches, such as informed much of the work of those associated with the ESRC PICT research programme of the early 1990s (e.g. Dutton 1996, Bekkers et al 1996) and a good deal of North American research (e.g. Dutton et al 1987, King and Kraemer 1991), remained strong. Thus, while there was an increasing recognition of the importance of agency as well as structure in studies of IS in the public domain, for many scholars of informatization it proved difficult to break their empirical research away from established approaches that tended to emphasise structures over agency, as much of

26

the research reported in Taylor et al 1997, Snellen and Donk 1998 and Hoff, Horrocks and Tops 2000 illustrates.

As discussed at the outset of this chapter, the author's preference was to use the opportunity that doctoral work presented to explore schools of thought that treated agency and structure in a more balanced way than those noted above. To address this issue, and to provide the necessary research 'tools' to explore and account for the complexity of the what, where, how, why and outcomes of IS development, what was required was a theoretical and methodological approach which recognised that structure and agency, and the properties and powers associated with them, have to be related rather than conflated (Archer 1995, Willmott 2000, Fleetwood 2004). Conflation is discussed in more detail below. Suffice to note here that by avoiding conflation it should become possible to analyse the processes by which *both* structure and agency shape and reshape one another over time so that we can account for the variable social outcomes of IS developments at different times.

The search for a non conflationary approach was inspired initially by a section of Donk and Snellen's Introduction to *Public Administration in the Information Age* (Snellen and Donk 1998) in which they state that in trying to formulate and develop theories of informatization it is crucial:

> ...to avoid the trap of technological determinism [by recognising that]: ICTs do not *cause* developments in public administration...The possibilities of technology function as *attractors* for aspirations that are already (or always were) existent in public administration, or are aroused by them.
> (Donk and Snellen 1998:9. Original emphasis)

Donk and Snellen go on to propose that a model that combines causal and functional reasoning that had been developed by van Parijs in 1981 can be used to 'show' the mechanisms associated with the potentialities (i.e. attractors) of ICTs and the social and technological outcomes. They conclude that by using such a model:

> Causes are, along this line of reasoning, prior conditions that are a necessary and sufficient condition for the appearance of a later state of affairs. The functional line of reasoning connects later states of affairs to prior situations in such a way that the (continuance of the) existence of prior situations is made understandable by the improvement they entail in later states of affairs. These kinds of reasoning are thus each other's mirror image in as far as the direction of explanation is concerned. Causal reasoning explains later occurrences by former ones, while functional reasoning explains former occurrences in the light of later ones.' (ibid:10)

When comparing this quotation with the brief discussion of critical realist views of causal powers and retroduction, and the morphogenetic approach, at the beginning of this chapter (Figure 1.1) it should be clear that it is possible to draw distinct parallels. For example, with the critical realist view that pre-existing structures condition and enable action in the present and are then reproduced or transformed as agents move into a new cycle of emergence – interplay – outcome. It was not until April 1998 however, that the author discovered an approach which was both non conflationary and appeared to provide sufficient tools (methods) to explore and document the complexity of IS development in public administration (i.e. the information polity). The initial introduction to Archer's morphogenetic approach was via the papers of McAnnulla (1998) and Johnston (1998) at that year's Political Studies Association annual conference. However, before commenting on the key reasons for choosing Archer's approach, it is appropriate to briefly outline how and why a good deal of the experience and practice of the PSTAG period (1993–1997) resonates with the later adoption of a critical realist approach for this book.

The dynamic nature of IS research in public administration in the 1990s, as well as the broad and eclectic mix of researchers from different scholarly and geographical/cultural traditions within the field at that time, meant that those involved in the various research networks were exposed to a wide range of theories and approaches. For example, it was argued above that a predominantly processual/pluralist tradition (usually referred to as institutionalist or neo institutionalist in the terminology of political science that is commonly used in public administration) could be identified in much of the IS research in public administration at that time. This leads institutionalists to focus less on the structures within technology and more on the social evolution of structures within human institutions (DeSanctis and Poole 1994). Consequently, researchers within the institutionalist tradition would regard technology as an opportunity for change, rather than a causal agent of change (Barley and Tolbert 1988, Orlikowski and Baroudi 1991). This is a point borne out by Donk and Snellen's (1998) reference to ICTs as 'attractors' or 'potentialities' discussed above, and is an important area of common ground between critical realists and institutionalists for two reasons. First, both are critical of schools of thought that tend towards technological determinism. And second, both adopt a very similar – broader – position on the role of technology in social systems.

Donk and Snellen's work also illustrate another commonality between critical realist and institutionalist approaches to social research – the study of technology and organisational change has to capture historical processes as social practices evolve. The focus is, therefore, on interaction and it follows that institutionalists tend to see the creation, design and use of new technologies as being inextricably bound up with the form and direction of social order. As the discussion in the following chapter demonstrates, this is, once again, an important dimension of a critical realist approach. Finally, in terms of research methods, both institutionalism and critical realism favour process orientated approaches over outcome studies. And there is a preference for interpretative accounts rather than heavily formulaic quantitative research designs.

As the subject for and design of the field research for this book built on and from the PSTAG and EGPA traditions it is not surprising that it incorporates many elements of a (neo) institutionalist approach, allied with features of the social shaping/construction schools that were, as discussed above, becoming increasingly popular in informatization research circles in the 1990s. Methodologically, therefore, the position taken for this research was interpretive and interactionist, reflecting the finding that: 'The focus of the interactionist approach...is on the institutional arrangement associated with IS development and use in organisations.' Thus, a goal of the interactionist approach is to '...shed light on the social issues surrounding organisational change and implementation of information systems' (Iivari, Hirscheim and Klein 1998:168). This was certainly a goal of many of those within the PSTAG/EGPA groups

Weak social constructivist influences also reinforced the interpretivist direction of the research that came from the author's institutionalist background. That is, that '...the important role played by discourse is accepted, with no further suggestion that discourse entirely constitutes, or exhausts, the world.' (Fleetwood 2004:44). From the discussion here and above, and as will become clear from Chapter 3, a researcher's ontological position bounds the methods used, hence the use for this book of multiple methods which enable a researcher to get close to their subject(s) and explore the detailed background and life history of the case.

Having associated the research on which this book is based with interpretivism, however, it should quickly be made clear that there were other philosophical assumptions at work that are generally not associated with such a stance. In general terms these points of departure can all be associated with what Morgan (1997) refers to as 'logics of change'. That is, beliefs about the nature of, and relationship between, systems, change and environments. Specifically this means that the tendency of an interpretive approach to ignore the conditions that give rise to certain meanings and experiences; omit explanations of the unintended consequence of action; underplay the structural tensions within society and organisations and the contradictions that may be endemic to social systems, and, finally neglect explanations of historical change (Orlikowski and Baroudi 1991), all ran counter to the institutionalist traditions and emergent commitment to critical realism of the author. Instead the preferred perspective, from the outset, was that:

> A particular element exists only in the context of the totality of relationships of which it is part, and the element and the whole are bound by an essential rather than contingent interdependence. This dialectical relationship between element and totality is understood to be shaped by historical and contextual conditions…Social reality is understood to be produced and reproduced by humans, but also as possessing objective properties which tend to dominate human experience.
> (Orlikowski and Baroudi 1991:19)

This is, as noted earlier in this chapter, the gist of critical realism, even though Orlikowski and Baroudi do not use such a term. Overall, then, my research was always inclined to be anti positivist and anti determinist, a trend noticeable amongst many of the scholars who were part of the EGPA and PSTAG groups, with the overarching aim of research being to increase understanding of the phenomenon under investigation within its cultural and contextual situation. Again this echoes Archer's approach and critical realism generally.

The structure/agency debate

Given the parallels between informatization and IS research from within mainstream management and organisation studies, it was to literature from that discipline that was used to continue to build up a knowledge and understanding of the structure/agency debate and the nature of conflation. Much that emerged differed little from the conceptual and theoretical approaches common to IS research and public administration, although often using different terminology. Nevertheless, what did become apparent was that there was a small body of work that linked concepts and theories of structure and agency to IS and technology generally (e.g. Barley 1986, 1990, Willmott 1987, Walsham and Han 1990, Orlikowski and Robey 1991, Gash and Orlikowski 1991, Orlikowski 1992, 1993, DeSanctis and Poole 1994, Barley and Tolbert 1997), usually, and with a few exceptions, (e.g. Mutch 1999a, 1999b), through what appeared to be use of a variant of structuration theory associated with the work of Giddens (1984).

Further research into the literature on structuration theory revealed, however, that when reviewing the work of Orlikowski (1992, 1993) and DeSanctis and Poole (1994) one of the leading advocates of Giddens' work had concluded that these authors had not employed structuration theory in their analysis and theorising at all, giving undue recognition, for example, to technology as a structure, as well as injecting a dualism rather than a duality into their work. And, specifically in the case of DeSanctis and Poole, that much of their work was '...directly contrary to Giddens' principles.' (Jones 1998:124). A more detailed discussion of these issues is contained in the discussion in Chapter 2 of technology as a structural form, where it becomes clear that Orlikowski for one does not regard technology as a structure but as a *structural property*.

There are, however, at least three issues that signal fundamental divides between critical realism/the morphogenetic approach and Giddens' variant of structuration theory. All have their roots in the different ontological conceptions and methodological injunctions that can and have been applied to social theorising, such as those that underpin critical realism and therefore the morphogenetic approach. It is only necessary to briefly discuss them here, as the first two are discussed in Chapter

2, while the third – conflation – is dealt with below. The first is that while Giddens' recognises that structuration occurs over time his models only implicitly reflect this. Thus, time is merely '...the unfolding of preferences instantiated in action.' (Hay 1997:13). The second concerns whether or not it is desirable to maintain an analytical distinction between structure and agency (as indeed Orlikowski and DeSanctis and Poole and other scholars of IS noted above had done). This is a point which approaches to organisation studies that are broadly referred to as postmodern (such as actor network theory and ethnomethodology) also emphasise. That is, in common with structuration theory they set out to dispense with the need to distinguish analytically between different levels or forms of reality as represented in the agency/structure distinction (Johnson and Duberley 2000). This puts these approaches squarely at odds with any theory that is built on the belief that as a matter of theoretical necessity analytical dualism must be maintained (Archer 1995, 1998b, Reed 1997, Fleetwood 2004).

The view supported here, and discussed fully in Chapter 2, is that the analytical collapsing of agency into structure has a '...debilitating effect on the explanatory power of any theory of organisation which remains sensitive to the stratified nature of social reality and its implications for social action.' (Reed 1997:37). The third area of fundamental disagreement concerns the way in which structure and agency are conflated one into the other - either up, or down, or, as with Giddens' structuration theory, centrally (Archer 1995, 1998).

Conflation in social theory

A range of reviews of extant literature on IS development (ISD), over several decades (Culnan 1986, 1987, Galliers 1991, Orlikowski and Baroudi, 1991, Hirscheim et al 1995, Iivari and Hirscheim 1996, Iivari et al 1998), demonstrate the accuracy of the claim of Ivari et al '...that there is a single set of dominant philosophical assumptions about the nature of ISD and what constitutes valid knowledge about the phenomena to be associated with ISD.' (Iivari et al 1998:165). Thus Iivari's (1991) earlier analysis of seven contemporary 'schools of thought' on IS development had shown that they:

> ...were predominately functionalist, sharing a number of common features. For example, they viewed IS as a largely technical system with social implications, conceived of information as descriptive facts, subscribed to a structuralist view of organisations, adopted a positivist epistemology, embraced mostly nomothetic and constructive research methods, and emphasised a means-end orientated view of IS conforming to organisation/management values.
> (Iivari et al 1998:166)

While some of these attributes do not necessarily imply conflation most do, and downward conflation in particular. Consequently, and as this is the form of conflation that has traditionally dominated across the social sciences this is the starting point for the discussion that follows.

Downward conflation

Downward conflation refers to the fact that action is treated as epiphenomenal to structure. This does not mean that agency entirely disappears from the equation however as theories built on downward conflation will often recognise that agency provides the motor for society and social change. Hence supporters of this approach may be led into making claims that are at odds with the ontological presuppositions on which downward conflation is based. That is, that ultimately action will only lead where structure allows it to go. People can only ever act as the agents of structure.

The impact of such a view on the temporal dimension of research, analysis and theorising is profound as social interaction cannot have any structural impact of magnitude, because agents are not granted the potential to generate intended, unintended, aggregate or emergent properties, then it (social interaction) is seldom

34

approached in analysis (Archer 1995). Thus, as Figure 1.3 illustrates, analysis stops after T2 because, from that point on, any future developments will be the result of structural tendencies that are already in the system.

The same conditions apply when exploring the historical dimension of any case, be it recent or otherwise: because action cannot create structure then at any point in history those structures must have emerged from some impersonal forces. In short, from a downwards conflationary stance, when researching and analysing the development of any type of social structure it is not social interaction we would be interested in, because social structures cannot have social origins. Instead research, analysis and theorising will be restricted to '...*the impress of structure upon agency in the present.*' (Archer 1995:84. Original emphasis).

Downward conflation underpins several of the theoretical approaches to technology and organisational change noted above. For example, it is to the fore in the underlying assumptions of the decision making school and, in particular, any approach that is built on technological determinism, as this automatically favours technology (as a structure) over agency. A tendency to downward conflation becomes less pronounced in the socio-technical and processual and pluralist approaches but is, none the less, still evident. As noted above, much of the research of those associated with the EGPA research group on informatization, tended to weak downward conflation. For example (and deliberately drawing on PSTAG work from this period as it has most relevance to this book) although the existence and role of 'project champions' – key individuals/groups who appeared to be critical to the development of IS – featured prominently in the work of Bellamy, Horrocks and Webb (1995) and Horrocks and Hambley (1998), ultimately the design and focus of the research and its conclusions favoured structures.

Upward conflation

Fairly obviously this is the reverse of downward conflation. Now agency is in the ascent: '...its prime function is to view so-called structural properties as reducible to the effects of other actors, which are in their turn always recoverable by agency.' (Archer 1995:84). All versions of upward conflation are underpinned by methodological individualism. Thus the social context is defined as no more than "other people", and no social situation exists that cannot be altered if a person has the know how (in the form of information) and the will. It follows that as with downwards conflation, the temporal focus here is on contemporary action, as history cannot be altered, and the structures of the future cannot be predicted as they will only emerge due to the actions of agents at a particular point in time. In short, any back reference to T1 and T2 (Figure 1.3) is ruled out. Nor can T4 be approached because, as Archer points out, by endorsing the 'autonomy of the present tense' advocates of upwards conflation have to truncate temporality, or otherwise admit that the unintended consequences of past action may have consequences (as emergent properties or aggregate effects) and thus that they represent new structural influences on future action.

As the discussion above of social construction, actor-network theory and social shaping showed, all of these approaches are built to some extent on upward conflation and therefore on overly voluntaristic accounts of the role of agency in the structure/agency dynamic. Or, specifically in relation to IS, how much power and interpretive freedom people have when faced with technological developments. Thus, one form of argument that would emerge from research built on the assumptions (implicitly or explicitly) of upwards conflation is that people are able to manipulate, 'misuse' (from a management perspective), or ignore IS when they are adopted into organisations. This is taken as demonstrating the power of agency over structure. These events/situations then become the focus of research attention, thus avoiding a broader analysis of the powers and inequalities that may be present.

In the context of the university at which I work, for example, academics are able to decide not to engage with a number of IS systems, such as the student registration and management system, that are available to all staff via the university's intranet. Nevertheless, both of these systems constrain and shape aspects of course design and operation, as well as many other aspects of the operation of the university in general, and thus impact, in some form or another, on the actions of academics, as they do on all staff. The extent of freedom within, and power over, these IS structures is therefore considerably less than an analysis informed by a theoretical perspective that endorses upward conflation would suggest.

Central conflation

Given the criticisms of upward and downward conflation noted above it might be assumed that central conflation is the obvious way out of such a bind. Indeed, the stated aim of many of those who work with structuration theory, and of Giddens himself, has been to try to overcome this situation of antagonism and divisiveness within social theory by substituting an 'ontology of praxis' (Archer 1995, 1998b). The result is that: 'Rather than seeing action and structure as counter-acting elements of a dualism, we should regard them as complementary terms of a duality, the "duality of structure".' (Thompson 1989:60).

Through the mutual constitution of structure and agency, and an ontology of praxis, Giddens aims to 'move social theory away from the reified notion (in his view) of emergent properties, as prior to and autonomous from action and the reductionist conception (in his view) of individuals, with personal properties which are independent and detachable from the social context of their formation and expression.' (Archer 1995:94). The consequence is that '...actual transcendence is held to consist in the assertion that a consideration of "social practices" suffices for analysis of all levels of the social world. Simultaneously, it re-valorizes the agent as someone with knowledgeable mastery over their social doings whilst eradicating the idea of external hydraulic pressures upon them.' (ibid:94).

37

The conflation/elision of structure into agency is held by advocates of structuration theory as one of the great strengths of the approach – a conceptual method where the detail of everyday life and of the structures which are reproduced or transformed through living always remain related and unified (Jones 1998). Thus, structuration theory has become the most modern and sophisticated version of central conflation (Sibeon 1999, Stones 2001).

Treating structure and agency as inseparable produces an ontology of social practices and it is these that elisionists (as Archer prefers to refer to them) such as Giddens argue we should exclusively focus on when seeking to develop practical social theory. Furthermore, as structure is inseparable from agency it cannot, therefore, be either emergent or autonomous from it, nor can it pre-exist it or be causally influential. Roles, positions and relations cannot exist except at the moment of instantiation and structure(s), which consist of rules and resources which manifest themselves through social practices, have no existence independent of these.

An example would be the general practioner (GP) service in the UK. To an elisionist this service only exists at the moment a person uses it and the rules and resources (i.e. structures) associated with the GP service also only come into being at that point. This clearly ignores the observable fact that were nobody to use any GP on any particular day the written and published 'rules' and resources (i.e. structures) that operate alongside actual human doctors would still exist, and will exist (in some form or another), after currently practicing GPs retire, and did exist (in some form or another), before currently practicing GPs came into being. Furthermore, even if no GPs were active, and no patients in their social system, the rules and resources that have been brought into being as part of this social practice and system would continue to condition and shape other agents and structures in other social settings – such as admissions to hospital and access to social services – both of which are conditioned and shaped to some extent by the rules and resources that apply to GPs.

Beyond conflation

At an ontological and methodological level, then, the fundamental argument between the supporters and opponents of elisionism is about the stratified nature of society: both social structures and people have emergent powers. This is a subject discussed fully in the following chapter. Nevertheless, it is appropriate here to briefly illustrate the nature and importance of the concept. The first point to note is that people are stratified: 'Since individuals, collectivities, corporate groups and populations have different emergent properties, [therefore] conflationist flattening of these severely jeopardises explanatory possibilities.' (New 2001:43).

The second point to note is that while a supporter of elision would recognise three strata when theorising the world – natural, biological and social – the critical realist view would be that there are at least two further layers: personal psychology (mind as emergent from body) and socio-cultural structures (structure as emergent from social relations). Each strata has its own distinctive, emergent and irreducible properties. Consequently, for those of a non-elisionist frame (referred to by Archer as emergentists because of their support for the view that there are emergent properties in society):

> …"the social" is not one and indivisible but made up of heterogeneous
> constituents. Because of this, examination of their interplay is central to any
> adequate form of social theorising (since the relative autonomy of each
> stratum means that its properties are capable of independent variation,
> combination and above all, influence).
> (Archer 1995:102).

Despite the criticism of central conflation noted above, the eliding of structure and agency, such as occurs in Giddens' variant of structuration theory, has become an extremely popular path to follow in social theorising, ('…scoring the retinas of five generations of students by now...' in Archer's view [Archer et al 1999:14]). It is worth noting, however, that there are some who question whether there is a fundamental difference between the duality of structuration theory and the dualism of critical realism (e.g. Stones 2001), but this is not a debate that lies within the scope of this book. The view supported here is that the emergentist ontology and non-conflationary theorising of critical realism leads to an entirely different conceptualisation of the problem of structure and agency than is employed by any type of social theory that endorses conflation. Furthermore, the use of analytical dualism (i.e. the separation for analytical purposes of structure and agency) provides us with a far more detailed account of the complexities of the interrelationship between structure and agency than would otherwise be the case (Archer 1995, Archer et al 1999, Willmott 2000, Fairclough 2005).

Having explained how and why this book developed as it did, and the ontology and epistemology that underpins it, it is now appropriate to discuss the claims for the originality of this work before concluding this chapter with a brief review of the structure of the remainder of the book.

Originality

When the writing of this book began one of the primary claims to originality for the work was that very few researchers within sociology, and even fewer across the social sciences generally, had even heard of critical realism, much less made use of Archer's work. This situation was borne out by Mutch (1999a and 1999b) who was the first scholar, as far as extensive research has been able to identify, to explicitly use Archer's methodology in a research field from within organisation and management studies. Consequently, if writing had gone to plan it was reasonable to expect that this book would have been in the forefront of the application of the morphogenetic approach within public administration and mainstream organisation and management studies research in general, as well as in the context of IS research in either discipline.

Unfortunately, writing went nowhere near to plan, leading to a suspension of work on this book until late 2001. One of the first things that became apparent at that point was that the popularity of critical realism was on the increase. This is due in no small part to the arrival of the International Association for Critical Realism and its journal, the *International Journal of Critical Realism;* the ESRC supported seminar series on social realism and empirical research of 2000 (see New 2001); as well as the body of literature which has been published by Routledge under the *Critical Realism: interventions* book series (e.g. Ackroyd and Fleetwood 2000, Danermark 2001, Carter and New 2004). All of these developments have raised the profile of, and increased access to, the field.

Across the social sciences the popularity of critical realism has continued to increase since 2001 (e.g. Scrambler 2001, Moren and Blom 2003, Skinningsrud 2005). This has been particularly marked in the field of organisation and management studies (e.g. Fleetwood and Ackroyd 2004, Fairclough 2005, Mutch 2005), with a heated debate taking place between the advocates of critical realism and post structuralism/social construction in the pages of one of the discipline's leading journals, the *Journal of Management Studies*, (e.g. Contu and Willmott 2005, Reed 2005a, 2005b). A number of the edited works that have appeared during this period have proved of particular relevance to this book (i.e. Ackroyd and Fleetwood 2000, Carter and New 2004, Fleetwood and Ackroyd 2004).

There have also been some relevant additions to the IS literature, such as Dobson 2001, Mutch 2002, and Carlsson 2004, all of which posit the relevance of critical realism to IS research. Nevertheless, in respect of Archer's morphogenetic approach specifically, by 2004 it remained the case that despite some recent attempts at its use in qualitative research '…its potential for empirical research had yet to be realised.' (Carter and New 2004:18). A very small number of examples of the use of the approach have appeared in print since, such as Thursfield and Hamblett's use of the morphogenetic approach to '…illuminate the factors and processes underpinning the development of HRM,' (Thursfield and Hamblett 2004:117), Hislop's (2006) use of the morphogenetic approach to reinterpret a previously reported case study of organisational learning, and Kowalczyk's (2004) case study of the causal processes associated with hospital mergers.

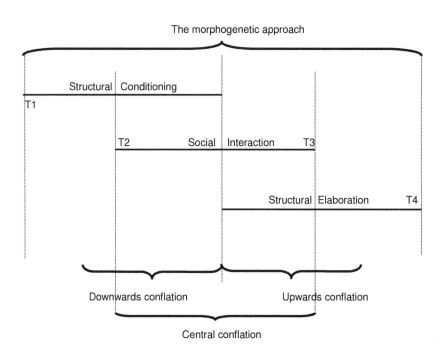

Figure 1.3 The limited time span of conflationary theories compared with the

morphogenetic approach

Archer 1995:82

Taking into account the discussion above and an ongoing review of critical realist literature, and of mainstream and public sector IS research, my conclusion is that the several (related) claims to originality of this book remain largely intact. The first is relatively straightforward: this work represents a critical realist account of IS development in public administration where none exists at present (i.e. to the end of

2007). The second is more fundamental given the situation with regard to the morphogenetic approach noted above: it represents one of the few comprehensive *applications* of the morphogenetic approach to empirical research currently available outside of Archer's own work, and thus a rigorous attempt to respond to Carter and New's observations, above, concerning its potential for empirical research. Specifically this is achieved through the application of the morphogenetic approach to a predominantly *micro level* longitudinal case study of IS development (framed within a broader setting of organisational change) in English local government – Council X.

The *approach* to this task is also original, for several related reasons. First, because it engages with *all three* morphogenetic/static cycles – structural, cultural and agential – and therefore with three types of emergent property and their related causal processes and powers (Figures 1.2). This contrasts with the approach taken by those scholars noted above, and others discussed in later chapters, who tend to focus primarily on one strata and/or type of morphogenetic cycle (i.e. cultural, structural, agential) and the relevant emergent properties and causal powers, when applying the morphogenetic approach, as Archer (1995, 1998c) does, for example, with culture, Kowalczyk (2004) does with structures and Moren and Blom (2003) do with agency.

Second, and as Figure 1.4 illustrates, this "holistic" approach – covering structures, mechanisms and events – represents an intensive programme of research which produces results of a depth and breadth not often seen in this kind of social science research (not least because of the resource constraints discussed in Chapter 7).

Finally, as well as the detailed account of the *application* of the morphogenetic approach to a specific case study, and of the findings and outcomes, given in Chapter 4–6, the concluding chapter of this book – Chapter 7 – reflects back on the use of Archer's approach and therefore presents a broader *assessment* of its potential (i.e. utility) for the type of empirical research reported here.

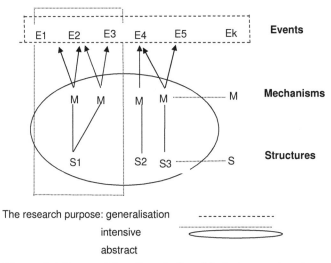

Figure 1.4 Researching the relationship between structures, mechanisms and events

Dobson 2002:13, from Sayer 1992

As noted at regular points throughout Chapters 4–6, and discussed fully in the concluding chapter, this intensive approach is not without its problems. Nevertheless, it will be argued (as Archer does) that the complexity of the relationship between structure, culture and agency '…remains hopelessly indefinite unless the interplay between them is unravelled over time to specify the where, when, who and how – otherwise we are left with the vagaries of mutual constitution.' (Archer 1995:274). Hence this book attempts to capture this 'interplay' by documenting and analysing the cultural, structural and agential domains over time, and thus produce new insights into the complexity of IS developments in local government and in what has been conceptualized, as noted above, as the 'information polity' (Taylor and Williams 1991, Bellamy and Taylor 1994).

How? The examples that follow are by no means exhaustive, as will become clear from the discussion in the next chapter, but are relevant as illustrations of how this book will progress. First, the stratified approach noted above, when applied to people, for example, enables the differentiation and analysis of the social interaction of people, whether as collectivities (i.e. as either or both corporate and primary agents); as actors (i.e. as individuals with roles within social structures); or as people (i.e. as individuals with a personal identity) and the different causal powers of each. For example, how do the causal powers of IS 'project champions' change as they move between roles as individual, actor and primary and/or corporate agent? A stratified analysis adds considerably to the granularity of analysis that is possible than if people are only considered as either actors or agents, and/or if the one is taken as synonymous with the other, as is a commonplace approach in a good deal of social science research.

Second, retroduction (i.e. the process of identifying which mechanisms and causal powers are active, where and when) should allow for a fuller account to be given of what – in terms of vested interests, opportunity costs, exchange and power – produces specific states and changes. As was made clear above, little attention is paid to this process, and thus to the identification of causal powers, in 'mainstream' social research where the focus is most usually on events/outcomes.

Third, the morphogenetic approach starts with the identification and analysis of the structural and cultural influences that condition and shape the ideational and discursive domains of agents, and thus their actions and strategic direction, at a specific point in time (in this case when field research began). This fully recognises the crucial claim of critical realism that structure and culture pre-exist contemporary action and therefore action in the present can only be fully understood by first examining the circumstances that confront people at the start of any empirical research. In addition, and importantly, the focus on complementarities and contradictions in any agency/structure relationship, and the way these are identified and analysed, allows for an account to be given of the conditions for morphogenesis or morphostasis (i.e. change or status quo) and the form of any change that may emerge. As the earlier discussion of conflation made clear, neither of these features are commonplace in 'mainstream' social research.

The final feature of this book to highlight is that although a morphogenetic approach is only applied here to one case it is likely that the analysis and conclusions drawn resonate with examples of IS development from other settings and environments. Consequently, it is argued that this book has a far wider applicability, value and importance, than for public administration alone. This is because IS development/informatization (in one form or another) remains part of a large-scale drive towards organisational change across governments and public sectors around the world. In fact, if anything, the importance of ICTs to organisational development and change, as well as to social and economic change generally, has increased since work on this book began. This was clearly evident from the discussion of contemporary developments in central government in the UK earlier in this chapter. Furthermore, as the so called information age progresses it is highly likely that organisational and institutional change will become even more closely bound to the availability and capabilities of IS/ICTs. There is no hesitation in claiming, therefore, that almost all examples of organisational/institutional change are now examples of IS development/informatization, even though few may recognise such a situation or use this term to describe it.

The structure of this book

The rationale and background to the research for this book and to the ontological, epistemological and methodological preferences that underpin it have now been set out in some detail. The next chapter introduces critical realism and then moves on to detail and discuss its 'methodological complement' – Archer's morphogenetic approach. This discussion then forms the basis for introducing and explaining how

Archer's methodology is applied to the Council X case study that forms the basis of this book.

Chapter 3 deals with the research strategy and methods employed for this research. The starting point for this exercise is a detailed review of the methods used, of the case study approach, and of the advantages and disadvantages and problems and issues that arose during the process of empirical research. This is then framed by a discussion of how the research approach that applied at the time of data collection was subsequently amended by the move towards critical realism and the application of the morphogenetic approach to data analysis.

Chapters 4 to 6 cover the presentation and analysis of data as it relates to the stages of the multi dimensional model of the cycle of change (the morphogenetic cycle) discussed at length in chapter 2. In other words, chapters 4 to 6 explore the way in which structural and cultural conditioning and ideational and discursive shaping took place (Chapter 4); how social interaction and ideational and discursive reshaping followed (Chapter 5); and, whether or not the outcome was morphogenesis or morphostasis (Chapter 6). In short, Chapters 4 to 6 represent the 'analytical narrative' (or history) that Archer (1995) argues should be a primary outcome of the application of the morphogenetic approach. Finally, and as noted above, Chapter 7 concludes the book by assessing the potential of the morphogenetic approach for the kind of empirical research reported here, and discusses some of the most significant outcomes and implications for future research of this kind.

2

CRITICAL REALISM AND THE MORPHOGENETIC APPROACH

Critical Realism

'Critical realism is a philosophy of social science, not a social theory...' (Sayer 2004:16), and therefore, as noted at the beginning of this book, it takes a specific ontological and epistemological standpoint '...that allows positivism and its empirical realist ontology to be abandoned without the researcher having to accept extreme forms of relativism and its strong social constructionist ontology.' (Fleetwood and Ackroyd 2004:3). The term 'realism' has acquired a variety of different meanings in recent decades, however. Therefore it is crucial to establish from the outset that a major distinction exists between critical realism and the most commonly cited variety of realism - empirical realism. Thus, while all '...realists are united by a rejection of the view that the world is created by the minds of human observers.' (Johnson and Dubberley 2000:149) *critical realists* would not subscribe to the view (of empirical realists) that '...what is real is only that which can be observed and measured – in other words, the objects of direct sensory experience.' (ibid:149). Instead the view is that:

> By 'concrete' we mean something real, but not something which is reducible to the empirical: we mean more than factual. The concrete object is concrete not simply because it exists but because it is a combination of many diverse forces and processes...It's important to note that whether the concrete is observable (and hence an empirical object for us) is contingent (i.e. neither necessary nor impossible). *The concepts 'concrete' and 'empirical' are not* equivalent.
>
> (Sayer 1998:123. Original emphasis)

Having clarified this issue it is now appropriate to examine the genesis of critical realism, which is widely recognised as having its origins in the work of Roy Bhaskar

(1975, 1979). *A Realist Theory of Science* (Bhaskar 1975) was published at a time of intense debate in western academia about the philosophy of science. The positivist conception of science – as monistic in its development and deductive in its structure – was under concerted attack. However, opponents of positivism found maintaining both a coherent critique, and, specifically, the argument for scientific change and for anti-deductivist approaches to research, difficult (Bhaskar and Lawson 1998). Consequently the positivist conception of science remained popular. Bhaskar's *A Realist Theory of Science* was highly significant in supplying the necessary explanation and coherence to the critique of positivism. Crucially, Bhaskar was able to demonstrate the need for a new account of, and ontology for, natural science, built on the rational insights provided by an anti-monistic and anti-deductivist philosophy of science. In fact, Bhaskar's work was so important that 'It necessitated...a reorientation of philosophy towards a non-anthropomorphic conception of the place of humanity in nature...that culminated in a new *realist* philosophy of science.' (ibid:3, Original emphasis).

Bhaskar continued his critique of positivism in *The Possibility of Naturalism* (1979). His primary aim here was to explore whether it was possible to study society 'scientifically'. That is, in the same way we study natural science. There were already two well established positions on this question – naturalist and anti naturalist. The former, represented by positivism, asserted that it could. The latter, represented by hermeneutics, argued that because of the uniqueness of the social realm it could not. However, both shared '...an essentially positivist account of natural science.' (Bhaskar 1998:xiv) If, as Bhaskar argued, this essentially positivist approach was incorrect, then there ought to be a third, 'critical realist'[2], position (Figure 2.1) which was '...a qualified, *critical* and non-reductionist, *naturalism*, based upon a transcendental realist account of science and, as such, necessarily respecting (indeed grounded in) the specificity and emergent properties of the social realm.' (ibid: xiv,

---

[2] The term 'critical realism' emerges from the synthesis of Bhaskar's terminology: transcendental *realist* and *critical* naturalist (Fleetwood and Ackroyd 2004).

Original emphasis).

This leads, in turn, to a critical realist conception of society as:

> ...both the condition and outcome of human agency and human agency both
> reproduces and transforms society...It means that agents are always acting in
> a world of structural constraints and possibilities that they did not produce.
> Social structure, then, is both the ever present condition and the continually
> reproduced outcome of intentional human agency. Thus people do not marry
> to reproduce the nuclear family or work to sustain the capitalist economy.
> Yet it is the unintended consequence (and inexorable result) of, as it is the
> necessary condition for, their activity.'
> (Bhaskar and Lawson 1998: xvi).

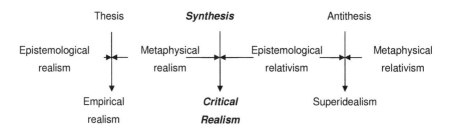

**Figure 2.1 Bhaskar's synthesis of realism and relativism creating critical
realism**

Johnson and Duberley 2000:153

What is apparent from the quotation above is that this conception of social structure
clearly differs from the most commonly held views in the social sciences of what
social structures are. Thus, as Porpora (1998) notes, they are not patterns of aggregate
behaviour that are stable over time (as exchange theory and some variants of
symbolic interactionism would argue). Nor are they law-like regularities that govern
the behaviour of social facts (as structural sociologists believe), or collective rules

50

and resources that structure behaviour (the position taken by structuration theorists). Instead, critical realists argue that social structure can best be conceptualised as:

> ...a nexus of connections [amongst human actors], causally affecting their actions and in turn causally affected by them. The causal effects of structures on individuals manifest themselves in certain structured interests, resources, powers, constraints and predicaments that are built into each position by the web of relationships. These comprise the material circumstances in which people must act and which motivate them to act in certain ways. As they do so, they alter the relationships that bind them in both intended and unintended ways.
> (Porpora 1998:344).

It is important to add, however, that the assumption that individuals will be motivated to act on the interests structured into their social positions is not a deterministic one since: 'Interests always represent presumptive motives for acting, but actors may fail to recognise their interests, and even when they do recognise them, they may choose to act against them in favour of other considerations.' (ibid:344).

Although critical realists would argue that Johnson and Duberley fail to fully represent the ontological, epistemological and judgemental rationalism of critical realism, Figure 2.2 does in broad terms illustrates the epistemological and ontological position of critical realism when compared to a variety of the common approaches to organisation and management research. Acceptance of subjectivist epistemology and objectivist ontology is significant in that it illustrates the rejection by critical realism of any attempt to collapse ontology and epistemology into one another (Archer 1995, 1998a, Collier 1998, Sayer 1998). Fundamentally, and as noted previously, this sets critical realism apart from many popular characterisations of realism '...since its adherents aim to be both anti-positivist and anti-relativist at once...' (Johnson and

Duberley 2000:151).

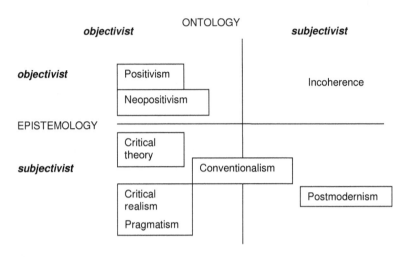

Figure 2.2 Objectivist and subjectivist assumptions about epistemology and ontology: distinctions between schools of thought

Johnson and Duberley 2000:180

From the discussion so far it follows that from a critical realist perspective science – whether natural or social – has two related tasks. The first is '...to explain the causal properties of each entity in terms of its internal structure...' and the second, '...to explain the occurrence of particular events in terms of conjunctures of the causal properties of various interacting mechanisms.' However, '...causation is not conceptualised in terms of a relationship between separate events "C" and "E", but in terms of the changes in each of "C" and "E" (Sayer 1998:124). Scientific "laws" are therefore not understood as well-corroborated, universal empirical regularities in patterns of events, but as statements about *mechanisms*: 'The essential characteristic of law-likeness is not universality but *necessity*.'(Sayer 1998:124. Original emphasis).

Causal properties, mechanisms and the nature of internal and necessary versus contingent relations are all discussed at length below. However, given this book

52

applies a critical realist method primarily to the point of contact between structures and agency *within* an organisation it is worth highlighting that: 'Central to this analysis *is the location of micro-level ethnographic descriptions of members' activities within the explanatory context of the complex interplay of macro-level structures which constrain members' activities.'* (Johnson and Duberley 2000:165–166. Emphasis added). The separability of structure and agency (i.e. analytical dualism) is indispensable to the fulfilment of this analysis because it allows us to:

(a) identify the emergent structure(s), (b) to differentiate between their causal powers and the intervening influences of people due to their quite different causal powers as human beings, and, (c) to explain any outcome at all, which in an open system always entails an interplay between the two. (Archer 1995:70).

Details of emergent structures and properties, of casual powers and mechanisms, of the powers and positions of people, and other essential detail of Archer's critical realist – morphogenetic approach – that was briefly outlined in Chapter 1, are discussed below, Subsequent chapters (4 to 6) then detail and discuss numerous examples of these structures, mechanisms, powers and so on, in the context of the case study organisation – Council X – such as the Local Government Review, and internal development such as organisational decentralisation and devolution and IS 'enabled' developments such as one stop shops. However, as analytical dualism is the basis of non-conflationary approaches to theorising the relationship between structure and agency, and therefore central to Archer's morphogenetic approach, it is to this that attention must now turn.

Analytical dualism

Three premises underpin analytical dualism. Two have already been noted above, that:

- there is full acceptance of a view of the social world as stratified, and;

- the emergent properties of structures and of agents are irreducible to each other and therefore are analytically separable.

The third:

- 'asserts that given structures and agents are also temporally distinguishable (in other words, it is justifiable and feasible to talk of pre-existence and posteriority when dealing with specific instances of the two), and this can be used methodologically in order to examine the interplay between them and thus explain changes in both – over time.' (Archer 1995:66)

Archer concludes therefore that: 'In a nutshell, analytical dualism is a methodology based upon the *historicity of emergence*.' (ibid: 66. Original emphasis).

At the core of analytical dualism sits the identification of emergent properties and what part these play in the shaping of agency. To do this what is required is a way to:

...identify structure(s) independently of their occupants and incumbents, yet of showing its effects upon them (establishing the reality of structures via causal criterion), whilst coping with the intervention of other contingent relations, and accounting for the eventual outcome which either reproduces or transforms the original structure.
(ibid:167–8)

As the discussion of conflation in Chapter 1 established, this contrasts with an approach such as structuration theory, where the two would be elided such that: '...material resources are confined to a virtual existence until instantiated by agency drawing upon interpretative schemes.' (ibid:175). However, the analytical and temporal separation of structure and agency means that the identification of structures, and of structural emergent properties, becomes possible because they predate agents. So, for example, except in rare periods of restructuring, in local authorities the committee and departmental structures predate the majority of the officers and councillors that function within them. This is, as Archer makes clear, why: '...Realists insist that agency does not create structure, but only reproduces or transforms it...' (ibid:168). Furthermore, Archer's proposition is that this dynamic creates 'morphogenetic[3] cycles' which, put simply, run: 'emergence – interplay – outcome'. The detail of these cycles, and of structural (and cultural) reproduction/transformation (i.e. morphogenesis/morphostasis) that is the outcome, is set out later in this chapter. It is sufficient to note here that Archer argues that four basic propositions underpin any practical application of the morphogenetic analysis to the structures that constitute any social system:

(i)   there are internal and necessary relations within and between social structures (SS);

(ii)   causal influences are exerted by social structures (SS) on social interaction (SI);

(iii) there are causal relationships between groups and individuals at the level of social interaction (SI);

(iv)   social interaction (SI) elaborates upon the composition of social structure(s) (SS) by modifying current internal and necessary structural relationships and introducing new ones where morphogenesis is concerned. Alternatively, social interaction (SI) reproduces existing internal and necessary structural relations when morphostasis applies. (ibid:168)

Four equivalent propositions apply when identifying and analysing properties that pertain to cultural systems:

---

[3] Archer notes that the term was first used by Walter Buckley in *Sociology and Modern Systems Theory* to signify processes that either change or preserve '...a system's given form, structure or state.' (Archer 1995: 75, from Buckley 1967:58).

(i)   there are internal and necessary logical relationships between components (i.e. ideas, beliefs, values and theories) of the Cultural System (CS);

(ii)   causal influences are exerted by the Cultural System (CS) on Socio-Cultural interaction (the S-C level);

(iii)   there are causal relationships between groups and individuals at the Socio-Cultural (S-C) level;

(iv)   there is elaboration of the Cultural System (CS) due to Socio-Cultural interaction (S-C) modifying current logical relationships and introducing new ones, where morphogenesis is concerned. Alternatively Socio-Cultural interaction (S-C) reproduces existing internal and necessary relations when morphostasis applies.

(ibid:168–9)

As noted above, the concept of morphogenetic cycles to which the two sets of propositions above apply are discussed in more detail below. Here, however, the task is to continue to explore emergence.

Emergence: properties, powers and mechanisms

Emergent properties are not the kinds of observable features or 'patterning' of social life that are usually presented in social research. Entities, such as socio-economic class, the military, or shop floor workers, are heterogeneous: '...made up of a mixture of taxonomic and aggregative and/or an admixture of people and positions...' (ibid:172). The weakness of applying this kind of categorisation to observables is, Archer argues, that it automatically discounts '...the real sources of phenomena, which may generate no manifest regularities, yet would show those detected to be conglomerations, that is contingent combinations of disparate elements from different strata which happen to manifest themselves at a given time.' (ibid:173).

Relations: internal and necessary versus contingent

Archer contrasts this with an emergent property, which is distinguished from the above by its homogeneity: '...the natural necessity of its internal relations, for what the entity is and its very existence depends upon them.' (ibid:174). The distinction between *internal and necessary* and *contingent* relations (the former often simply stated as *necessary* in critical realist literature) is a crucial one for critical realists when exploring and analysing causation, as the quotation from Sayer (1998), above, on the essential characteristic of law-likeness being *necessity* rather than universality should have made clear. Nevertheless, it is also an area of disagreement. Elder-Vass, for example, questions the view of critical realists, such as Archer, who claim that a prerequisite of emergence is the existence of internal and necessary relations between entities, or parts of an entity: 'The whole conception of internal relations as "necessary relations", however, is problematic...' (Elder-Vass 2005: 324). However, at the time of writing Elder-Vass had not published an explanation of this problematic. Consequently, as the stated intention of this book is to adopt Archer's approach it is her conception of internal and necessary relations that feature prominently in the relevant sections of this book.

Put briefly, while entities can be contingently related and exert influence over each other, if there are no internal and necessary relations then ultimately the entities could exist on their own. Furthermore, where relations are internal and necessary they may be symmetrical or asymmetrical '...as in the case of the state and council housing, money and the banking system in which the former object in each pair can exist without the later but not vice versa.' (Sayer 1998: 127, after Bhaskar 1979). From a critical realist perspective therefore, it is precisely because of the importance of the exploration of whether relations between entities exist, and of what type, that histories of emergence are so important. The question which Archer then poses is how is it possible to differentiate between emergence and other relations?

The crucial distinguishing property [of an emergent property] itself being a relational property [is that] it has the generative capacity to modify the powers of its constituents in fundamental ways and to exercise causal influences *sui generis*. This is the litmus test that differentiates between emergence on the one hand and aggregation and combination on the other (Archer 1995:174).

It is also clear that while generative/causal mechanisms are *always* emergent properties of social relations (i.e. interaction) they are not simply reducible to *any* interpersonal relationships. Archer uses the example of Adam Smith's social relations of pin makers: increased productivity was an emergent property of the division of labour. Womens' knitting circles are also an example of social relations but there are no emergent powers. (Archer 1995).

Causal power may be exercised or un-exercised, or may be obscured at the level of events. For example, a potential rise in the price of petrol due to insufficient supply of crude oil being offset by a country making use of its oil reserves. The morphogenetic approach is, therefore, directed at:

> ...analysing the generative mechanisms potentially emanating from structures (and cultures) as emergent properties and their reception by people, with their own emergent powers of self and social reflection. Outcomes never simply mirror one another, but are the products of their interplay.' (ibid:175).

A variety of examples of internal and necessary and contingent relations are identified and discussed throughout the three analytical chapters (4–6), including, in Chapter 4, inter governmental relations, before the focus moves firmly to *intra* organisational relations in the later stages of Chapter 4 and through Chapter 5. Examples of emergent properties and powers[4], such as policies for community governance and the formation of new vested interest groups, also feature prominently

---

[4] Elder-Vass (2005: 317) takes the view that since a property '...is some intrinsic aspect of an entity that can have a causal impact on the world...Properties and powers may therefore be regarded as synonyms.'

in these chapters. Outcomes of specific relevance to IS development, such as the emergence and growing acceptance of ideas for 'joined up' organisational change premised on the properties of new ICTs, and the development of networked organisational structures – such as one stop shops – are discussed in Chapter 6. At this point, however, the focus of the book remains on detailing and discussing the theory of these concepts.

Causal or Generative Mechanisms

The concept of 'mechanisms', their identification, and the analysis of their effects, is not restricted to Archer's work as they are a key feature of a number of realist approaches to social research. For example, Pawson and Tilley employed the concept in their criminology research in the mid to late 1990s and popularised it in *Realistic Evaluation* (1997). Their definition of mechanism equates to 'appropriate ideas and opportunities' (Harrison and Easton 2004:200). However, as Kowalczyk (2004:298) points out, Pawson's and Tilley's approach: '...does not encourage the researcher to consider what exactly mechanisms or context are.' Archer, however, emphasises the importance of the detail of both, as well as the temporal dimension and of 'feedback' within a causal process (Figure 2.3).

While Archer's approach is more fine grained and nuanced than Pawson's and Tilley's it is important to note that critical realist terminology is rather imprecise when it comes to the concepts of 'causal powers', 'causal mechanisms' and 'generative mechanisms' (Sayer 2004). It is not uncommon, therefore, to find the three terms being used interchangeably. Sayer helpfully points out the distinction between a power and a mechanism: 'The meanings are very close ...causal or generative mechanisms are perhaps more suggestive of *the way of working* of these capacities or powers (Sayer 2004:19. Original emphasis). However, no clear agreement seems to exist over the exact definition of mechanism.

As the definition of a causal mechanism that a researcher adopts is clearly fundamental to both the application and outcome of any critical realist methodology it is appropriate to state unambiguously at this point that the intention here is to work to and with Archer's definition. The outcome of this choice as well as an assessment of a range of different viewpoints, and their implications for empirical research, is discussed in Chapter 7.

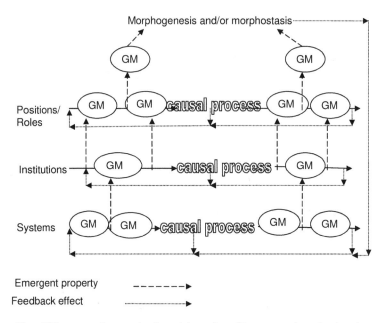

Key: GM = generative mechanisms (also referred to as causal mechanisms)

Figure 2.3 The relationship between strata, causal processes and generative mechanisms/emergent properties

Utilising Archer's definition emergent properties – whether structural, cultural or agential (see below) – are products of (some of the) social relations of the causal processes at work at the different levels of strata and act on the next 'level' of the strata, while not being reducible to the strata from which they emerged (Figure 2.3). That is, 'Emergence occurs when the properties of one stratum [system, institution, role, position] engender, through interaction with other properties, properties on a different stratum.' (Thursfield and Hamblett 2004:120).

Collier (1998) and Moren and Blom (2003) also draw attention to the operation of mechanisms across strata, with the latter drawing on Hedstrom's and Swedberg's (1998) typology of three types of social mechanisms: *situational* – macro to micro; *action-formation* – micro to micro; and *transformational* – micro to macro – to illustrate this relationship. When this typology is applied to Council X the emergent properties/generative mechanisms of the cultural and structural systems of the European Commission and British central government (which were the outcomes of social relations at those level), in the form of ideas about local government as an enabler of services not a provider, and policies for electronic service delivery and the contracting out of services, for example, represent situational mechanisms. These then exert causal powers that condition and shape the context of agents at the level of roles and positions within the Council (i.e. action formation mechanisms) leading, as will be demonstrated in later chapters of this book, to further cycles of morphogenesis or stasis – transformational mechanisms.

Emergent Properties: structural, cultural, agential
Archer argues that there are three types of emergent property. The next task is to highlight the main features and characteristics of each.

Structural emergent properties (SEPs) can be differentiated from other emergent properties because of their '… *primary dependence upon material resources*, both physical and human. In other words, the internal and necessary relations between its constituents are fundamentally material ones: these make it what it is and without them it could not exist as such or posses the causal powers which characterise it.' (Archer 1995:175. Original emphasis). SEPs take the form of roles, institutional structures and social systems. Furthermore, it is important to note that it is SEPs and structural relationships that lead to, and explain why, different people find themselves where they are in society: '…and in turn will condition those with whom they are and are not objectively predisposed to collaborate.' (ibid:178).

Cultural emergent properties (CEPs) need to be separated from what Archer refers to as the 'cultural system' (CS) and cultural agents. This separation occurs by differentiating between logical and causal sets of relations. Thus: '…there are *logical* relations prevailing between items constituting the Cultural System, whereas it is *causal* relations which maintain between cultural agents.' (ibid: 179. Original emphasis). Causal relations therefore relate to people: for example, the influence that the ideas of one person or group can have over another person or group. In other words, causal relations rely on 'agential instigation'. Archer provides the example of teachers on pupils or one generation of thinkers over another. This she refers to as 'causal consensus':

> Causal consensus tends to be intimately allied to the use of power and influence, whereas logical consistency is entirely independent of them since it exists whether or not it is socially exploited or concealed and regardless of it being recognised. Therefore, causal relationships are contingent (they *may* pertain) whereas logical relationships *do* obtain, and when internally and necessarily related they constitute cultural emergent properties (CEPs).'
> (ibid:179. Original emphasis).

In short, when Archer refers to the Cultural System (CS) she is specifically referring to: 'relations between the components of culture' (i.e. theories, ideas, beliefs and values). This is intentionally differentiated from Socio-Cultural (S-C) interaction, which solely concerns 'relations between cultural agents.', although both '…overlap, intertwine and are mutually influential.' (ibid:180). The CS is therefore emergent from the S-C, or to be absolutely precise, from socio cultural interaction that predates the period being studied. However, and crucially, from a critical realist perspective:

62

'Like structure, culture is a human product but it too escapes its makers to act back upon them.' (ibid:181).

The Local Government Review (LGR), a central government policy initiative which features prominently in Chapter 4 and is subsequently identified as one of the most significant features for the morphogenesis of IS/organisational change in Council X in later chapters, provides some excellent illustrations of emergent properties. For example, logical relations between a variety of ideas and beliefs in the cultural system of British local and central government about the tiered system of local government in England and Wales (parish, district, metropolitan district, county, metropolitan county) being too complex for the general public to understand led to the emergence of a range of CEPs (ideas, theories and beliefs), all of which centred on a reduction in the number of tiers of local government. Interestingly, but in line with the discussion of CS and S-C above, the CS and CEPs of LGR were clearly emergent from socio-cultural interaction that predates 1991: namely the widespread dissatisfaction amongst many vested interest groups with the reform of local government in 1974.

The LGR also led to the emergence of a range of SEPs, the most prominent of which was the body which carried out the Review, The Local Government Commission, and the structures and mechanisms associated with it. However, the Review also led to the emergence of SEPs within local government as local authorities sought to respond to the Review. As we shall see in Chapter 4, 5 and 6, as these developments were mediated by people so the Review also impacted on the last category of emergent property – PEPs.

The two defining features of *people's* emergent properties (PEPs) are that: '...they modify the capacities of component members (affecting their consciousness and commitments, affinities and animosities) and exert causal powers proper to their relations themselves vis-à-vis other agents or their groupings (such as association, organisation, opposition and articulation of interests).' (ibid:184). The point has already been made about what predates which and in this case PEPs are '...the outcome of prior interaction in anterior socio-cultural contexts during previous morphogenetic cycles.' (ibid:184).

As explained above, critical realists insist that the world is stratified for both structures and agents, as Figure 2.3 illustrates, and although this phasing across time means that the two are analytically separable there is a double morphogenesis at work: agents transform and acquire new powers as they struggle to reproduce and/or transform structures. The illustration of morphogenetic cycles later in this chapter demonstrates this (Figure 2.4). Thus, through such cultural and structural struggles:

> ...collectivities are transformed from primary agents into promotive interest groups; social selves are re-constituted as actors personifying roles in particular ways to further their self defined ends; and corporate agency is re-defined as institutional interests promote reorganisation and re-articulation of goals in the course of strategic action for their promotion or defence. *All of the above processes are reinforced or repressed by the overall state of systemic integration, whose incompatibilities foster actualisation and whose coherence serves to contain this transformative potential of agency.*' (Archer 1995:191 Emphasis added).

Examples from Council X of systemic integration/divergence, such as the outcome of privatisation and decentralisation, feature prominently in subsequent chapters, while a discussion of the significance of these features of social systems to morphogenetic cycles occurs towards the end of this chapter. First, however, the task is to continue exploring the significance of the tripartite division of agency into persons, agents and actors.

Differentiating actors, agents and people

In theories of social systems based on the conflation or elision of structure and agency it is common to find person/people, individual, agent and actor being used interchangeably. However, as both the quotation above and ten point list of propositions below, illustrate, agency is not static – people in different settings have different emergent properties. Therefore, Archer argues that a stratified distinction, between humans as individuals, as people with roles and positions, and as groups and collectivities who may be more or less 'powerful' in decision making situations, needs to be advanced (Archer 1995, 2002). How many strata is determined by the incidence of emergent properties, thus Archer argues that personality emerges from consciousness, which emerges in turn from mind.

For the purpose of this book the relevant strata are: agent(s), actor(s) and person/people. Agent(s) are further differentiated into corporate and primary categories. The detail of, and reasons for these categorisations are set out below. Suffice to note here that in the context of a micro level study of an organisation such as Council X this allows the identification of, and clear distinctions to be drawn between, the actions of actors as individuals and as members of a variety of interest groups with more or less influence over and within causal processes. For example, in the latter stages of Chapter 4 two key vested interest groups (i.e. corporate agents) in the IS domain of Council X are identified: the Information Systems Strategy Sub Group (ISSSG) and the Partnerships Project Group (PPG). The nature of the relationship and interaction between these two groups, and between them and other corporate and primary agents and actors is then analysed (Chapter 5) and the outcome, vis a vis the morphogenesis/stasis of IS, detailed and discussed in Chapter 6.

Agents

Agency emerges as the end product of the double morphogenesis of structure and agency:

...in which collectivities of human beings are grouped and re-grouped as they contribute to the process of reproducing or changing the structure or culture of society. In this way, they also maintain or change their collective identities as part and parcel of maintaining or transforming the socio-cultural structures which they inherited at birth. (ibid:255).

From a morphogenetic perspective, then, reference to *agents* and *agent* always means that we are referring to collectivities. Thus to use the term in the singular indicates reference to a specific group while use in the plural indicates reference to groups. Furthermore, agents cannot have a strict identity. Nevertheless, what *is* crucial is to register the distinction Archer draws between primary and corporate agents. At any given time *primary* agents can be distinguished from corporate agents because the former '...lack a say in structural and cultural modelling...they neither express interests in nor organise for their strategic pursuit, either in society or a given institutional sector.' (ibid:259). This does not, of course, preclude people who are primary agents in one context/environment being corporate agents in another at the beginning (T1) of a morphogenetic/static cycle (Figure 2.4). This is because '...these categories are *not fixed but mobile* over time.' (ibid:259. original emphasis). Furthermore, lacking a say in the organisation or reorganisation of systems does not mean that primary agents have no systemic effect:

...but the effects are unarticulated in both senses of the word – uncoordinated in action and unstated in aim. Collectivities without a say, but similarly situated, still react and respond to their context as part and parcel of living within it. Yet similarities of response from those similarly placed can generate powerful, though unintended aggregate effects which are what makes everyone an agent.
(ibid:259).

It is *corporate* agency that shapes the context in which all actors operate. Again, this is usually not in a way that any particular agent would prefer but as a consequence of corporate interaction. Meanwhile: 'Primary Agency inhabits this context but in responding to it also reconstitutes the environment which Corporate Agency seeks to control. [Primary agency then] unleashes a stream of aggregate environmental pressures and problems which affect the attainment of the latter's promotive interests.' (ibid:260). Of course, whether or not morphogenesis or morphostasis then occurs depends entirely upon such interaction, which, simultaneously, also determines the morphogenesis or morphostasis of agency.

Archer distils the relationship between primary and corporate agency into a list of ten 'basic propositions' which it is worth reproducing in full as an exploration of this dimension of the morphogenetic approach is an important feature of the analysis of Council X that follows in later chapters:

1. All agents are not equal: the initial distributions of structural and cultural properties delineate Corporate Agents and distinguish them from Primary Agents at the start of each cycle;
2. Corporate Agents maintain/re-model the socio-cultural system and its institutional parts: Primary Agents work within it and them;
3. All agents are not equally knowledgeable because of the effects of prior interaction upon them;
4. All change is mediated through alterations in agents' situations: Corporate Agents alter the context in which Primary Agents live and Primary Agents alter the environment in which Corporate Agents operate;
5. The categories of Corporate and Primary Agent are redefined over time through interaction in pursuit of social stability or change;
6. Actions by Corporate and Primary Agents constrain and enable one another;

7. Action by Primary Agents constitutes atomistic reaction, uncoordinated co-action or associational interaction, depending upon the extent of their participation in a given institutional context;

8. Interaction of Corporate Agents generates emergent properties: actions of Primary Agents produce aggregate effects;

9. The elaboration of Social Agency (societally or sectionally) consists in the shrinkage of the category of Primary Agents, who become incorporated or transformed into Corporate Agents, thus swelling this category;

10. Social change is the resultant of aggregate effects produced by Primary Agents in conjunction with emergent properties generated by Corporate Agents and thus does not approximate to what anyone wants.[5] (Archer 1995:265)

Actors

Actors emerge from the morphogenesis of agency which condition who occupies which of many social positions. In other words, who becomes an MP, school teacher, policeman and so on. Sets of social roles are based on 'internal and necessary' relations. For example, the existence of students demands the existence of lecturers or teachers; the existence of prisoners demands the existence of prison officers; and the existence of voters within a representative democracy demands "politicians" who represent them. Of course, some of these relations obviously depend on other sets of relations: students require educational establishments, which require funding and HE policy and so on. In short, roles do not operate in isolation but in sets and the dependency between them may be symmetrical or asymmetrical.

Archer also makes clear that the distinction between social agent and social actor is only temporal and analytical. They are the same people and therefore actors '…cannot be understood without reference to agency.' It was noted above, however, that when referring to agent(s) this always denotes a collectivity or collectivities.

---

[5] Archer's argument is that the consequences of the conjunction between corporate and primary *action* are always unintended outcomes given that neither variant of agency has sole control of *both* the context and environment in which they operate. This is an argument I question in the concluding chapter of this book.

Actor is always in the singular, as with person, but an actor is distinguished from a person by their social roles and positions and therefore the interests that come with whatever role/position they have. In short, actors '…are role incumbents and roles themselves have emergent properties which cannot be reduced to the characteristics of their occupants.' (ibid:276).

This is a crucial argument as far as Archer is concerned because her approach is predicated on not bundling all of the interests of people as agents into roles: '…but allowing that some interests pertain to Social Agents (privileges being the broadest way of construing these).' She goes on to point out, therefore, '…that as Social Agents, groups and collectivities of people confront problems which are interest-related but not role-related. Secondly, that as Social Agents they engage in promotive activities when tackling these problems, which are too innovative to be construed as '…"games" – since they follow no regulative rules and embody no constitutive rules.' (ibid:278).

People

It may seem that the extensive definitions of actors and agents, above, leaves little or nothing to attach to human being as person. However, Archer's position on this is unambiguous: 'From birth, part of being in the world is to be a Social Agent and part of living in society is to learn how to become one kind of Actor rather than another (and to decide which of these, if any, a person can and will adopt as their own social identity). Important as all of this is, it still does not exhaust our humanity.' (ibid:281). What remains is personal identity – a 'knowing subject' with particular interests and certain opportunities that will have been influenced and conditioned by parentage and social context but whose future is certainly not determined. Persons then become agents (ie. members of collectivities, such as the middle or working class) before they become actors (ie. take on roles). The final point to note is that people remain 'active and reflexive' throughout their lives and thus always retain the '…properties and powers to monitor their own life, to mediate structural and cultural properties of society, and thus contribute to societal reproduction or transformation.' (Archer 2002:19).

Analytical dualism, emergence, mechanisms and the differentiation of agency have now been introduced and explained. Thus the 'tools' for examining under what conditions, and in what location or domain, morphogenesis or morphostasis may occur, are now in place. Bhaskar's term for this is domain is the 'mediating system' – a system that consists of positions that are filled by individuals and practices/activities. Archer synbookes the component parts to come up with the term 'position-practice system': '...where position refers not only to roles occupied by individuals, but also the situations and contexts in which they find themselves.' (Thursfield and Hamblett 2004:119). However, before exploring how agency is conditioned and shaped and provided with directional guidance within this system it is now appropriate to return to a subject that was introduced in Chapter 1 and discuss Archer's concept of morphogenetic cycles.

Morphogenetic cycles
Archer argues that the morphogenetic approach provides the means to operationalise analytical dualism and thus bridge the methodological gap between the '...explanatory power of practical social theory and the ontological strength of the realist philosophy.' (Archer 1995:192). The outcome is a three stage morphogenetic/static cycle covering structure, culture and agency '...each of which has relative autonomy and yet interacts with the others.' (ibid:193) and where how they '...*emerge, intertwine* and *redefine* one another...' over time (ibid:76, emphasis in original) becomes an overarching concern of researchers. Broadly speaking the steps in understanding this cyclical process are to:

- Establish which systemic relationships (i.e. structural and cultural emergent properties) condition action, how they do so and the range of possible reactions to such constraints.

70

- Explore the socio-cultural interaction leading to actual responses.
- Identify the systemic consequences of action and the processes by which these modify the system in turn.

(Archer 1988:144)

Although analytically and temporally separable the three interrelated cycles of emergence – interplay – outcome are continuous and therefore, '…when studying any given problem and accompanying periodisation, the projection of the three backwards and forwards would connect up with anterior and posterior morphogenetic cycles.' (Archer 1995:76). The delineation of the cycles is according to 'the scope of the problem in hand.' (ibid:274), with each cycle containing the same three core stages.

Figure 2.4 illustrates the three stages of the three cycles. As noted in the introduction, Archer claims that by following the morphogenetic approach it is possible to set out clearly '…the conditions under which morphogenesis versus morphostasis ensues from particular chains of socio-cultural interaction, as conditioned in a prior social context [and] the form (though not the substantive content) of social elaboration to take place.' (ibid:294). In short, the approach offers the means not for predictive formulae '…but rather an explanatory methodology…namely the analytical history of emergence.' (ibid:294).

Directional guidance

The first phase of the cycle focuses on mediatory processes. In other words, structural and cultural conditioning is not direct but is mediated through people (whether as people, actors or agents) whose exercise of agential power is in itself potentially affected by '…the social forms in which they are developed and deployed…The difference then between the two kinds of entities and their respective powers is not one of relative influence but of mode of operation, where the effects of the 'parts' are necessarily mediated, whilst the agents stand as mediators.' (ibid:196). Archer concludes, therefore, that a precise definition of how mediation takes place is: '…as an *objective influence which conditions action patterns and supplies agents with strategic directional guidance.*' (ibid:196. Original emphasis). This means that in all situations and settings structural and cultural properties (SEPs and CEPs) provide not only the 'objective limitations' to action but also what projects are '…conceived, entertained and sustained…'. (ibid:197).

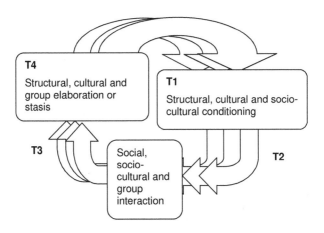

Figure 2.4 The three cycles of morphogenesis
Archer 1995

Figure 2.5 draws on material from Chapter 4 to illustrate this in the specific context of IS and the agents and actors of Council X. This, as Archer makes clear, means that the first step for identifying the morphogenetic cycle (T1): '…is to supply an account of how the powers of the 'parts' condition the projects of the 'people' – involuntaristically but also non-deterministically, yet none the less with directionality.' (ibid:201). It is worth adding, however, that although this is an involuntaristic action Archer rightly reminds us that there are a range of factors that come into play which impact on how agents react to the structured and shaped situations in which they find themselves.

The first is, as noted above, that people have reflexive powers, which means that conditioning is not a 'law' or a 'force' but a reason and that we enjoy interpretative freedom in respect to this. (ibid:208). However, in exercising this freedom, and therefore in responding to the 'directional guidance' that structural and cultural conditioning brings into being, we are influenced by two further factors – vested interests and opportunity costs – which '…condition both interpretation and action.' (ibid:209). Each of these requires a brief summary to illustrate what role they play in this dynamic.

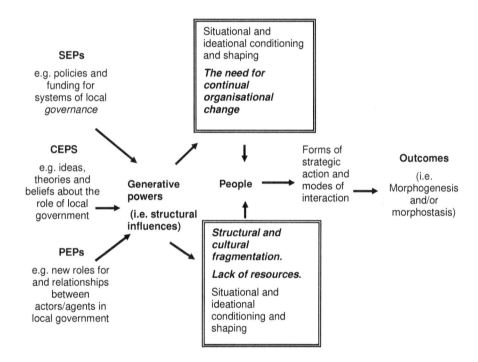

Figure 2.5 An illustration of the objective limitations, directional guidance and processes of mediation within Council X

Vested interest and opportunity costs

Everyone has vested interests as these are a product of the situations in which we find ourselves and, as such, they predispose us '…to different courses of action and even towards different life chances. [interests are] embedded in *all* socially structured positions.' (ibid:203). When people move from position to position, so their vested interests change. However, people do not act on vested interests because they are some kind of invisible social force, or because people are slaves to some hidden law in this respect, but because ignoring vested interests means also '...ignoring the costs that attach to either advancing or defending those interests.' (ibid:205). The bottom line here is that the opportunity costs of any project differ between people depending on their situation in society. Furthermore, '...differential opportunity costs not only affect the ease or difficulty of undertaking the same course of action for groups which are differentially situated, they also condition which projects are entertained by them and thus serve to explain why it is that these can be systematically and diametrically opposed.' (ibid:208).

When pursuing their vested interests, groups in society are predisposed to act either *defensively, concessionally, competitively* or *opportunistically* in their interaction with other groups (Figure 2.6) because there are '...premiums or penalties associated with following or ignoring them [courses of action], which are again cashed in through their positive or negative impact upon vested interests.' (ibid:216). Furthermore, attempts to protect or destroy vested interests represent concrete examples where the pursuit of one or other course of action will contribute to morphogenesis or morphostasis. Thus, when agents seek protection of vested interests they knowingly or unknowingly 'contribute to morphostasis' while attempts at destruction contribute knowingly or unknowingly to morphogenesis.

Reference to vested interests and the opportunity costs of certain courses of action provides clear evidence that agents are not totally 'free' when making choices about forms of strategic action and modes of interaction, and responding to the objective limitations and strategic guidance of SEPs and CEPs. This is only part of the story, however, for the different ways in which systemic properties are related also impacts on how the situations of agents are shaped. This differs depending on whether these

74

relationships are between first, second or third order emergents. Figure 2.6 illustrates this dynamic, while the discussion that follows the figure explains the process by briefly drawing on examples from Council X, as Figure 2.5, above, did.

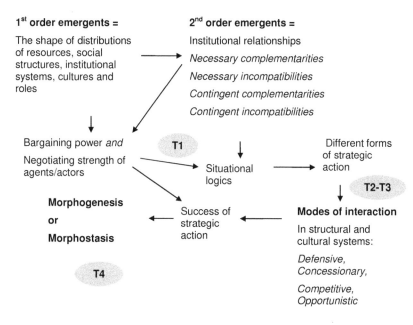

Figure 2.6 The relationship between first and second order emergents, interactions and outcomes

Systemic and cultural integration/disintegration

The final factor that comes into play when considering how emergent properties shape the situations of agents – and thus whether morphogenesis or morphostasis will occur in any social system – is: '…whether such emergent properties are characterised by tensions between their component elements or coherence between them.' (ibid:214). 'Incongruence[6] represents a systemic fault line running throughout the social structure. Whether it is split open remains unpredictable, but its existence will condition strategies for its containment versus its actualization amongst different

---

[6] Incongruence and incompatibility, congruence and compatibility, and integration and divergence, are all used interchangeably by Archer when discussing whether systemic and cultural integration is strong or weak.

sections of the population.' (ibid:215). In short, these compatibilities/incompatibilities and strains and variations are all '...themselves *relational properties*: they have nothing whatever to do with optimal or sub optimal conditions for attaining some super-ordinate goal, but simply refer to congruence or incongruence as the state of affairs resulting from the historical elaboration of socio-cultural structures whose various operations then have to coexist.' (ibid:214–215).

It needs to be emphasised at this point that contradictions (as Archer notes that Marxists would refer to them) apply to *both* the structural and cultural systems because of '...the relative autonomy of structure and culture.' (ibid:215). Thus, there may be congruence in the 'structural domain' while there is incongruence in the 'cultural realm', in this case creating a situation where structures would be in morphostasis while cultures would undergo morphogenesis. In addition, Archer is clear that it is '...the relationship between second-order emergents [that] are of particular relevance to morphogenesis or morphostasis, since the incidence of complementarities serves to identify the potential loci of systemic reproduction and the occurrence of incompatibilities the potential loci of systemic transformation.' (ibid:215). Focusing on second order emergents therefore provides us with '...the bridge between real but unobservable systemic properties (complementarities and incompatibilities) and their impact upon daily experience at the level of events.' (ibid:215). Second order emergents are, therefore, concerned with the realm of the 'actual' in so far as the stratified nature of reality preferred by critical realists is concerned. That is, they are experienced as '...operational obstructions and practical problems, frustrating those upon whose day-to-day situations they impinge, and confronting them with a series of exigencies which hinder the achievement or satisfaction of their vested institutional interests.' (ibid:215).

For the critical realist researcher whose concern, as here, is on morphogenesis/stasis within organisations the focus of attention therefore becomes the position-practice systems of the case study organisation(s): the roles occupied by individuals and the situations and contexts in which they find themselves. Furthermore, what is of primary concern when analysing this mediating system are the four *institutional relationships* between complementarities and incompatibilities that second order emergents create: necessary complementarities; necessary incompatibilities, contingent complementarities; contingent incompatibilities (ibid:216), and whether or not they are contingently or necessarily related. The significance of these relationships is discussed below (and illustrated by Figure 2.6). The important point to highlight here is that these relationships produce different *situational logics* which then motivate agents to pursue the four different *modes of interaction* that have already been noted: defensive, concessionary, competitive and opportunistic (Figure 2.6).

As the opening sections of Chapter 4 demonstrate, when applied to the example of Council X it becomes clear that the first order emergents (structures, systems and roles/positions and the bargaining power of collectivities of agents) were largely caused by the generative powers of the SEPs and CEPs created by the policies and practices of the EC and British central government. For example, the privatisation of public services and the review, and subsequent revision, of the structure of local government in 1974. These policies were more often than not conditioned and shaped by more general changes in the cultural and structural systems at international level, such as the rise of neo-liberal economics.

Second order emergents within Council X arose from the complementarities and incompatibilities brought into being by first order emergents. The imposition by central government of cuts in the funding of local government, at the same time as implementing other policies that demanded local authorities took on more responsibilities (e.g. the human and material resources that had to be diverted into responding to the government's Local Government Review), would be one such example. The resulting institutional relationships created situations which meant that corporate agents had far less scope – both ideationally and structurally – to pursue strategic actions to develop policies that required resources, and this, in turn, impacted on the modes of interaction corporate agents employed within the Council (T2–T3 Figure 2.6).

Not being able to replace the aging mainframe computer with networked PCs, thus creating 'operational obstructions and practical problems' for both corporate and primary agents is another example from Council X. From a critical realist perspective, then, third order emergents not only affected agents as events (the actual) but also empirically, because the *experience* of being a local government officer became far less comfortable, secure and rewarding than had been the case prior to the early 1990s.

Exchange and power

The final factor in the success or failure of any strategic course of interaction undertaken by agents, and therefore of morphogenetic/static outcomes, is the relative power (i.e. bargaining power and negotiating strength) of groups. Thus, as Figure 2.6 illustrates:

> Power itself is profoundly influenced by relations between first and second order emergents: that is between the shape of distributions (first order) which determine the bargaining power of those groups involved in compatibilities or complementarities (second order) and their negotiating strength vis and vis each other.' (ibid:217).

What this means is that stages one and two of the morphogenetic cycle are connected by the distribution of *vested interests* and the *different situations* that confront agents when they try to attain these. Stages two and three are connected through *exchange and power*. The latter is an important distinction because Archer's argument is that concentrating solely on power ignores that there are in fact:

...three sources of elaboration arising from interaction – the confluence of desires, power-induced compliance and reciprocal exchange. [Therefore] ...exchange transactions and power relations are both responsible for social elaboration. Moreover, they are inextricably linked with one another and jointly account for the emergence of either reciprocity or control in the interaction between different groups. [All processes of exchange and power involve] the use of resources, namely political sanctions, liquid assets and expertise. [With] the differential availability of different resources to various agents...providing the bedrock of bargaining power. (ibid:296–297)

At the start of any analytical cycle of the morphogenetic approach the primary concern is, therefore, the identification, where possible, of the '...the institutionalised distribution of *wealth, sanctions and expertise.*' (emphasis added). However, the distribution of resources is not a static phenomenon because different independent factors constantly influence this distribution. Consequently, Archer makes clear that tracking changing resource distributions and how these influence the relations and transaction between vested interest groups is of ongoing importance when analysing interaction. To this end the position of groups vis a vis other groups can be assessed by their position on a scale constructed by reference to the distribution of each of the three resources. Moreover, although the bargaining positions of interest groups can be seen as a unilateral concept (ibid:301) negotiating strength is a relational one. Thus negotiating strength '...is not a generalised capacity, possessed by some groups but not by others, but pertains to interactions itself.' It is a second order emergent and thus '...refers to the emergent "resources and relations" of Corporate Agents vis a vis one another...' (ibid:302). This dimension of the interaction of corporate agents features prominently in the case study of Council X, as the discussion in later chapters demonstrates.

Morphogenesis or morphostasis?

The outcome at the third stage of the three morphogenetic cycles is structural and cultural differentiation/diversification versus reproduction/reinforcement respectively due to the emergence or not of SEPs and CEPs and regrouping, or not, at the level of agency due to the emergence of PEPs. However, the point has been made on several occasions above that all three types of emergent property are relatively autonomous. Consequently, it may or may not be the case that structural and cultural morphogenesis/stasis are synchronised. This is another feature of Council X which emerges strongly from the analysis in later chapters, with some examples outlined briefly below. Archer's proposition is that when morphogenetic/static cycles of structure and culture are synchronised then there are 'reciprocal influences' between them and when they are out of sync one will be '...more consequential for the other, temporally and temporarily.' (ibid:308). By theorising what the condition and interplay of structural and cultural morphogenesis/stasis is at any given time Archer argues that it becomes possible to explain '...what actually results under various conditions of conjunction and discontinuity [of institutional relationships], due to what agency does in different circumstances.' (ibid:308).

Structural and cultural stasis

Archer is quick to point out that this is not on "ideal type" but almost certainly an extreme type, since it is found in reality only rarely. Here structural and cultural morphostasis coincide, with no opposition at the ideational level (i.e. within the cultural system) and with this accompanied by the '...continued reproduction of ideas amongst a unified population...' at the socio-cultural level. In short: 'The force of hegemonic ideas imposes itself on stable social groups and the fortune of the dominant groups reinforces the stability of ideas, the two thus working together for maintenance of the status quo.' (ibid:310). As the discussion in Chapter 4 demonstrates, it is possible to argue that somewhere approaching this type of morphostatic arrangement applied to post-war local government in England (and Britain generally) at least until 1974 and probably within many local authorities until well into the 1980s.

Cultural stasis/structural change

As was the case with the previous combination, culture remains in a morphostatic state which means '…that Syncretism is being made to stick or that Systemisation is well protected by cultural power.' (ibid:313). However, change has occurred in the structural domain taking the cultural and structural out of sync. This means that in terms of the interactional element of the cycle (i.e. emergence – interplay – outcome) the result will be '…a substantial growth in the differentiation of material interest groups.' while one powerful cultural agent maintains. Consequently: 'Culture provides no spur to the *group differentiation of corporate agents which is the genetic motor of structural change, but acts as a drag upon it.'* (ibid:313 Original emphasis). The analysis presented in Chapter 4 clearly indicates that this was the combination of morphogenesis/stasis that applied to the majority of Council X following the implementation of the policies of decentralisation, devolution and privatisation in the early 1990s. Chapter 6 discusses how, in the context of IS development, this model altered over time.

Cultural change/structural stasis

This is the reverse of the last combination, thus Archer argues that the divide is between one powerful structural agent '…and a number of corporate agents that have become culturally differentiated.' That this situation has arisen indicates that as a result of 'internal cultural dynamics' pluralism or specialisation has occurred, with the latter leading to the 'progressive diversification' of ideas, and the former, 'conflict between' ideas, both of which affect the socio-cultural level of interaction fairly immediately. Cultural morphogenesis has the potential to be a particularly powerful motor for more widespread change, Archer suggests, because although it occurs in the cultural domain '…its effects do not stop there because cultural actors are also structural agents. Thus, cultural change leads to the reconstitution of structural subjects.' (ibid:317). In short, the overall effect of cultural change on structural stasis is, as might be expected, '...that ideational change stimulates social regrouping. Chapters 5 and 6 detail and discuss why and how this combination of morphogenesis/stasis developed around IS developments, such as one stop shops and intranets, and amongst vested interest groups, such as the PPG and the ISSSG, noted above, and how and why it coexisted with the previous model within Council X.

Cultural and structural change

The defining feature of this combination is, Archer claims, the rapid transformation of primary agents into '...new, varied and more powerful interest groups...more and more groups acquire the characteristics of corporate agency – namely organisation and articulation.' (ibid:318). As with the first combination, Archer again argues that morphogenesis of both the structural and cultural domains is likely to be an extreme type as the likelihood of the precise temporal alignment of structural and cultural change will be rare. The 'melee' of corporate agents in both the structural and cultural domains, all pursuing divergent and probably competing agendas, ensures that any move to try to reproduce the former '...syncretic formula or resumed reproduction of the traditional systematised conspectus are simply not on...Hence, social interaction and S-C interaction reinforce one another, leading to morphogenesis after intense competition, diversification, conflict and reorganisation in the two domains.' (ibid:322). As will be seen, the analysis of the outcome of the policies of decentralisation and devolution (Chapter 4) indicates that by the mid 1990s (some five years after the initial implementation of these policies) some Departments of Council X had come close to achieving this degree of synchronisation.

It is worth noting that Fleetwood and Hesketh (2006) argue that *explanation* of a particular phenomenon can lead to what they refer to as 'tendential prediction'. That is, while a causal mechanism may not always bring about certain effects it always tends to. A tendency is therefore '...the typical way of acting of the ensemble of structures, powers and relations.' (Fleetwood 2001: 10). Once an understanding of a

82

particular tendency generated in a particular context has been gained it is then possible to make a 'tendential prediction' as to the outcomes that may arise under similar circumstances elsewhere. Hence:

> To the extent that we can successfully retroduce to the causal structures that govern some observation (and there is no gain-saying the difficulty of this), we have a theory that explains this observation. To the extent that we have a theory and an explanation, we have an understanding of the tendencies generated by these structures. To the extent that we understand these tendencies we can make claims about how the structures are likely to govern the actions of the humans agents that draw upon them. We hesitate to call this a prediction...Nonetheless, it is a prediction of some kind, albeit heavily qualified, and we call it *tendential prediction.*'
> (Fleetwood and Hesketh 2006:239–240)

Specific examples of tendential prediction relevant to IS development within Council X are discussed in the latter sections of Chapter 6.

The emergence of critical realism as a philosophy, or meta-theory, of social science and its core principles have now been outlined, and the nature of Archer's morphogenetic approach detailed and fully discussed. However, given that the main aim of this book is to apply the morphogenetic approach to a case study of IS development, albeit set within a broader scenario of general organisational change, and that technology – in the form of ICTs – are a fundamental feature of this, the final section of this chapter discusses where and how technology features in this approach.

Technology as structure

As noted in chapter 1, a number of scholars have argued for the relevance of critical realism to IS research (e.g. Mutch 1999a, 1999b, 2002, Dobson 2001, 2002, Carlson

2004). However, of these only Mutch attempts to make explicit the role of technology in the agency/structure dynamic. Thus, in his latter work he states that '...for those with a social realist approach, the power of technology to reinforce existing structural patterning is an important one.' (Mutch 2002:492). Unfortunately he does not elaborate further as to whether this power is exercised as a material resource, causal mechanism, SEP, etc.

In his discussion of four modes of reality (material, ideal, artefactual and social) Fleetwood (2004, 2005) shows no such ambiguity. He is clear about exactly what kind of entity new technology is: 'The term "artefactually real" refers to entities such as cosmetics and computers. Computers are a synthesis of the physically, ideally and socially real.' (Fleetwood 2005: 201).

When we move beyond literature that is specifically labelled critical realist to that which focuses more generally on IS and the agency/structure dynamic we do find more explicit expositions of the role of technology in the structure/agency relationship (e.g. Barley 1986, 1990, Barley and Tolbert 1997, Desanctis and Poole 1994, Orlikowski and Robey 1991, Orlikowski 1992, 1993, Walsham and Han 1990). Orlikowski, for example, is in no doubt '...that it [technology] be considered as one kind of structural property of organisations developing and/or using technology.' (1992:405). Thus ICTs enable the performance of certain kinds of work, but at the same time they also structure, or restrict, our performance to within set parameters and applications.

Orlikowski, like Archer, does not define this 'structuring' in a deterministic way because she argues that human agency is always needed to use technology, with the obvious implication of the possibility of rejecting its prescribed uses and rules. It follows, therefore, that technology cannot determine social practices, 'it can only condition them.' (ibid: 411). Furthermore, although technology can be both enabling and restraining Orlikowski argues that which of these conditions dominates depends

84

on multiple factors, such as the institutional context in which the technology is embedded, the power and autonomy of users, and external and internal environmental factors, such as resources, politics, and so on.

Importantly, and another similarity with the work of Archer, is Orlikowski's recognition of the temporal dimension of the structure/technology relationship. Specifically, she points out that there is a time-space discontinuity relating to the design and implementation of technology. In other words, the design of a technology usually takes place in a different place and at a different time from the implementation, or use, of a technology. Thus, when studying the development of a technology what is needed is an analytical model which clearly allows us to see that the stages in a technology's life cycle are not disconnected, and artefacts, just as much as the people and institutions in which they are used, are potentially modifiable throughout their existence. Therefore the division between human interaction with technology, in the design and use mode, which directs and informs many studies of technology in organisations, is a false one. In reality the two processes are 'tightly coupled' and highly iterative (ibid:406).

Orlikowski also notes two further influences which she argues are particularly important when studying the use of technology in organisations. The first concerns the situated nature of human action, which is therefore shaped by organisational contexts. In other words, humans are influenced by the institutional properties of their setting, drawing on existing knowledge, resources and norms to perform their work. These influences often go unrecognised and therefore largely remain unquestioned and unchallenged. The reverse of the above has to be the way in which human action (through the use of technology or not) acts upon the institutional properties of the organisation. Typically this reinforces these, although, to a substantially lesser extent, transforming them. In other words, the construction and use of technology is conditioned by an organisation's structures and the adoption and use of technology implies the change or reinforcement of these institutional structures (Figure 2.7).

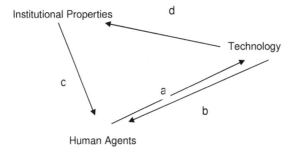

Key: a. Technology as a product of human action; b. Technology as a medium of human action. c. Institutional conditions of interaction with technology; d. Institutional consequences of interaction with technology.

Figure 2.7 A structurational model of technology
Orlikowski 1992:410

DeSanctis and Poole, meanwhile, argue for recognising the importance of technology in the agency/structure relationship by highlighting both the structural and cultural dimensions of technology. The former are familiar to most people – these are the specific capabilities of a given ICT. The cultural dimension of technology DeSanctis and Poole (1994) refer to as the "spirit" the '…normative frame with regards to the behaviours that are appropriate in the context of the technology.' (ibid:126). When considering spirit DeSanctis and Poole argue that we are more concerned with what a system promotes, in terms of goals and values, than what it actually consists of in terms of technical capacity and hardware. Second, taken together '…the spirit and structural feature sets …form its structural potential, which groups can draw on to generate particular social structures in interaction.' (ibid:127).

As noted in Chapter 1, Orlikowski and DeSanctis and Poole both attach a 'structuration' label to the work cited above. However, even on the basis of the brief review given here it is clear that their work exhibits an analytical dualism rather than a duality. This is an important point to note because, as was also made clear in Chapter 1, a leading advocate of Giddens' work (Jones 1998) notes that too often the approaches of Giddens and Archer are combined when in fact they cannot be as they stand in opposition. In fact, Jones specifically highlights the work of Orlikowski and DeSanctis and Poole as two examples of this practice. Thus, amongst other things, he points out that: 'To suggest that structure may be somehow fixed into technology is to separate it from agency and hence turn Giddens' carefully constructed duality back into a dualism.' (ibid:127). As this separation is at the core of Orlikowski's model it is clear that she is certainly not able to claim to be working to structuration theory. Furthermore, Jones' conclusion is that she gives undue prominence in her model to technology, whereas in true '...structurational terms, however, technology is a minor aspect of social practice, if indeed considered at all.' (ibid:127). Insofar as DeSanctis and Poole's work is concerned, Jones notes, amongst other things, that various key concepts of their work, such as 'structure within technology', 'independent sources of structure' and a 'dialectic of control' '...are all directly contrary to Gidden's principles.' (ibid:124).

It is precisely because Orlikowski and DeSanctis and Poole make use of analytical dualism, and therefore that they *do not* adhere to the central tenets of structuration theory, that their work has been highlighted here. As per Archer they argue that the properties of structures and of agents are irreducible to each other and are therefore analytically separable. They then move one step further by arguing that, for the purpose of analysis, it is possible to separate out technology and then set about the task of evaluating what role technology plays in enabling or constraining action, and conditioning and shaping discourse, interaction and elaboration. Fleetwood's position on technology as being artefactually real also allows a similar position to be taken. Given the focus of this book clearly these approaches are all of considerable interest. However, for two reasons extreme care will be taken not to overstate the case for technology here. First, because IS are far more than simply combinations of ICTs, as was established early in Chapter 1. Therefore, all relevant structural and cultural features need considering when analysing the development of IS. Second, because the morphogenetic approach is central to data analysis for this book it is necessary to be absolutely clear about where Archer stands on the technology issue. Unless her views run counter to the discussion above then to remain consistent with the morphogenetic approach it will be to Archer's position that is adopted here.

It has to be said from the outset that technology is seldom mentioned explicitly in any of Archer's work. Nevertheless, it is clear that 'technology development' occurs as 'a *result* of morphogenesis' (Archer 1995:79) and that technology is a systemic *property*, (as it is for Orlikowski), which, in the context of technology use, I take to mean at both the level of social systems and institutional structures. From the standpoint of the morphogenetic approach, therefore, technological and IS development, and organisational change in general, represent the aggregate *consequences* of past actions elaborated over time (and subject to whatever objective limitations, directional guidance and processes of mediation apply to a particular context) which then exert causal influences on subsequent interactions. In other words, IS development would not be the intended outcome, or form, which any one interest group wanted, because, as is the case with structural elaboration in general, it would be the aggregate result of a range of outcomes from various strategies pursued over the same time period by a variety of interest groups. In addition, since ideas, theories and beliefs about the role of technology in organisations, and society generally, are also features of the cultural system clearly technology can also be a cultural property and therefore can and does feature in cultural morphogenesis/stasis.

When this conceptualisation of ICTs/technology is allied to the morphogenetic approach the outcome is that when accounting at T1 for the pre-distribution of systems, structures and roles (SEPs); the pre-constitution of ideas, theories and beliefs (CEPs); and the pre-grouping of vested interest groups (PEPs), and the relative power, negotiating strength, and types of relationships they enjoy, then attention should be paid to where, when, how and why IS, and/or technology specifically, feature in the causal processes of social systems. In other words, and in the specific context of this book: how, why, when and where were IS implicated, in conjunction with other structural, cultural and agential properties, in conditioning and shaping the 'projects' of the staff of Council X at the point at which field research for this book started. Additionally, analysis of the social and systemic contradictions and complementarities, and the extent of synchronisation of morphogenetic/static cycles, should act as a guide to whether the outcome of the socio-cultural interaction observed during the course of the 15 months of field research (i.e. between T2 and T3) results in cultural and structural morphogenesis and thus, whether IS development which supports this is also a likely outcome at T4.

Discussion of the nature and role of technology within a critical realist/morphogenetic approach to IS research, and the resulting statement of the direction from which this book approaches the issue, signals the conclusion of the current chapter. It is appropriate now to move on to review and discuss the overall research strategy and the specific design and methods employed for field work and data collection. The chapter concludes with the re-introduction of the morphogenetic methodology as a framework for data analysis.

3

DATA COLLECTION AND ANALYSIS

Methods: some opening remarks

Research methodology has been described simply as defining '...how one will go about studying any phenomenon.' (Silverman 2000:79). Mason (1996:19) for example, suggests that a researcher's '...intellectual puzzle, and the research questions which express it, represent a large part of your overall research strategy and methodology'. Whilst Miles and Huberman (1984:42) suggest that: 'Knowing what you want to find out leads inexorably to the question of *how* you will get that information.' In short, the clear message from much of the literature on social research methodology is that researchers should select methods appropriate to the investigation of the research questions suggested by the theoretical approach employed (Silverman 2000, Burns 2000). This reflects a similar point made in previous chapters that a researcher's ontological standpoint affects their methodological approach and thus the techniques adopted for data collection and analysis. The task of this chapter is, therefore, to explain the methods that were deemed appropriate for data collection and analysis for the research on which this book is based. An important point to note at the outset, however, is that as the initial stages of (iterative) analysis preceded the adoption of the morphogenetic approach a discussion of the relationship between the initial methods used and those that were subsequently adopted is included where relevant.

Qualitative and quantitative methods

The first issue to engage with, albeit only briefly, is to summarise the qualitative versus quantitative methods debate so as to make plain my own position. The considerable literature on social science research methodology highlights broad criticisms of both quantitative and qualitative approaches, although focusing more heavily on criticisms of the latter than the former. These criticisms have been extensively debated in research methodology literature (e.g. Alveson and Skoldberg

2000, Silverman 2000, Burns 2000) with the crux of the debate, from the qualitative perspective, encapsulated by Borman, Le Compte and Goetz (1986:5, quoted in Berg 1989:9), who contend that criticism of qualitative approaches arises out of 'an erroneous equation of the term "empirical" with quantification, rather than with any real defect in the qualitative paradigm itself.'

Proponents of quantitative approaches frequently point to subjectivity and lack of validity as fundamental flaws in qualitative techniques. However, the existence of strengths and weaknesses in *both* approaches led one prominent scholar of research methods to conclude that: '...the whole qualitative/quantitative dichotomy is open to question...' and to argue persuasively that: '...ultimately, objectivity should be the common aim of all social science.' (Silverman 2000:11). Support for this view is proffered by Hammersley (1992:182) who argues that: '...the process of inquiry in science is the same whatever method is used, and the retreat into paradigms effectively stultifies debate and hampers progress.' Both of these viewpoints are supported here, as is the view that the quantitative/qualitative debate is in fact one aspect of the wider concern with epistemology and ontology, and the nature of conflicting paradigms within social science (Symon and Cassell 1998, Johnson and Duberley 2000).

For some people their paradigmatic position – adopting a more interpretivist, contructivist or deconstructionist stance – means that they have a clear affinity for qualitative methods. For others the choice of methods is simply a pragmatic, technical matter concerned with selecting the most appropriate techniques for the job (Trouth and O'Connor 1991, Symon and Cassell 1998). The ontological and epistemological assumptions at play in the research reported here were clearly spelled out in the relevant sections of the previous two chapters, as were the paradigmatic positions. It was due to experience of a *range* of the latter that the choice of methods for data collection for this book was almost entirely pragmatic. This approach was reinforced because this research shadowed a larger evaluation study. Consequently, the wide ranging nature of that research, combined with the institutionalist beliefs and traditions that informed it, meant that both quantitative and qualitative methods were adopted to ensure a wide range of data was available.

The primary sources of quantitative data were twofold. First, a wide ranging survey of attitudes to, and perceptions of, ICTs/IS amongst staff and councillors of Council X, discussed below. Second, usage data from the Officers' and Members' ICT Pilot Project (OMPP, also discussed below). Qualitative data was largely gained by deploying three separate methods: i. historiographical analysis of a wide range of documentary material; ii. semi-structured face-to-face interviews with a wide range of personnel occupying a variety of positions within the organisation, all of whom were in some way involved in the processes of IS development under investigation; iii. What Alveson and Skoldberg (2000) define as a general ethnographic orientation. That is, close contact with practitioners within the case study organisation over an extended period. In practice this was achieved through participant observation (through day to day work within the organisation, such as attending a wide range of meetings and briefings and generally working on data analysis and reports in the offices of Council X's staff), and involvement in social activities (such as lunch and after work drinks).

By adopting this mixed methodology approach the research reported here treads a middle path between Denzin's and Lincoln's (1994) exhortations to adopt multiple methods and Silverman's (2000:100) advice to 'choose simplicity and rigour rather than the...illusory search for the "full picture". Furthermore, by drawing on the two families of methods it is possible to satisfy the requirements of critical realism, where the use of both qualitative and quantitative methods is regarded as crucial when trying to produce explanations of '...the context in which events take place and the meanings attributed to events by key actors and groups of actors.' (Fleetwood and Ackroyd 2004:131).

A range of important methodological issues that underscore social research have now been outlined and their relevance to this research discussed. It is now appropriate to move on to discuss the specifics methods and techniques used for data collection.

The case study approach

Case studies are commonly used in a wide range of research settings, including policy studies, political science, education and health studies, organisation and management studies and city and regional planning. They have also been successfully applied to IS research (e.g. Calloway and Ariaz 1991, Ledington and Heales 1993, Orlikowski 1993, Mutch 1999a). They are widely accepted as being particularly important to the development of both practice and theory in public administration (Agranoff and Radin 1991), with Bailey (1994:193) arguing that: '...public administration theory could not have developed as it has without the theory building derived from case studies.' Furthermore, when reviewing critical realist research methods Ackroyd (2004:157) explicitly notes the value of case studies, as they provide the context in which generative mechanisms and causal processes work, with context(s) being '...indispensable to the identification of mechanisms.'

In practice many case studies employ multiple research methods, such as interviews, observation, surveys and archive work. It is for this reason that it may be more appropriate to consider case studies as a research strategy rather than a method (Yin 1994). Thus: 'The strength of the case study approach is that it enables the capture of "reality" in considerably greater detail than is possible with most other research approaches.' (Galliers 1991:334).

In general, case studies are relevant when, as with this research, '...how and why question are being asked about a set of events over which the investigator has little control.' (Yin 1994:9). In other words, the distinctive design and need for case studies arises out of a desire to understand complex social phenomena and to allow an investigation to retain the holistic and meaningful characteristics of real life events (Eisenhardt 1989, Yin 1994). Therefore, case studies may be defined as:

- an empirical inquiry that investigates a contemporary phenomena within its real life context especially when,
- the boundaries between phenomena and context are not clearly evident. and
- copes with the technically distinctive situation in which there will be many more variables of interest than data points, and as a result,
- relies on multiple sources of evidence, with data needing to converge in a triangulating fashion, and as a result,
- benefits from the prior development of theoretical propositions to guide data collection and analysis.

   (Yin 1994:13)

Case studies can be explanatory, exploratory or descriptive, critical or interpretative, problem solving or theory building. Single or multiple case studies are possible, depending on the nature and aim of the research. The main reasons for using multiple case studies (i.e. comparative case studies), Yin argues, is to achieve replication in one form or another. That is, cases can be selected to predict similar results – i.e. literal replication – or, produce contrasting results for predictable reasons – i.e. theoretical replication. There are also 'embedded' case studies – the study of a case within a case – perhaps better considered as multiple units, or levels, of analysis. The approach adopted for this book is the latter. The primary focus is social interaction within the position-practice system of a single local authority. However, as the morphogenetic approach is also concerned with how first and second order emergents (e.g. social structures, institutional systems and institutional relationships) condition and shape interaction, and this is therefore a concern of this book, a case study of the position-practice system of Council X therefore represents an embedded case. At an institutional level, however, it represents a single case (i.e. only one local authority is being studied). Yin (1994) cites three main reasons for using single case studies:

- Critical case: where a single case exists which can be used to confirm, challenge, or extend an existing 'theory'
- Extreme/Unique case
- Revelatory: where a previously inaccessible case becomes open to observation and analysis.

Both critical and revelatory case examples are relevant here, for the following reasons. First, at the time field research took place Council X was one of a small number of local authorities who were in the forefront of adopting radical policies for the restructuring of local government and the delivery of public services; or re-invention of government as it was often labelled at the time (Wilson and Game 1998, Stoker 1999). For example, and as the following chapter details, by 1990 Council X had already privatised, decentralised and devolved a wide range of services. Unusually for a local authority at that time this occurred very largely in advance of central government legislation. A significant point here is that these initiatives were all to become integral to the Conservative government's aggressive attempts to reform local government, and move – or force if necessary – local authorities from direct providers of services to an 'enabling' role (Burns, Hambleton and Hoggett 1994, Young and Rao 1997).

Although there was widespread resistance to these policies amongst local authorities at that time, it was clear that change was largely unavoidable as central government had both the power and the will to force through change, as had already been the case with the imposition of compulsory competitive tendering (CCT) – discussed more fully under the section on inter governmental relations in Chapter 4. Thus, the study of developments and events within Council X as a pioneering, and thus revelatory case of 're-invention', should prove valuable in terms of providing a historical comparison to developments elsewhere in local government in Britain. Furthermore, and as Chapter 1 made clear, as the Labour government from 1997 was as committed as its predecessor (Conservative) administrations to reinventing local government (and central government and public services generally) and organisational change premised on the "transformative power" of new ICTs, then the value of the case study remains high.

The second reason that both critical and revelatory case examples are relevant here is that the morphogenetic approach is designed to provide a very detailed, holistic account of the events it is applied to. Therefore its application to Council X represents a critical case because the fine grained nature of the study can be set alongside the majority of less detailed studies of IS in public administration and can therefore be used to confirm, challenge or extend existing 'theories'. Furthermore, the way in which data was collected and analysed (even though the former was not done under the explicit guise of critical realism), in an attempt to understand the deeper *causal processes* that were active in the case study setting, ought to produce outcomes that can be used to *inform* research in other, similar, settings.

Use of *inform* rather than 'generalise' is deliberate, given that it should be clear from the discussion of critical realism in the previous two chapters, and of the morphogenetic approach specifically, that the positivist thinking that underpins arguments for generalisability as the main aim of research are unacceptable. This is a view that is not restricted to critical realism however, with a number of well known and respected scholars arguing that precise replicability is unachievable and impractical in view of the innumerable variables that may influence events within a case study. Denzin (1983:133–134), for example, claims that: 'Every instance of social interaction…represents a slice from the life world that is the proper subject for interpretive inquiry…Every topic…must be seen as carrying its own logic, sense of order, structure and meaning'.

In summary, the focus of this research, as with critical realism in general, is on providing explanations of what produces change – and thus on how causal processes work – through the identification and explanation of the causal mechanisms that link events and how these operate on various levels (i.e. within a stratified social world), while subscribing to the view that: '...social reality is context-dependent, and causal mechanisms are contingent on time and location (Thursfield and Hamblett 2004: 115). However, as previously discussed, *explanation* of a particular phenomenon can lead to what Fleetwood and Hesketh (2006) refer to as 'tendential prediction'. That is, while a causal mechanism may not always bring about certain effects it always tends to (Fleetwood 2001). Once an understanding of a particular tendency generated in a particular context has been gained it is then possible to make a tendential prediction. This is akin, of course, to Archer's argument that certain conditions are likely to produce morphogenesis and others morphostasis and leads directly to the discussion of the outcomes of the causal process associated with IS within Council X in Chapter 6.

The Case: selection

Chapter 1 briefly outlined how the focus of this book changed from a specific concern with electronic democracy to a broader concern with IS development in public administration in general, and how this led, in turn, to Council X becoming the case study for this research. It is now appropriate to expand further on this topic.

Since the late 1980s Council X had been engaged in the full range of activities that were defined in Chapter 1 as informatization: the Council had widely adopted ICT and redesigned internal and external structures and processes that related to this; built up specialist expertise in information processing; had well developed internal and external information relations; and adopted internally and externally relevant information policies. In fact, it was the pioneering nature of some of the Council's IS developments that first brought Council X to the notice of those involved in the PSTAG research project at Nottingham Trent University. Specifically, and as noted above, this related to the Council's development of what PSTAG researchers referred to as either Community Information Systems (CIS) or Electronic Public Information System (EPIS). The latter pretty much describes what such a system is: an ICT based system that allows the public to access a wide range of information (on council services, local events, news, etc), via free standing terminals and kiosks, from a variety of locations within the geographical area covered by a Council. As one of the main aims of PSTAG research was to explore innovative ICT/IS developments by government contact had been made in 1994 with relevant staff within Council X and their CIS had subsequently featured in some of PSTAG's published research (e.g. Bellamy, Horrocks and Webb 1995, Bellamy and Horrocks 1995).

In early 1995 a representative of Council X approached PSTAG with a proposal that we become involved in evaluating two specific IS projects, both of which were part of a broader information management programme. One was a one stop shop (OSS) which was in the exploratory stages of development – an initiative that had emerged from the Council's work through 1993–1995 on the Local Government Review. The other was a pilot project to provide councillors and officers with online access, via the internet, to Council X's email system and information resources, such as committee papers, reports, news, etc. As the research fellow for PSTAG the author was to take day to day responsibility for this work in conjunction with a full time research assistant, and under the supervision of the two senior academics associated with PSTAG.

As the preliminary stages of the PSTAG research progressed through 1995 it became clear that the two projects to be evaluated formed part of a much wider policy initiative aimed at promoting 'local governance '(i.e. the implementation of policies that it was hoped would bring the council "closer" to its customers/citizens by improving accessibility, accountability and responsiveness). A fundamental feature of this policy initiative was that is was largely premised on the availability and capabilities of new ICTs. In other words, certain actors/corporate agents were

98

engaged in the initial stages of what appeared to be a wide ranging process of IS development, which they suggested and/or believed would reengineer and reinvent the organisation in line with much of the rhetoric of the "information age" that was popular at that time. These developments are discussed fully in the following chapter.

When, in early 1995, it became apparent that the case studies of electronic democracy on which the fieldwork element of the initial research for this book was based had not materialised, and as it did not appear that the situation would change in the short term, an obvious course of action was to seek permission to use Council X as a case study of what was at that time often referred to as informatization and/or an example of the information polity. Given the nature of IS developments in Council X, and that access to the Council and a good working relationship had developed as a result of the PSTAG IS evaluation that was already underway, this appeared to be a wise move. There were other important benefits: It enabled the coordination of doctoral and PSTAG field research; access had been granted; and it reduced the travel and subsistence overheads.

Following negotiations with Council X over such things as ownership of outputs and anonymity for participants, permission was given for the Council to become the case study organisation and the fieldwork for this book duly began in October 1995, concluding at the end of December 1996. It is worth noting that an additional two months of planning and "ice breaking" for the PSTAG evaluation studies took place over the late summer of 1995, and the publication and presentation to representatives of the Council of the final two PSTAG research reports took place in January and February 1997. Data from these additional periods of contact has been incorporated into this book where relevant.

Methods and techniques

The point has already been made that case studies typically combine multiple data collection methods, and that the multiple methods employed in undertaking this research were both qualitative and quantitative. In addition to the case presented below for an ethnographic approach when undertaking social research, it is worth briefly highlighting two further points that serve to underscore the value of designing research in such a way. First, the research focused primarily on topics of context. That is, agents and actors and the structural and cultural situations that conditioned and shaped social, socio-cultural and group interaction (i.e. morphogenetic cycles of emergence – interplay – outcome in Archer's parlance). It was therefore important to use methods that enabled the collection of a comprehensive range of historical and contemporary data on a wide range of organisational events and issues. These included the structures, cultures, personnel, management, systems, resources, ICTs, policies and policy making of Council X.

As the relevant sections of Chapters 1 and 4 illustrate, data was also collected and analysed on more general developments in IS within the public sector and more widely, as well as on developments and policy initiatives from central government that had, or were likely to impact on, local government in England. Second, the use of multiple methods created the opportunity for the triangulation of data and thus more rigorous analysis. This improved the accuracy of the interpretation of data and subsequent conclusions. Finally, it is important to make clear that data collection and analysis was iterative rather than linear. In practice this meant that the early stages of the research were more open-ended than the latter stages, by which time a range of 'concepts' (discussed below under data analysis) had begun to emerge and it was therefore possible to be more targeted with data collection.

Ethnography

The nature and scope of IS developments within Council X at the point at which field research began in October 1995 had already been established via the PSTAG IS evaluation research which had begun earlier that year. Thus, for example, and as Chapter 4 discusses, since 1990, in one form or another, IS had been a key feature of an environment of wide ranging organisational change driven by policies of decentralisation, devolution and privatisation. What was also clear, and something which sat well with the ontological, epistemological and research traditions which underpin this book, was that any attempt to get at the "deep" data that would be necessary to develop a comprehensive understanding of the causal processes behind IS development, and the processes of organisational change in which it was located generally, would benefit from the adoption of an ethnographic approach (Shein 1991, Fielding 1993). In practice this involved establishing a presence within Council X as close to the one described by Adler and Adler (1987:67) as 'complete membership', where '...researchers study settings in which they are already members.' This approach, described as '...auto-ethnography, the cultural study of one's "own people"...' (Hayano 1979:100) is derived from an existential sociological perspective, which posits that most people, when referring to their activities, present a "front" to outsiders that may differ from reality. Thus Adler and Adler (1987:21) argue that people: '...manage the impressions they give to others...' and that as a result researchers '...must penetrate these fronts to find out about human nature and human society.'. They conclude that: 'The only way to penetrate people's individual and group fronts is to become an insider, thereby gaining deep and personal experience in their worlds.' (ibid: 21).

Of course, becoming a complete insider within Council X without being an employee of the Council meant there were limitations on how far 'membership' could be achieved. There were, however, a number of factors that went at least some way to compensating for this. The first was the author's involvement in previous PSTAG research into Community Information Systems/Electronic Public Information Systems (CIS and EPIS) which had featured Council X and which had reported favourably on their activities (Bellamy, Horrocks and Webb 1995, Bellamy and Horrocks 1995). This meant that PSTAG personnel were well regarded within the Council. In fact this had been a significant factor in the origins of the second reason for acceptance within Council X: the PSTAG IS evaluation, which, as noted above, was already in progress by October 1995, meaning that the researchers involved – of which the author was one – were recognised figures in and around the Council. Third, was my background in and experience of local government. This provided a source of familiarity with the structures and operations of Council X and, perhaps more importantly, meant the author was 'culturally attuned' (i.e. empathised) with many of the situations facing the actors of Council X. The last point is particularly important because Schein (1991:312) suggests that in order for a researcher to understand 'much of what goes on in...organisations' he/she should come from the same 'host culture'. Overall, therefore, it will be maintained here that for the reasons noted above the position achieved was as close as realistically possible to 'complete member' status and thus '...share and grasp the meaning of the members' world as members themselves feel it, as opposed to hearing members recollect and interpret their experiences.' (Adler and Adler 1987:82).

What should be fairly obvious to anyone familiar with social research is that there are strong similarities between the approach outlined above and what is generally termed action research. The origins of both can be traced back to a desire to apply the tools of anthropology to a wider variety of social science disciplines (Stringer 1996, Alveson and Skoldberg 2000). However, a primary concern of action research as it has evolved from the seminal work of Kurt Lewin in the 1940s (who invented the term), through what is often referred to as 'new paradigm research' and/or 'fourth generation research' (e.g. Reason 1988, Guba and Lincoln 1989) is that it should be collaborative and participatory. That is, researchers and practitioners should both be fully involved in the definition and process of research and in the implementation of any recommendations that follow from it (Stringer 1996, Burns 2000). Indeed, and in common with developments elsewhere in the social sciences, it is for these reasons that action research became popular in organisational studies (e.g. Clark 1972, Margulies and Raia 1978), with a resurgence of interest in the 1990s (e.g. Baskerville and Wood Harper 1996, Maruyama 1996). In fact, the previously discussed PSTAG IS evaluation research is an example of action research. However, despite a research orientation towards close contact with practitioners within the case study organisation (i.e. the position-practice system of Council X) over an extended period (i.e. what Skoldberg and Alveson [2000] define as a general ethnographic orientation, hence the discussion of ethnography above), this book cannot be similarly classified as it was not collaborative or participatory to the levels required of action research.

As with most research methods the 'complete membership' approach is not without its drawbacks. The main criticism relates to a researcher's objectivity. As was made clear earlier in this chapter, this is an issue that has broader relevance as our beliefs, values and assumptions can distort any type of research and its findings. Thus a researcher's biases can produce 'scientific tunnel-vision' (Crano and Brewer 1986:211), where the researcher fails to distinguish between known information and new information. Furthermore, the 'complete membership' approach does have the added tension that a researcher may 'go native'. Nevertheless, while Adler and Adler (1987:81) concede that the 'complete membership' role may diminish objectivity, they contend that: 'While researchers may sacrifice some detachment, the depth of the data gathered via this role is a valuable compensation. Complete membership researchers are able to gain the full openness of their subjects to an extent unknown by any other kind of fieldworker.' (Adler and Adler 1987:81)

Given the aims, nature and scope of the research endeavour on which this book is built ethnographic methods such as above, which deliver in depth data, proved crucial to ensuring that the history of emergence, and thus explanation of the conditioning and shaping of agency, were adequately explored and documented as required by the morphogenetic approach. A stance of 'critical subjectivity', which, it is argued, enables a researcher to recognise their own subjective views and experience without allowing themselves to be overwhelmed or swept along by them (Reason 1994) was also adopted. This process involved initially recognising that the desired state of complete neutrality and objectivity was unrealistic and then consciously attempting to raise self-awareness of this issue by engaging in 'critical self-scrutiny' (Mason 1996). An outcome of this process was the production of a research paper that set out to explore the relationship between researchers and researched in the specific context of Council X (Horrocks and Hambley 1996).

Historiographical

Chapter 2 explained why a key objective of the morphogenetic approach is to account for the situations that condition and shape agency at T1 (i.e. the point at which field research begins, and which also signifies the beginning of the morphogenetic cycle under review for that particular piece of research. Figure 2.4). In other words, provide a comprehensive account of the context in which actors and agents operate at a particular point in time and how this came to be. As the schedule and discussion set out at the end of this chapter illustrates, the objective is to account for the pre-distribution of material resources, such as systems and technologies; the pre-constitution of ideational sources, such as theories and beliefs; and the pre-grouping of agential features, such as vested interest groups and corporate agents and the relative power of these (Archer 1995). Historiographical research is bound to be of primary importance when fulfilling this objective. It is also worth adding at this point that as an institutionalist perspective also emphasises the importance of historical data there was no mismatch between the methods used for data collection and the morphogenetic methodology later applied to data analysis.

There are two main ways in which historical data can be collected – verbally and in printed form. Both proved straightforward, for two main reasons. First, and as the following section on observation makes clear, opportunities to discuss both the contemporary and historical features of the Council were numerous and staff at all levels were generally very forthcoming with information. Second, the nature of local government means that any council produces a wealth of printed material recording its activities and decisions, such as minutes, briefing papers, reports and committee papers, as well as a range of material to publicise services and activities. This situation was enhanced further because local government in the area in which Council X was located had been subject to the Local Government Review for some

104

years prior to fieldwork commencing (coincidentally the Review concluded in the same month as fieldwork began and, as the next three chapters will show, is a prominent feature of the causal processes associated with IS development). As a result, Council X had produced a wealth of information about its functions and activities such as publicity leaflets, newspapers and pamphlets, as well a promoting and enhancing access to Council papers and archives.

The author's lead involvement in the PSTAG evaluation of the one stop shop (OSS), which included both a feasibility study and cost benefit analysis, was also a significant opportunity to collect both historical and contemporary data. The scope of the evaluation meant it was necessary to develop a comprehensive understanding of the range policies and developments that underpinned this initiative in an attempt to understand how it had come about, and to ensure the regular reports from PSTAG to the Council on the OSS were historically accurate[7].

The outcome of the situations noted above meant that apart from minor issues, such as having to wait for the delivery of some documents from the Council X archive, no problems were experienced in obtaining documents of any type that had some element of historical (or indeed, contemporary) significance. In fact, it was more usual for staff to volunteer background papers. On occasion these included internal papers which had restricted access, such as reports and briefings to the senior management group, consultant's reports, and so on.

The ease of availability and plethora of background paperwork and historical documentation, allied to what was emerging from verbal communication, did create

---

[7] These were: *One Stop Shop evaluation and benchmarking* (January 1996); *One Stop Shop: the development stage* (July 1996); *Communities in Partnership: the case for change* (July 1996); *Beyond Information Technology: an interim report* (October 1996); *Communities in partnership: options and issues* (November 1996); and *Evaluating the One Stop Shop Initiative: main issues and recommendations* (February 1997). And jointly with Neil Hambley (PSTAG research assistant): *Information Management Programme Phase 1: Members' survey, interim report* (March 1996); *Information Management Programme Phase 2: Officers' survey, interim report* (August 1996); *Information Management Programme: Final report* (January 1997).

some problems with ordering and managing data and then checking/deciding on relevance. For example, where similar data (i.e. dealing with the same activity/issue) emerged from different sources was it consistent with other data? Did it supplement a "story" when taken together with other data? If this was not the case why? And was it necessary to undertake further data collection to fill perceived and/or real gaps in potentially relevant lines of inquiry that emerged as data collection progressed? The reality was that in attempting to address these issues more data was collected than was subsequently necessary to construct the analytical history of emergence (relevant to Council X) that ultimately emerges from the application of the morphogenetic approach. However, as data collection would have proved increasingly difficult as time passed from the original fieldwork this transpired to be an advantageous position to be in.

One further point worth registering at this point is that as the author was immersed in Council X research of one type or another for a considerable period of each week, with the opportunity for regular discussion of both my work and that of PSTAG, in reality analysis of historical data, as indeed with all data, was not too onerous. Furthermore, and as discussed below, the frequency with which Council X was visited meant that where it was deemed necessary to collect further data, whether documentation or verbal, opportunities were numerous.

Observation
Observation took two main forms. First, participation as an observer in a variety of regular and one off meetings at which various aspects of IS development/organisational change, and related policies, were discussed and debated. The two most significant of the regular meetings were the Partnerships Project Group (PPG) and the One Stop Shop (OSS) development group. Meetings of the former took place every month and were attended by a nominated officer from each department of the Council. The OSS project largely fell under the remit of the PPG, although as the detailed analysis of agential interaction in Chapter 5 makes plain,

other agents were also closely involved. Nevertheless, the OSS remained a development priority for the PPG for the course of this research and the author was co-opted onto the PPG in his capacity as the PSTAG researcher responsible for the OSS evaluation. The management group of the OSS pilot project met monthly and included an officer from the council that owned the building in which the OSS would be located and of another from the council that would also provide some of the services. Consequently, attendance at the OSS group meetings provided valuable insights into the agency/structure dynamic between Council X and other councils, and was therefore a significant aid to the process of identifying which causal powers were active in these situations.

Involvement in the social interaction of the groups noted above meant close and regular contact with staff from most of the departments of the Council, as well as some key external actors/agents. One of the most valuable outcomes of this (apart from helping to establish and maintain my variant of complete membership) is that it often allowed for observation of people operating in the stratified way that was discussed in Chapter 2. This is a subject discussed in the latter sections of Chapter 4 and analysed in full in Chapter 5. It is, however, worth briefly illustrating the significance of this point here. Although it was clear from the outset (i.e. when employing an institutionalist perspective) that the PPG and its members occupied an important role within Council X with regard to the Council's community governance policies and initiatives, such as the OSS, and thus they had a considerable interest in IS developments, it was not until the application of the stratified approach to the analysis of the role of people that the full extent of the role and importance of this group, and its interactions and relations with other groups vis a vis IS developments, became clear. This showed, for example, that the PPG's members collectively constituted an important *corporate agent* within the IS domain. That is, collectively they were able to shape the context in which other actors operated, particularly in respect to IS developments. In addition, as *actors* they were instrumental in processes of discursive and ideational reshaping that took place via other arenas for social interaction than the PPG. This meant they had a key role in the morphogenesis/stasis of IS at departmental and unit level across the Council.

Importantly, several of these actors had been heavily involved in the Local Government Review (LGR), a significant event for Council X, as it was for all English local authorities at that time. Again, the morphogenetic methodology made it possible to analyse how this event conditioned and shaped agency, and IS developments in particular, across the Council, endowing certain actors/agents with specific material and ideational resources (i.e. emergent powers) that were subsequently drawn on in social interaction. As previously noted, the role of LGR in the conditioning and shaping of agency, and how this fed through into IS development, is discussed at length in Chapter 4, while a detailed analysis of social interaction and ideational and discursive reshaping is the subject of Chapter 5.

The second form of observation was less targeted than the above but nonetheless provided crucial insights into, and information about, Council X. It consisted of lengthy periods of time spent at the main offices of Council X (hereafter referred to as Council Hall) in between interviews, meetings and other activities. The majority of this time was spent in and around the Chief Executive's Office, or other departments located at Council Hall. Again this provided an ideal opportunity to try to develop Adler and Adler's ideal of complete membership of the organisation. In practice these periods of quite and unobtrusive observation provided a valuable opportunity to speak with administrative and other support staff, to observe the day to day interactions and relationships between staff, and, perhaps more importantly, between the staff of different units, sections and departments, and to observe, listen, and generally get a "feel" for the agential and cultural dimensions of the organisation. It is worth noting at this point that the amount of time spent at Council X was not insignificant, averaging four to six days per month for at least eight months of the field study, with an average of 2–3 days per month at the beginning and end of the study.

Interviews

Structured, semi-structured and unstructured interviews are recognised '...as major tools in the qualitative researcher's pack.' (Burns 2000:423). Seale (1998:202), for example, argues that: 'The researcher can...use an interview to find out things that cannot be seen or heard, such as the interviewee's inner state and the reasoning behind their actions and their feelings'. The most common way of differentiating between types of interview is by the extent to which the format of the interview is structured.

Semi Structured

The semi-structured or semi-standardised interview allows a researcher to ask each interviewee a consistent set of questions and to explore similar topics, whilst affording the freedom to digress and pursue unexpected areas of inquiry that arise during the interviews but that had not been considered beforehand. This approach has been described as '...an attempt to understand the complex behaviour of members of society without imposing any a priori categorisation that may limit the field of inquiry.' (Fontana and Frey 1994:366). These two arguments underpin why semi structured interviews were judged to be one of the most appropriate methods for data collection in the context of Council X.

There are two further reasons why this approach was generally preferred to more formal or rigid interviews. First, the need for data covering a wide range of events, both past and present, meant that interviewees varied widely, both in terms of their location within Council X and their role and position. When taken together with the requirement for specific information from each interviewee (discussed below), these factors militated against the use of a standardised approach. Second, attempting to gain complete membership status meant that there needed to be room for a higher or lower degree of informality in the way that interviews were conducted, depending on my familiarity with the interviewee. For example, I was acquainted with several of the interviewees from prior research activity into CIS and/or from their sponsorship of the PSTAG research. When this factor is combined with the extended period over which both the PSTAG and doctoral research took place this meant that a close working relationship began to develop with certain employees of Council X. In these circumstances a formal interview would have been highly artificial. In other words, it was important that if the circumstances required interviews appeared naturalistic, perhaps even ad hoc, as this gave the impression of something more akin to a conversation than an interview. In general this resulted in a franker and more insightful, and thus useful, interview.

Interviewees were selected on the basis of their membership of *either* groups which were taking the lead in formulating and implementing IS developments, often under the umbrella policy of community governance, and/or people who were outside these groups but could be classified as 'key' staff. That is, their name emerged from interviews/conversations and/or reports and other council papers as playing an important role, in some way or another, in IS developments. The Council's Records Manager is an example of someone who was identified in this way. As I noted above, the application of the morphogenetic approach allowed for the subsequent differentiation of this aspect of the research, and thus the identification of specific actors, interest groups and corporate agents and of their roles and causal powers in the causal processes under review.

A programme of semi structured interviews was devised and implemented through 1996. Interviews were usually scheduled to last between 45 to 90 minutes, depending on the role and position of the individual to be interviewed and thus the range of questions and topics it was assumed would need covering. In reality, nearly all interviews averaged 90 minutes, and sometimes more, as it was commonplace for interviewees to elaborate at length on topics they felt strongly about – which was often a good deal, given the extent of organisational change staff had witnessed since

1990, as well as the ongoing agenda for change that central government was imposing on local government in general at that time.

Thirty staff at various levels, including the Chief Executive, a Deputy Chief Executive, two Assistant Directors, three principal policy analysts, and various project, section, and unit managers from nearly all departments were interviewed initially. A number of other staff working at more junior levels and capacities within the organisation, but who fell within the 'key' criteria listed above, were also interviewed later, as was the IS consultant who had been working within the Chief Executives Office for a considerable time. In addition, and as I noted above, during the course of the year, and because of the frequency of visits to Council X, there were numerous occasions when it was possible to have informal discussions on any number of matters with a wide range of staff. This proved particularly valuable for developing an understanding of IS developments within the Council from the perspective of *primary agents*.

Structured interviews

Data collected in the course of the PSTAG evaluation of the Officers' and Members' ICT Pilot mentioned earlier in this chapter, which was contained in three reports[8], was also drawn on for this book where appropriate. Although this dimension of the PSTAG research was largely the day to day responsibility of the PSTAG research assistant, my limited involvement was valuable as it brought me into contact with Council X's councillors. Through the resulting conversations it was possible to gain an insight into the views and opinions of Council X from the perspective of the Council's party political wing, who generally had much less knowledge of IS development within the Council. In addition to this informal contact, fifteen councillors were formally interviewed for PSTAG research, with roughly equal

---

[8] *The Information Management Programme Phase 1: Members' survey, interim report* (March 1996*); The Information Management Programme Phase 2: Officers' survey, interim report* (August 1996*); The Information Management Programme: Final report* (January 1997).

numbers from each of the main political parties, plus the sole councillor from the Green Party. In addition, twelve people (eight officers and four councillors) participated in focus groups to discuss the general theme of ICT, networking and community governance. These interviews were structured (although time was allowed at the end of each session for any additional comments the interviewees would like to make) as the aim was to test out some of the findings of the wide scale survey of officer's and members' attitudes to ICT/IS (see below), as well as to tease out issues that had emerged from the survey but had not been answered by it. For example, we were keen to find out where people were getting their information on ICT developments – TV, press, colleagues, etc.

The protocol for dealing with all interviews was the same: interviews were taped and then transcribed by a member of the administrative staff at Nottingham Trent University. Additionally, and importantly, the interviewers own observations and opinions concerning individual interviews were dealt with in two ways. First, initial impressions, key points and possible leads or further lines of inquiry were recorded in note form during or as soon after an interview as possible. On the occasions where two researchers had been present at Council X then this could be done via a debrief on the return journey to Nottingham. On those occasions where the author worked alone observations were recorded on the drive home and then notes made from the tape the following day. Observations and issues which emerged over the course of several interviews with different people were noted and cross referenced. Where there was a discrepancy this was followed up, where possible, by reference back to the relevant people. Observations and information from other sources, such as meetings and informal discussions, were also noted and/or taped and data subsequently matched, where appropriate, with relevant interview transcripts.

Surveys

A central feature of the Information Management Programme noted above was an extensive survey of attitudes to and knowledge and use of ICT in the workplace. The questionnaire was distributed through the spring of 1996. For the officers' survey a process of stratified random sampling was used to ensure that the ratios of variables, such as age, gender and department would be as close to that which applied to Council X as a whole. The questionnaire was subsequently circulated to 250 officers above senior officer scale 2 (i.e. those officers with managerial responsibilities of some kind or another) and 197 questionnaires were returned, which represents a response rate of 78.8%, which is exceptional. The same questionnaire was sent to all 70 councillors. There were 55 responses, which represents a 78.5% response rate, which is again exceptional. There was a correlation between those who did not respond and political party, with a higher response from Labour and Liberal Democrat councillors.

Although the surveys were not directly designed to aid and elaborate on the research for this book the results did prove valuable in a number of ways. First, in informing the design and targeting of interviews by, for example, providing evidence of which departments appeared to be more or less in favour of ICT/IS developments. Second, in providing an invaluable insight into the cultural dimension of the Council, and thus of the pre-constitution of ideas, theories, beliefs and values of agents that applied in the early stages of my research. Data from several other surveys was also made available during the course of my fieldwork. For example, as part of Local Government Review Council X had carried out extensive surveys of the information and communication needs of parish and town councils. Also, a survey of departmental communications needs. Both provided useful additional data.

The Officers' and Members' ICT Pilot Project (OMPP)

This research was based on the provision of a package of off-line and on-line PC based applications (specifically email, file transfer, access to the internet and a range of information resources on disc) to a sample group of officers and members (16 of each) over a six month period in 1996. The pilot was constructed to allow evaluation on a number of levels: weekly monitoring of use and the investigation of any problems and issues that emerged; an assessment of whether and to what extent the pilot raised the awareness of participants and other staff of the 'potential' of new ICTs; and, finally, an assessment of costs and benefits.

Put briefly, the results of the pilot showed that once technical issues had been resolved both staff and councillors soon realised the benefits of the new technologies made available to them, and their awareness of the potentialities increased accordingly. However, the pilot also highlighted a range of issues relating to such things as technical support, training and education, security, and, perhaps most importantly, the ability of the Council to adequately resource such a project at a time of deep financial cuts imposed by central government. Furthermore, the operation and subsequent findings of the pilot highlighted a range of organisational and managerial issues which were also beginning to feature prominently in data from other sources such as interviews. Many of these issues appeared to stem from the policies of privatisation, decentralisation and devolution that had been adopted in the early 1990s. Subsequent analysis of this data using the morphogenetic approach, reported on fully in Chapter 4, strongly suggests that this is evidence of systemic contradictions and discontinuities within Council X and that these play a prominent part in conditioning and shaping agency at T1.

The methods used for the research for this book have now been set out and discussed. Before moving on to detail how data analysis was undertaken one final point remains to be made. The nine PSTAG research reports on Council X produced between January 1996 and February 1997 (for details see footnote above) document a pioneering attempt by Council X (or, more specifically, certain actors and agents within the Council) to explore the threats and opportunities inherent in the emerging ICT/IS systems of the time, and the organisational, managerial and political issues associated with such developments. Importantly, it was precisely because of the nature of the PSTAG research, and the insights it produced, that convinced the author that there was value in adopting a methodology that allowed a more comprehensive

114

analysis of the complexity of the structural and agential relationships of Council X and thus of the causal processes behind IS development. The result, as discussed in Chapter 1, was the adoption in 1998 of Archer's morphogenetic approach and its application, from late 2001 onwards, to the ordering and analysis of case study data. Of course, this begs the question of what was the basis for analysis prior to this date.

Data analysis pre the morphogenetic approach

The approach to data analysis used prior to the explicit adoption of the morphogenetic approach was based on grounded theory (e.g. Glaser and Strauss 1967, Turner 1983, Martin and Turner 1986, Strauss and Corbin 1990). The reasons for being attracted to analytical techniques framed by grounded theory were threefold. First, a major premise of grounded theory is that to produce accurate and useful results the complexities of organisational context have to be incorporated into an understanding of the phenomena, rather than simplified or ignored (Martin and Turner 1986, Guba and Lincoln 1989, Pettigrew 1985, 1990, Stringer 1996). Second, grounded theory '…facilitates the generation of theories of process, sequence, and change pertaining to organisations, positions, and social interaction.' (Glaser and Strauss 1967:114). Third, grounded theory takes both an iterative and comparative approach (requiring a steady movement between concept and data and a constant comparison across types of evidence) to control the conceptual level and scope of the emerging theory. It is particularly appropriate to this book, therefore, because '…this provides an opportunity to examine continuous processes in context in order to draw out the significance of various levels of analysis and thereby reveal the multiple sources of loops of causation and connectivity so crucial to identifying and explaining patterns in the process of change.' (Pettigrew 1989:14).

The specific technique used for data analysis was a form of content analysis based on open and axial coding (Straus and Corbin 1990) which clearly complements a grounded theory approach and which has been successfully used for IS research (e.g. Toraskar 1991, Orlikowski 1993). Open coding consists of identifying possible concepts and their dimensions and properties, with the primary objective being that data is read and categorised into concepts suggested by the data rather than imposed from outside. Once this has been done axial coding takes place; concepts are organised by recurring themes which link a number of associated concepts. In other words, connections are made between concepts and/or groups of concepts in an effort to construct a more comprehensive schema. The outcome is the generation of a set of themes, categories and associated concepts that describe the critical elements (conditions, events, experiences and consequences), their linkages, and how they interact.

As noted above, data collection, coding and analysis proceed iteratively. In practice this meant that the early stages of the research were more open-ended than the later stages, by which time a range of concepts had begun to emerge and it was therefore possible to identify further data needs and decide on what methods were required to satisfy them. Some of the strongest concepts to emerge at a relatively early stage (bracketed, where appropriate with examples of their dimensions/properties) were:

- Party political divides (e.g. no party had an overall majority on the Council)
- Division of responsibility (e.g. who should be taking the lead on IS development?)
- Internal politics (e.g. devolution had increased departmentalism)
- Loss of in house ICT (e.g. privatisation had undermined the quality and autonomy of ICT/IS development)
- Financial cuts (imposed by central government)
- Lack of IS strategy (e.g. privatisation had created a vacuum in this area, as had other internal developments)
- Community governance (e.g. how to respond to this emerging policy direction)
- ICTs as Trojan Horses (e.g. using new technology to "launch" other types of organisational change)

- The Local Government Review (e.g. dealing with the bad blood created by the process, particularly with other local authorities, and what polices should be pursued once the Review was over).

Later joined by such things as:

- Lack of IT skills (e.g. funding cuts and privatisation had undermined training provision)
- Information Management (e.g. what to do about it)
- Disparate systems (e.g. as a result of organisational change).
- Loss of ICT intelligence (e.g. due to privatisation of the ICT/IS function)
- The 'centre' versus departments (e.g. as a result of organisational change)
- The divide within the CE's office (e.g. as a result of organisational change)
- Networks (e.g. internal and external. Complexity)
- The intelligent client (e.g. responding to the privatisation of the ICT/IS function)
- Partnerships (e.g. who with? Why? Internal and external)
- Accountability (e.g. why? Responding to the LGR)
- Duplication (e.g. lack of leadership and strategic management)
- Security (e.g. of the internet)
- Accessibility (e.g. for the public, for members)

Once the concepts had been organised the recurring themes that emerged were:

- Decentralisation (organisational)
- Devolution (organisational)
- Contracting out (of functions and services once provided in house)
- Technological solutions (to organisational issues)
- Organisational relations (intra and inter)

These "sub" themes can then be set within three overarching themes of:

- The need for continuing organisational change (cultural and structural)
- Organisational fragmentation (cultural and structural and how to rectify this)
- Resources (how to do more with less)

Before further discussion of the next stage of analysis two points require elaboration. First, the emergence of some key (or core) concepts at a relatively early stage in the research process is not uncommon: Martin and Turner (1986), Eisenhardt (1989), Toraskar (1991), and Orlikowski (1993), all note such an occurrence from their own research. Second, this occurrence early in the process of data collection should not be taken to imply a narrowing of focus, or loss of flexibility in the research process. As Martin and Turner (drawing on Glaser and Strauss 1967) note, this is because… 'As one's theory emerges, more useful concepts will remain and less helpful ones will fall into disuse. If a concept is useful, one (typically) discovers it often and members of the organisation under study can recognise and relate it to their experiences…The grounded theory methodology encourages the researcher to take steps, through the rotating cycle of collection and analysis to determine if one's theory is genuinely useful for addressing the phenomena under study.' (Martin and Turner 1989:149). In other words '…no construct is guaranteed a place in the resultant theory (Eisenhardt 1989:536).

In fact work on this book was suspended for several years. On returning to the project it was encouraging to see that in the intervening years more had been published by Archer and others on the morphogenetic approach specifically, and critical realism in general, as the discussion towards the end of Chapter 1 illustrates (e.g. Archer 1998b, 2002, Mutch 1999a, 1999b, 2002, Carter and New 2004). Consequently, a major task on restarting this book was to become (re) acquainted with the relevant literature. This proved to be a considerable enterprise in its own right, as it became increasingly obvious that to fully understand Archer's work, and thus be confident in the application of the morphogenetic approach, it was necessary to be more deeply immersed in critical realist literature. However, undertaking this work simply underscored the belief that the morphogenetic approach offered the depth and rigour, and met the preferred ontological and epistemological criterion, for it to be the approach adopted here.

Applying the morphogenetic approach

Full details of the morphogenetic approach were discussed in Chapter 2 and so there is little to be gained from repeating that material here, except to be reminded that: 'The end-point and the whole point of examining any particular cycle is that we will then have provided an analytical *history* of the emergence of the problematic properties under investigation. (Archer 1995:91, Original emphasis).

The staged nature of the morphogenetic approach provides the basis for identifying what data is needed and how it should be sorted and ordered. Therefore, when evaluating data for its relevance and significance at the start of research (i.e. T1) what is of interest is material that throws light on:

- the pre-distribution of structural emergent properties (SEPs): i.e. social systems, institutional structures and roles.
- the pre-constitution of cultural emergent properties (CEPs): i.e. ideas, theories and beliefs.
- the pre-grouping of peoples' emergent properties (PEPs): i.e. vested interest groups/corporate agents, and the relative power [i.e. bargaining power = liquid assets, political sanctions and expertise; plus negotiating strength] and types of relationships [i.e. internal and necessary or contingent] of these).

(Archer 1995)

Furthermore, when undertaking this task further direction as to what may or may not be "in scope" can be gained by keeping in mind that the primary objective at T1 is to account for the situations in which actors and agents find themselves at that specific point in time. Establishing this baseline then allows movement to the next stage of data analysis, T2–T3 (below). Evidence of social and systemic contradictions/complementarities or conjunction/discontinuity is also being sought at this stage as this should provide a guide as to whether morphogenesis or morphostasis will be the outcome at T4 (Archer 1995).

Similarly for T2/T3 the focus when ordering and analysing data is:

- Identifying how interaction takes place, where, why and by which of the groups identified at T1.
- Tracking the changing resource distributions of different vested interest groups and how these influence the relations and transactions between them.
- Identifying the different forms of interaction (i.e. defensive, concessionary, competitive, opportunistic) between different groups.

(Archer 1995)

Again, when undertaking this task further direction as to what may or may not be "in scope" can be gained by keeping in mind that the key objective at T2–T3 is the analysis and evaluation of the different courses of action open to agents and how the opportunity costs of each are confronted and played out through social, socio-cultural and group interaction.

Finally, at T4 the objective is to evaluate what the outcome of interaction has been in terms of structural, cultural and group elaboration (i.e. morphogenesis or morphostasis, or, in plain English, reproduction or change) as well as an analysis and evaluation of whether the outcome of the social and systemic contradictions/complementarities or conjunctions/discontinuities identified at T1 was as surmised. Therefore, analysis focuses on:

- Examples of the morphogenesis or morphostasis of structure, culture and agency, with specific reference to IS development, and explains these outcomes.
- The contradictions/complementarities or conjunctions/discontinuities brought into being by the changed or reinforced SEPs, CEPs and PEPs?
- The possibilities for future morphogenesis/stasis.

(Archer 1995)

Because of the wealth of data collected by the application of multiple methods to the Council X case study, and the very detailed analysis and ordering of this data produced by the form of coding used, there was no lack of material when it came to re-evaluation from a morphogenetic perspective. The main task was, therefore, to work backwards from the concepts and themes identified in 1996–97, and the research reports and articles that emerged during this period, and deconstruct these in line with the schedule and objectives of the morphogenetic approach set out above. This was time consuming and often complex work, usually involving several iterations of any findings. This was largely because the author was grappling with developing his own understanding of many of the concepts of Archer's work, such as generative mechanisms, internal and necessary versus contingent relations, and the general commitment to society as stratified rather than aggregated, as I explained in Chapter 2. Nevertheless, the fact that all the material on Council X collected through 1996, including interview transcripts, notes and diaries from that period, were still available meant that data was on hand to be reanalysed when required.

It is worth adding at this point that the increasing popularity of critical realism in the discipline of organisation and management studies noted in Chapter 1, and the small but increasing number of scholars who have begun to work with the morphogenetic approach, proved valuable as an opportunity to cross reference the author's understanding and application of Archer's work while writing up of this book.

Occasionally this proved both helpful *and* challenging, as was the case with Fairclough's (2005) work on a critical realist approach to discourse analysis in organisation studies. Specifically in this case the challenge arose for two reasons. First, because throughout this book discourse is taken as a dimension of the cultural system and given a relatively 'light' touch. This is entirely in keeping with the approach adopted by Archer (1995). In other words, although discourse is given prominence throughout the relevant sections of this book (e.g. regular reference to discursive reshaping) its various dimensions (e.g. language, texts, etc) are not explicitly "unpacked". The second is that although discourse analysis is not specifically identified as a method employed for data collection and analysis here, it is clear from Fairclough's arguments on the nature of critical realist discourse analysis that it is, in fact, a central feature of the analysis on which this book is built. Thus:

> The objective of discourse analysis, in this view, [critical realism] is not simply analysis of discourse per se, but analysis of the relations between discourse and non-discoursal elements of the social, in order to reach a better understanding of these complex relations (including how changes in discourse can cause changes in other elements).
>
> (Fairclough 2005:924)

Consequently, as the material presented in the next three chapters will evidence, and as has already noted, a "weak" form of critical realist discourse analysis is a feature of this book. No doubt subjecting the data to re-analysis using Fairclough's detailed suggestions would produce some further valuable insights. However, that remains a possibility for future research. For now, the next three chapters detail and discuss the outcome of the re-analysis of the case data through the application of the morphogenetic methodology, and, collectively therefore, document the movement from T1 to T4 of the morphogenetic cycle as it applies to IS development in Council X. Each chapter is devoted to one stage of the cycle. The next chapter commences this process by exploring material that relates to stage T1: those structural, cultural and agential features of Council X that predate the start of this research but which, nevertheless, conditioned and shaped the situations of the staff of the Council with regard to ICT/IS at that point in time.

4

CONDITIONING AND SHAPING

The parts, the people and information systems development

The aims of this chapter are twofold. First, to explore and explain how the 'parts' of Council X that predate the empirical research for this book (i.e. the outcome of prior morphogenetic/static cycles), and the properties of the systemic and institutional environment in which the Council existed, conditioned and shaped the IS 'projects of the people' at T1 – October 1995. This equates to the elements of the morphogenetic cycle grey shaded in Figure 4.1.

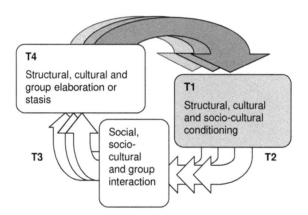

Figure 4.1 Morphogenetic cycles at T1: conditioning and shaping

The second task is to analyse the degree of social and systemic integration that applied to Council X at that time and the implications of this for the morphogenesis/stasis of ICT/IS specifically. As the discussion in Chapter 2 made clear, Archer's proposition is that this type of analysis, allied to an assessment of whether or not structural and cultural morphogenesis/stasis is synchronised or not, should act as a guide to whether the outcome of the social, socio-cultural and group interaction observed between T2 and T3 of any cycle of change (which in this case

124

represents a specific 15 month period of field research) results in either structural morphogenesis or morphostasis at T4.

It is important to emphasise that the second task is taken as integral to the first and therefore analysis and discussion of systemic contradictions and complementarities occurs at appropriate points throughout the chapter, not as a separate activity. It is also worth reiterating here a number of points covered in earlier chapters, as they affect the structure and content of this chapter. The first is a reminder that the primary focus of this book is the position-practice system within Council X. Consequently, the majority of the material that follows concerns the staff of Council X (whether as actors and/or agents) and the roles, situations and contexts in which they found themselves at T1. The result is exactly the '...micro-level ethnographic descriptions of member's activities within the explanatory context of the complex interplay of macro-level structures...' that Johnson and Duberley (2000:165) note is central to critical realist explanations of organisational behaviour. However, as society is stratified and causal mechanisms operate across strata, as discussed in Chapter 2, then it is important to start the process of retroduction by reviewing the systemic and institutional context in which Council X operated. That is, what were the first and second order emergents – social structures, institutional systems, roles, distributions of resources, and types of institutional relationships – and the resulting bargaining power and negotiating strength of entities, that were causally efficacious in central/local government relations at that time, and thus conditioned and shaped the strategic actions and modes of interaction of agents at the level of the position-practice system of Council X.

The second issue concerns data analysis. As the discussion at the end of the previous chapter made clear, the material presented in this chapter, as with Chapters 5 and 6, is based on revisiting the results of an earlier content analysis and reanalysing this material using the morphogenetic methodology discussed in Chapter 2. The intention is not, therefore, to present a running critique on the appropriateness, or otherwise, of the application of the morphogenetic approach to this research. Comments concerning that aspect of this book are reserved for the concluding chapter.

Finally, it is important to remember the discussion in the previous chapter of the interpretive nature of this research, and the implications of this for the material presented in this and the next two chapters. Thus, with the exception of the next section of this chapter, which deals with significant features of the inter governmental environment, the subjects this chapter details and discusses are those which emerged from data analysis as causally significant and not necessarily what the author would have considered significant based on his own knowledge and experience of English local government and IS developments. Figure 4.2 summarises these.

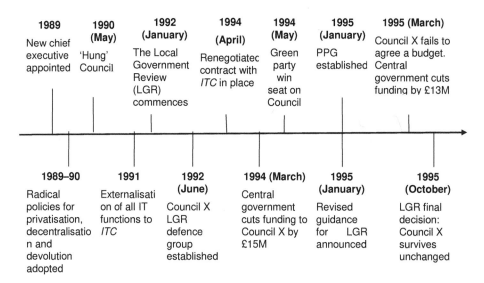

Figure 4.2 Primary causal processes and mechanisms shaping the situations of actors/agents in the IS environment of Council X at T1

First and second order emergents: a brief history of inter-governmental relations in England

Local authorities in England have two roles. They are political institutions constituted '...for the expression of local voice on the needs and concerns of local communities. [And] they are agencies for the delivery of services prescribed by national legislation.' (Leach, Stewart and Walsh 1994:16). Consequently, under a unitary system of government, such as applies to the UK, central government is able – should it so wish – to control almost every aspect of the activities of local government. This applies even where devolution has taken place, as with Scotland and Wales, as the respective Assemblies of both countries are constitutionally subordinate to Westminster. From a critical realist perspective, therefore, the relationship between central and local government is internal and necessary and asymmetrical, rather than contingent. That is, local government could not exist without central government, although the reverse is possible. Crucially, and as Figure 2.3 and its accompanying discussion illustrates, this also means that causal processes and mechanisms at the level of central government have the capacity to modify the powers of local government in fundamental ways, although as with any causal power these may or may not be exercised (Archer 1995).

The second dimension to central/local government relations in England (and Britain in general) concerns the extent to which complementarities and contradictions/incompatibilities apply. Between 1945 and 1964 central/local relations largely exhibited *complementarities*, which is not surprising as it reflects the general level of systemic and social complementarities that largely epitomised the post-war consensus in British politics and society at that time. For British local government this was also a significant time as it signalled a period of continuous expansion of expenditure, services and personnel. The basis of the central/local relationship was also its undoing, however, with the collapse of the post-war consensus in the mid 1960s inextricably linked to the decline of local government (Young and Rao 1997).

By the late 1960s the institutional relationship between central and local government had begun to shift and incorporate some significant necessary *incompatibilities*. The most significant of these was largely the result of the agitation of a variety of vested interest groups who wished to reform the structure of local government. The outcome, the Local Government Act of 1972, was in line with Archer's argument of what is usual for social change. That is, as the result of the aggregate effects of the interaction of the various interest groups it did not approximate to what any one group wanted. It was of little surprise, therefore, that: '...within three years the former county boroughs were straining to break out of the constraints of county government.' (Young and Rao 1997:194). Furthermore, despite another lengthy review between 1991 and 1995 (a causal process, which, as was noted in Chapters 1 and 3, features prominently in this book), and subsequent changes to local authority structures in some parts of England and Wales, it appears that the structure of local government remains an issue for central government.[9]

The 1980s: central government takes control

1979 signalled the beginning of the most significant changes to the balance between the necessary complementarities and incompatibilities of central and local government, with the arrival of a Conservative government which began to exercise causal powers that had previously largely remained unexercised. As ideas, theories and beliefs based on what would come to be known as neo-liberal economics gained the ascent over the Keynesian economics of the post-war consensus (Armstrong, Glyn and Harrison 1991, Self 1993), significant changes began to occur in the cultural system at state and local level. The resulting drive to create a 'free economy and a strong state' (Gamble 1987) saw central government accuse local government of embodying all that was bad about bureaucratic, big government (Clarke and Stewart 1992, Gray 1994). Driven on personally by the Prime Minister, Margaret

---

[9] On the 1st January 2005 *The Guardian* reported that if Labour won a third term in office in 2005 it would seek to abolish two tier local government in England for similar reasons to those cited by central government in 1991. By June 2006, however, there was little evidence that this remained a pressing concern of the Labour government.

Thatcher, who '…unusually for a Conservative…harboured a strong distaste for local government, and was unabashed by the prospect of central intervention to liberate people from local authorities.' (Young and Rao 1987:265), central government departments produced a steady stream of SEPs and CEPs – in the form of green papers, legislation and policy initiatives – the causal powers of which impacted heavily on the cultural and structural domains of local government, and thus on the internal working of local authorities, their role as service providers and their relationship with central government (Elcock 1994, Wilson and Game 1998). In short, post 1979: 'Tension between central and local government [became] endemic…' (Elcock 1994:6).

Three examples from amongst many serve to illustrate these changes. First, functional change as a result of successive legislation forced local authorities to put specified services out to competitive tender on terms and time scales imposed by central government. At the forefront of this policy of privatisation was compulsory competitive tendering (CCT): 'Of all the changes introduced by the 1979–97 Conservative Governments, perhaps the most fundamental and far reaching were those associated with compulsory competitive tendering (CCT).' (Wilson and Game 1998:124). There is little doubt, therefore, that the emergent structural and cultural properties and powers associated with contracting out were powerful enough to force significant structural and cultural change onto local government, and thus were also highly significant from a specifically IS perspective. Unsurprisingly, this is a subject that features prominently in the discussion of Council X below.

The Community Charge (or Poll Tax) of 1990 and the Right to Buy legislation, part of the Housing Act 1980, were also both implemented despite the opposition of most local authorities and, in both cases, strong evidence from scholars and other policy analysts to suggest that the policies would have a detrimental impact on local communities (Wilson and Game 1998). In both cases local authorities had no power to resist the legislation. Nevertheless, this did not stop agents in many local authorities, particularly those that were Labour controlled, from exploiting the fact that all cultural and structural properties and powers are mediated through people (Archer 1995 and Figure 2.5) and therefore agents and actors were able to influence the implementation of both policies. Where this did occur, however (and as was also the case with rate capping between 1985 –1991), central government was swift to use political sanctions (such as the disqualification from office of councillors) and the actual or threatened withdrawal of funding to enforce compliance. In fact, the Rates Act of 1984 gave '...central government complete control for the first time over the spending and taxing policies of some and potentially all local authorities.' (Wilson and Game 1998:188), and thus represents one of the most graphic examples of the exercise of causal powers that had, prior to 1979, seldom been exercised. It has become a power that has been used consistently by both Conservative and Labour governments to control local government ever since.

The view of local government as an unnecessary bureaucracy softened somewhat in central government thinking after November 1990 when John Major (a former local councillor) became Prime Minister (Flynn 1997). Thereafter the scale and speed of change generally diminished, although some major changes continued. For example, and as noted above, in a series of consultation papers produced in 1991 further structural reorganisation was proposed. This subsequently featured as a prominent pledge in the 1992 Conservative Party manifesto, and, following the Conservative's election victory of that year, reorganisation duly became a policy objective.

Despite the slight improvement in the relations between central and local government post 1992 what is clear is that the changes to social structures, institutional systems and institutional relations that occurred from 1979 represent the causal effect of the increasing dominance of ideas and beliefs about free market economics. Promoted by powerful interest groups these CEPs, such as the emergence of the idea of the 'nanny state' and Thatcher's stated belief that there was no such thing as society only individuals, appeared to resonate with a significant percentage of the general population of the UK. Once mediated by agency the causal powers of CEPs then contributed to the morphogenesis of structures, and thus the emergence of the type of new structural and institutional forms discussed above, because as Archer notes and I discussed in Chapter 2: '...cultural change leads to the reconstitution of structural subjects.' (Archer 1995:317).

The 1990s: from government to governance

By the early 1990s local government in England, as in Britain generally, had been the subject of a decade of near constant and often radical change that was more far reaching than in any other country that had adopted the mantra and associated practices of 'new public management' (Flynn 1997, Stoker 1999). However, a further development in the cultural systems of government and public administration of Western democracies in the early 1990s was about to impact on both central and local government. This was the debate which emerged initially in academia, and was subsequently taken up more widely, concerning the distinction between government and *governance,* and the ideas and theories that emerged concerning the nature of the latter (Kooiman 1993, Clarke and Stewart 1994).

Stoker (1994:11) notes that: 'Government is the term conventionally used to refer to a formal institutional structure with authoritative decision-making powers.' By contrast, governance was increasingly adopted as a catch all term to refer to the new process(es) of governing which emerged in many parts of the world during the 1990s which were built upon self organising, inter-organisational networks of organisations from the public, private and/or voluntary sector (Rhodes 1996, 1999). Thus, local or community governance became the term: '...used to distinguish this more fragmented, multi agency pattern of local government from [the] earlier, "near monopolistic council" model.' (Wilson and Game 1998:82). Clearly, the more 'fragmented' and 'multi agency' local governance became, the more the potential for both complementarities and incompatibilities in institutional relations increased (as with any social structure/institutional system). Furthermore, and as Figure 4.3

illustrates, while the relations between central and local government post 1979 became almost entirely internal and necessary and 'top down', at the level of local governance inter organisational relations became increasingly complex.

Put briefly, prior to the reforms discussed above the system of institutional relations at the local level was extremely hierarchical and had been largely stable, barring boundary changes and the local government reorganisation of 1972–74, since the late 19th century (Alexander 1982, Elcock 1994). By virtue of the distribution of resources that came with this institutional system, and thus their bargaining power and negotiating strength, county and metropolitan county councils sat at the top of a hierarchy of metropolitan district councils, then district/borough councils, and, finally, town and parish councils. The responsibilities of each tier of local government were largely self contained and therefore the relations between the tiers of local government were largely contingent and complementary (although hostilities between the agents of the different tiers were often commonplace). Furthermore, what few services local authorities did not provide themselves were usually provided through 'grant aid' to local or national voluntary organisations, such as Age Concern, MIND or Shelter, or voluntary groups that had been initiated and were then financially supported by local authorities. In many cases this funding was so extensive that the relationship between the voluntary group and local authority was almost entirely internal and necessary.

It is appropriate at this point to bring forward evidence from Council X to illustrate this situation. Under the system of institutional relations described above, corporate agents from Council X had been able to take the lead in defining the aims and objectives of projects undertaken jointly with other local authorities/organisations. However, the advent of local governance, allied with the increased control of the activities of local government by central government, reduced the relative power (i.e. negotiating strength and bargaining power) of these corporate agents, and thus undermined their influence over structural and cultural modelling both internal and external to the Council. A key example of this, to which I return later in this chapter, was the Partnerships Project initiative. A senior officer responsible for this initiative expressed their exasperation with the decline in the relative power of Council X's corporate agents when they told me:

> Here we are struggling desperately with absolutely no money to try and make this wonderful initiative [Partnerships Project] happen. So part of the problem - and this isn't just for PP - is that we are totally reliant on the partners [other councils and organisations with which the Council works] to actually take us forward…Because we are so reliant on others to actually do it then we don't put in the objectives. We say, "We can't possibly do that because it would dictate things". [i]

Despite the fact that local authorities across England (and Britain generally) were faced with similar challenges to those set out above different models of local governance did emerge, both within and between local authorities (Clarke and Stewart 1994, Holman and Tizard 1995, Lowndes 1999). Three of the pre-eminent scholars of local government of the time, Leach, Stewart and Walsh (1994), argued that broadly speaking alongside the traditional bureaucratic local authority were three emerging governance models. The common feature of them all was the concept of enabling – or 'steering not rowing' – as Osborne and Gaebler (1992), two of the leading U.S. exponents of the new public management had snappily put it. This simply meant that local authorities, and any other layer of government for that matter, *facilitated* the delivery of local services by other organisations, preferably from the private or voluntary sectors. The three models were: the *residual enabling authority*, which was simply 'a provider of last resort'; the *market-orientated enabling authority*, which was similar to the residual model in terms of the (lack of) services it delivered but which took '…a stronger and more active role in relation to the economic future of its area.' (Leach, Stewart and Walsh 1994:241) and the *community orientated enabler*. The last model was based on a broader interpretation of the enabling role and on a re-emphasis of the democratic role of local government.

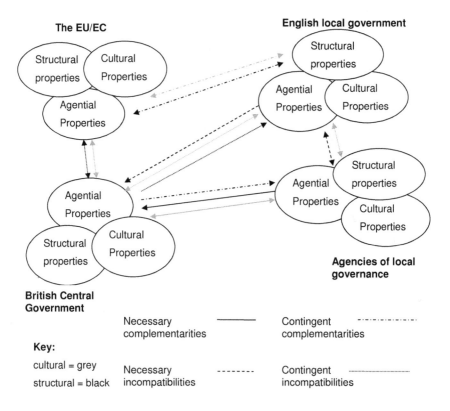

Figure 4.3 The primary institutional relations for English local government in 1995 (within global social and institutional systems)

Leach, Stewart and Walsh were clear that the underlying values of different local authorities would influence which of the models they pursued. From a morphogenetic perspective, also, values – along with other features of the cultural system – would play an important role in the emergence of different models of local governance. Consequently, where cultural morphogenesis was based on free market ideas, beliefs and values, then structural change would reflect this. Fundamentally, however,

Archer also makes the point that whether, and in what form, morphogenesis occurs also reflects the balance between *necessary* complementarities/incompatibilities and *contingent* complementarities/incompatibilities within and between institutions, particularly with respect to the cultural system, as Chapter 2 explained.

Information systems and local governance: the morphogenesis of the cultural system

The discussion so far has centred on the features of the systemic and institutional strata (i.e. first and second order emergents) that exerted causal powers on local government, and therefore played a significant role in conditioning and shaping the organisational environment in which the actors and agents of Council X operated from the 1980s. Turning now to IS developments specifically, what was clearly significant at that time (and remains the case) is that the successful forging of systems of local governance was/is heavily dependant on the capacity of actors/agents to develop and manage the increasingly complex and flexible networks of relationships noted above. Enabling these flows (allied with the more obvious processing of information) would be where ICT played an increasingly crucial role because it could facilitate the redistribution, dissemination and sharing of information (Horrocks and Bellamy 1997).

Unfortunately, many of the public sector management reforms espoused in the 1980s and 1990s by advocates of the free market, such as Ridley (1988) and Osborne and Gaebler (1992), focused on intra-organisational control and management objectives (Carter 1994, McKevitt and Lawton 1994) rather than developing management practice which promoted and enabled the 'management of networks' (Rhodes 1996, 1999). Likewise, interest in new ICTs primarily focused on intra-organisational developments: financial and management information systems, departmentally specific databases, geographic information systems (GIS), and so on. Nevertheless, in response to the increasing dominance of ideas and beliefs about new public management and the enabling role of government and the role of the G7 and EU in promoting and resourcing actual structural developments (discussed below) the IS agenda had broadened by the early 1990s. A dominant theme emerged in the cultural systems of governments across the developed world which emphasised the increasingly pivotal role that new ICTs could play in the *delivery* of public services. Particularly important, it was argued, was that ICTs would provide the technology and networks to manage and deliver the intelligence of a range of organisations to front-line staff. This would be crucial when trying to deliver 'joined up' public services (such as the type of 'one stop shop' noted in Chapter 3 and which is a prominent feature of later chapters) and/or when supporting the reengineering of business processes (Davenport 1993, Hammer and Champy 1993, Taylor et al 1997), or in enabling new forms of participation in local democratic processes (Horrocks and Webb 1994, Percy-Smith 1995, Kinder 2002). As Chapter 1 established, these themes are nowadays even more important to policy makers than in the early to mid 1990s.

The fragmentation and reformulation of systemic and institutional relations, and the complexity of the inter-organisational relationships that emerged, further fuelled ideas and beliefs about the increasing importance to local governance of information flows, and of the ICTs that might enable them. Crucially, this also placed the agenda for local governance within a cultural framework provided by the concept of the 'information society': the argument that ICTs could provide the tools for dramatic social, economic and institutional change. This was an increasingly widely held view of the time (e.g. Castells 1996, Handy 1991, Mosco 1996, Castells 2000), questioned by relatively few (e.g. Lyon 1988, Mansell 1993, Winston 1998). Furthermore, the rapid development and growing availability of technical innovations, such as cable and satellite TV, CD-ROM, multimedia applications, electronic mail and bulletin boards, computer conferencing and video phones, and remote on-line telecomputing (which at that time were beginning to make possible applications such as telemedicine and telelibraries – now a commonplace), was rapidly creating a climate in the cultural systems of the developed world where more and more people expected to be both participants in, and beneficiaries of, the 'information age'. As the discussion in Chapter 1 showed, the result was that national governments world-wide rushed to follow the lead of the USA in formulating strategies for developing national information infrastructures. In this way they hoped to ensure that their countries were not only equipped to compete successfully in the global information economy but also to reap the civic, cultural and social benefits of the information society.

Contingent compatibilities: looking to the EC/EU

At a European level publication in 1994 of the Report of the High-level Group on Europe and the Global Information Society (usually referred to simply as 'The Bangemann Report') became one of the most important contributions to the development of ideas and theories about the information age, and thus IS developments, in Europe. Although the report reflected the EU's preoccupation with industrial policy and economic development, which was to be expected given the nature of the vested interest groups involved in its preparation, it nevertheless served as a wake up call to European governments on the possibilities of using new ICTs for organisational and institutional 'transformation'. Subsequent developments at European level – such as the establishment of the Information Society Forum – laid growing emphasis on ICT applications capable of strengthening democratic values and widening access to public services, especially at the local level, but also, and crucially, became important for the socio-cultural interaction necessary to propagate these ideas and beliefs to a wider audience.

An indicator of how the CEPs that emerged as a result of this interaction then began to impact, through the actions of agents, on structures was the promotion and funding throughout Europe of the range of 'digital city' initiatives that were discussed in Chapter 1. Although in the very early stages of development during the period of the field research for this book a crucial aim of these developments was to stimulate the deployment of new approaches to the provision of more citizen orientated and efficient public services and more and more on-line information. In short, they were able to take advantage of the morphogenesis of ideas, theories and beliefs (i.e. the cultural system) to begin to promote and pursue structural morphogenesis. From a local governance perspective these developments were highly significant as it was convincingly argued by their supporters that they would bring citizens into closer contact with their administrations (Hoff and Stormgaard 1991, Bekkers, Koops and Nouwt 1996, also various authors in Dutton 1996). Interestingly, this was an idea/belief which struck a chord with the head of the Local Government Commission (as noted previously, the body undertaking the LGR), and as the discussion later in this chapter demonstrates, this subsequently had significant implications for IS in Council X, as well as for other councils that were under review.

The development of the digital city initiatives illustrates how the properties of the morphogenesis of the institutional systems of the EC, initially in the cultural domain but later structural in form, such as new criteria for funding IS developments, gradually fed down to impact on the institutional relationships of the lower strata of organisations involved in local government and governance across the EU (Figure 4.3). This certainly applied to actors/agents within Council X through their involvement in project planning for applications for funding for a range of IS pilot projects under a variety of EU initiatives. Although often not successful, data collected from Council X shows that the EU connection played an important role in increasing the awareness of the *potential* of new ICTs amongst key actors/agents.

Reference to the potential of ICTs is deliberate and important, for in almost every case it was not the actual capabilities of a new ICT that were the defining point in reshaping ideas and beliefs about new ICTs, because these were hardly ever witnessed, but the potentialities; ideas, theories and beliefs about what *might* be possible. It is clear therefore, that socio-cultural interaction via the process of collaboration with agents from other local authorities across the EU proved invaluable in producing the CEPs necessary for cultural elaboration within Council X (T4, Figure 4.1). Furthermore, although limited in number, on the occasions when actors/agents from the Council were involved in *actual* EC supported IS projects the exchange of ideas and values, and the injection of resources in particular, meant that EU policy and practice became increasingly influential, both in shaping the ideas and discourse of key agents within the Council and for IS as a structural property (Figure 4.3).

Given the few examples where there was any exchange of resources for IS development between Council X and the EC it is unsurprising that relations were overwhelmingly *contingent*. However, strong *complementarities* developed at the level of cultural systems, as discussed above, both in terms of IS specifically and more broadly regarding ideas and beliefs about the nature and purpose of local government. The dominant view of local government amongst actors/agents within the EC was that local authorities were important and should be largely autonomous democratic institutions. This is a view based on the models of local government that prevail across most of Western Europe (Chandler 1993). For the agents of Council X, with its recent history of strained and domineering relations with British central government, there was much to find attractive in the EC view. It was not surprising therefore, that for Council X, as for other British local authorities, there was an increasing attraction in closer ties to the EC and, through these, to continental local authorities, and an increasing tendency to use this as the means to attempt to counteract the policies and practices of British central government. However, this did not go unnoticed by central government. Consequently, it was not long before a number of central government departments became actively involved in the processes of 'vetting' applications from English local authorities to the EC, reserving the right to veto these.

The causal powers and unintended consequences of central government actions: the view from Council X

The demise of historical political structures and power

Despite boundary changes and the reorganisation of local government in 1974 Council X had remained a Conservative controlled authority since the late 19th century. This situation ended in 1990 as a result of the public furore over the Poll Tax/Community Charge which saw the Tory Party punished through the ballot box at the local government elections of that year. The result was that the Conservatives lost control of Council X to Labour and the Liberal Democrats and from 1990 through the period of this research Council X remained a 'hung' council (i.e. no one party had enough councillors to take overall control), usually controlled by an anti Tory alliance between Labour and the Liberal Democrats.

Given the nature of local government this type of power-sharing/no overall control of a council usually has a considerable impact on the operations of the organisation (Leach, Stewart and Walsh 1994, Burns, Hambleton and Hoggett 1994) and Council X was no exception. One of the most important was the volatility of the power sharing arrangements, allied to the different and frequently changing agendas of the political parties. This created an environment in which it would appear that councillors became unable/unwilling to provide leadership and strategic management, to the extent that at T1 it was largely non existent in most areas of policy and practice within Council X.

It is relatively commonplace in local government to find that, where political power and influence is weak, the relative power and ideational significance of agents from the officer side of a council increases. However, the evidence strongly suggests that this did not occur within Council X, primarily because a rapid and wide ranging process of structural morphogenesis, initiated with the arrival of a new chief executive in 1989, created a situation where the structural and cultural domains were significantly out of sync. The result, as the morphogenetic approach would predict, was that select politicians and senior managers – in the form of the Strategy and Resources Committee – continued to fulfil the role of the dominant cultural agent, accompanied by a fairly rapid growth in material interest groups. These then became more interested in protecting their interests than in the general interests of the organisation. This, in turn, had a profound impact on system and social integration, with an increase in both necessary and contingent *incompatibilities*. However, before exploring this dimension of the case study in detail a specific example of the actions of central government will be explored as this was cited by the staff of Council X as primarily responsible for the loss of political leadership (as well as causally relevant to other developments, as we shall see). Of course, although discussed entirely from a Council X perspective here the causal powers of these events can be traced back to the wider developments in the political economy of the UK, discussed earlier in this chapter, and to the changed relations between central and local government that emerged as a result.

The power of material resources: central government takes revenge

Whether by coincidence or design, relatively soon after the Tory Party lost control of Council X the authority began to be penalised financially through the SSA (Standard Spending Assessment) formula imposed by central government. The SSA therefore represents the causal mechanism, with the actual cuts being the causal powers. The result was that for 1994–95 the Council was forced to make cuts in spending of approximately £15m, followed by a similar amount in 1995–96, and a further £13m for 1997/98. The causal powers of the SSA impacted on the Council in three related ways. First, relations between central government and Council X deteriorated significantly, such that the Labour/Liberal Democrat alliance that controlled the Council at that time failed to agree a budget within the amount and time allowed by central government in both 1995 and 1996. Second, the amount of time spent dealing with the political infighting and other issues related to the budget undermined the ability of political actors/agents to give time and thought to other policy and managerial issues, and thus to the leadership and strategic direction of the Council.

Third, both of these developments then acted to seriously constrain the actions of actors/agents and shape their interactions at the position-practice level.

The primary dependence of structures and structural emergent properties on material resources meant that cuts in funding, and the impact this then had on material and human resources generally, was one of the three overarching themes (i.e. lack of resources) that emerged from the data analysis reported towards the end of Chapter 3. Furthermore, another of the three themes – the need for organisational change – was also largely a response by agents to the causal powers and processes emergent from the impact of financial cuts at the institutional level. Consequently, it is unsurprising that both of these themes and the contradictions they appeared to bring into being, underpin many of the specific IS and organisational developments that conditioned and shaped the actions of agents, and that are discussed in this chapter.

Agents respond: events and actions in the position-practice system

In January 1997 the author gave a presentation to officers and councillors on the provisional results of the Officers' and Members' ICT pilot project being undertaken by PSTAG. During the post presentation discussion conversation turned to network security and the importance and cost of firewalls. A leading Liberal Democrat councillor, who was highly supportive of the need to press ahead with a new phase of IS development for the Council, asked: 'Which councillor is going to stand up and vote for expenditure on a firewall at the same time as teaching posts are under threat'. No one gave him an answer.

This example of the impact on the ideas and attitudes of agents of the causal powers emergent from the SSA illustrates how significant these were in conditioning and shaping the actions of actors/agents at the level of positions and practices. In fact, it was obvious from my frequent presence at Council X that the vast majority of staff were acutely aware of the financial position of the Council, and therefore of the possible implications for themselves, regardless of whether they were corporate or primary agents. This fed through into quite commonplace organisational behaviour, such as (not) being able to offer hospitality to visitors (i.e. tea and coffee) and whether or not to continue funding the in-house newsletter. The upshot was that something akin to a "siege mentality" developed amongst both officers and councillors.

Promoting morphogenesis: the electronic phone book, opportunity or threat?
Developments that were genuinely unrelated to funding cuts also became enmeshed in the unstable ideational and structural environment that had been created. For example, as part of the ongoing development of the Council's electronic public information system (EPIS) the small team that ran the project got the backing of senior management in the Chief Executive's Office to use the database technology they had at their disposal to launch an e-phone book. This would supersede the existing paper based directory which had to be updated incrementally and laboriously every year. Once implemented this system would allow any movement of personnel within the Council to be noted electronically and the database would update accordingly. However, the senior management team (i.e. a corporate agent) of one department which had suffered considerable job losses through a previous 'rationalisation' exercise, stemming from central government imposed cuts in funding, believed that these cuts had been based on a "trawl" of numbers of staff and their roles from the internal telephone directory. Consequently, they were only prepared to release extension and contact numbers to the e-phone book development team, rather than a full list of staff, and chose to ignore the arguments that this would seriously undermine the value of the e-phone book.

Whether or not the e-phone book would have been used in the way outlined above is an open question. Nevertheless, the stonewalling of this development continued for at least the duration of my study, with the EPIS team unable to convince the management of the renegade department to change their attitude. To complicate matters further, other causal powers were at work as a result of the implementation from 1990 of radical policies of decentralisation and devolution (discussed fully below); namely the extent to which relationships between departments had become structurally and culturally *contingent* and *incompatible*. This situation was gradually becoming ever more pronounced as similar changes in occurred in the cultural domain (but more slowly). These relationships and the situational logics they create impact on the modes of interaction employed by corporate agents, both in the structural and cultural systems. As the example above and those that follow illustrate, within Council X this meant that in most cases interaction between corporate agents became primarily defensive. However examples of competitive and/or opportunistic behaviour did emerge from time to time when this served the interests of certain agents, as the evidence and discussion of forms of interaction set out in Chapter 5 demonstrates.

Archer (1995) is clear that the success or failure of any strategic course of interaction pursued by any interest group is conditioned by the bargaining power and negotiating strength of that group. In the example above the group promoting the e-phonebook – the EPIS development group – had very little of either, because of their limited resources (i.e. liquid assets, political sanctions and expertise), and because their institutional relationships were largely restricted to other groups within the relatively powerless CE's office. In fact, the only resource they did have at their disposal was IS expertise, which the renegade department was not interested in. It is not surprising, therefore, that they failed to get the corporate agents of the renegade department to tow the line. However, they also failed to appreciate that what seemed like a relatively straightforward technological "fix" (using ICTs as a structural property to initiate a limited form of morphogenesis. A positive development as they saw it) carried the potential to alter the balance of material resources, and thus impact on the interests, of a variety of actors and agents, all of whom were more influential and powerful than they were.

Legacy systems: taking on the systemic properties of ICTs

A far more common situation than that of the potential for morphogenesis presented by the e-phone book was that the structural properties and cultural 'norms' of previous cycles of IS development (nowadays referred to as legacy systems) within Council X assisted in structural morphostasis. The example that follows serves to highlight this more than most and is also highly relevant because the causal powers and structural and cultural effects of cuts in funding again feature prominently. However, and perhaps most importantly, the example also provides further evidence of how the emergent properties of one stratum, often as Archer (1995) would argue in the form of the unintended outcomes of actions, can exert powerful causal powers on another stratum.

Until the early 1990s a particular software system called Office Power had been used throughout Council X. By 1995 however, only Committee Services and the Fire Service (because of the existence of a national network for fire services based on Office Power) continued to use this system. Despite its overwhelming rejection across most of the Council the fact that all reports and papers to all committees and sub committees of the Council had to be prepared by Committee Services meant that all other departments, including other sections of the Chief Executive's Office (of which the Unit was a part) had either to maintain an Office Power facility, or alternatively, manually copy documents from their original format to the Office Power format. The fact that it was widely recognised that this was a waste of human and material resources was not enough to overcome what appeared to be a widely held view that in a period of severe cuts in funding new investment in IS development was not a risk worth taking. The head of Committee Services confirmed this when he stated:

> There is an attitude problem...the mere fact of trying to achieve some
> kind of enhancement (of IT) when in all other fields of council activity
> we are retrenching I think doesn't really help. Unless there was a very

clear vision of material advantage...I guess I shouldn't be talking about this attitude problem as if I didn't participate in it, because I do feel it as well. I have always felt that, "why the hell are we mucking about with this (new IT) when it is all we can do to keep the ship going as it is". [ii]

In 1994–95 an unintended outcome, insofar as any of the corporate agents of Council X were concerned, of a planned event, provided the catalyst to challenge this cultural and structural impasse. With the exception of the Green Party, the election to Council X of a Green Party councillor appeared to be a relatively minor political event. However, the 'hung' nature of the Council meant that staff had already adopted systems and practices to ensure there was no suspicion of bias to one party or another by providing support and advisory services equally to all political parties. This meant that Committee Services staff, with their responsibility for most of the interaction with councillors, saw it as their duty to provide the same level of support to the Green Party councillor as they did to members of the three main parties.

The additional burden this placed on material and human resources was almost immediately problematic given the cuts that had already been imposed on the Unit. Unfortunately, more were to follow in 1995/96, when Committee Services were ordered to reduce their budget by a further 30% without any reduction in the services they provided. The result was that the arrival of a fourth political party onto the Council became a generative mechanism, the causal powers of which finally prompted serious questioning of the design and function of Committee Services from *within* the unit. This applied not only to the activities of actors/agents, but, crucially, extended to finally questioning the unit's use of ICT and the significant constraints that the properties of the unit's technologies placed on other structures and people. The results of this change of attitude – the beginnings of the morphogenesis of the cultural system as it applied to the actors and agents of Committee Services – fed through into the second stage of the morphogenetic cycle (interaction) and are therefore dealt with in the next chapter.

While the morphogenetic approach, as with critical realism generally, is clear that the situations in which people find themselves are conditioned and shaped by pre-existing structural and cultural properties it is equally the case that this is not a deterministic assumption (Archer 1995, Porpora 1998). Consequently, as Chapter 2 established, even if actors/agents do recognise their interests '...they may chose to act against them in favour of other considerations.' (Porpora 1998:344). The examples presented so far illustrate how this conditioning and shaping can occur and how a range of responses may emerge that may be regarded as more or less clearly associated with the specific interests of a particular interest group/corporate agent.

Having explored evidence of the way in which the properties and causal powers emergent from the cultural and structural morphogenesis of the institutional strata impacted on agency at the level of the position-practice system of the Council, and therefore how the actions of agents were conditioned and shaped at T1, the next task is to undertake the same exercise with regard to morphogenesis/stasis that occurred from within.

Organisational change in Council X: the decline of systemic and social integration

Decentralisation and devolution

Prior to 1989 the structure and function of Council X followed the traditional hierarchical model of service departments and matching committees that was at that time common to almost all local authorities in the UK. The management of Council X was similarly structured, with service departments, such as education and social services, presided over by a central services department which incorporated, and was steered by, a powerful central policy unit. A Policy and Resources Committee had the ultimate say over the allocation of resources, which were then controlled and allocated through the Chief Executive's office.

As noted above, 1989 saw the arrival of a new chief executive with progressive ideas concerning the structure and management of local government, and although little evidence emerged from data collection and analysis that the reforms were ideologically driven, it is clear that they did resonate strongly with the thinking of the Tory government of the time and of the Conservative majority that controlled Council X until 1990. The result was the implementation, in early 1990, of two strands of structural reform:

- An aggressive and comprehensive policy of decentralisation and devolution.
- A rapid and extensive programme of contracting out and privatisation largely *in advance* of central government legislation.

The programmes of decentralisation, devolution and privatisation – the three policies went hand in hand – appear to have met relatively little resistance from members and were implemented rapidly. Consequently, by late 1991 structural morphogenesis was well advanced, with almost all responsibility for intra departmental policy making and resource allocation transferred to corporate agents within service departments. In addition, many of the functions which had traditionally been treated as corporate activities – such as IT support, strategic planning, etc. – were contracted out, abolished, or downgraded, because they were no longer considered crucial to the operation of the new structure. The result, as the Chief Executive was keen to point out, was that: 'The Council's voluntary contracting-out programme is acknowledged by the District Audit Service to be among the foremost in the country.'[iii]

In terms of the three different approaches to organisational change that Leach, Stewart & Walsh (1994) identified at that time as being adopted by British local authorities ('dynamic conservatism', 'indiscriminate fashion following' and 'selected response') the rush to change adopted by Council X strongly suggests that much that was pursued fell into the category of 'indiscriminate fashion following'. Or, to elaborate slightly, an '…over-response [to external pressures in the fields of] strategies, structures, systems and staff management.' (Leach, Stewart & Walsh 1994:11). Unfortunately, the evidence presented in this book suggests that in adopting such policies Council X failed to heed the warning that the danger of such an approach was '...one of an unconsidered embracing of this whole range of current managerial fashions, without a proper appraisal of what is appropriate for the specific circumstances of the particular local authority...' (ibid. p.11).

Reshaping the bargaining power and negotiating strength of agents

It was noted at the end of the section on *the demise of historical structures and power* that the policies of decentralisation and devolution created a situation where for several years contradictions and incompatibilities existed between the cultural and structural systems, and that at T1 these remained largely unsynchronised. The result, as the morphogenetic approach would suggest, was that the difference between the morphogenesis of SEPs and CEPs led to some patchy and uneven developments insofar as PEPs were concerned (Archer 1995). Thus, while the relative power of corporate agents at departmental level rapidly increased, that of corporate agents associated with what had been the Central Services department and Chief Executive's Office decreased just as rapidly. The nature of social relationships and interaction also changed, because, in most cases, departmental agents and actors were no longer dependant on their corporate colleagues for resources. Thus, relationships that pre 1989 had been internal and necessary now became largely contingent, or reversed, as the example of the lack of support for the in-house programme to enhance service quality and effectiveness, discussed below, illustrates. The unfolding of these power relationships are discussed in detail in Chapter 5.

As might be expected, however, corporate agents that had a strong affinity to the new structural forms were keen to promote acceptance of these changes by encouraging cultural morphogenesis, although the evidence was that this was largely directed at other corporate agents, and even here acceptance seemed to be a slow process, as the examples discussed below will illustrate. By T1, therefore, the extent of cultural morphogenesis was noticeably less in many parts of the Council and appeared particularly so amongst primary agents, with the result that many lower grade staff appeared hostile, or, at the least, ambivalent to the policies of organisational change. This is an unsurprising situation, however, when we remember that although corporate agency shapes the context in which all actors operate it is the environmental pressures and problems that primary agency unleashes '…which affect the attainment of [corporate agents] promotive interests.' (Archer 1995: 260). Consequently, convincing primary agents of the need for structural morphogenesis needed to be a much higher priority than it was. Furthermore, many actors and agents continued their social interaction through interest groups that had existed pre 1989 and this also played a key role in slowing cultural change and the emergence of CEPs, as well as masking the extent to which relative power had shifted within the Council. Finally, and as discussed later in this chapter, from 1992 the Local Government Review bolstered the diminishing power of the centre, with, as we shall see at the end of this chapter, a surprising outcome for the structural and cultural morphogenesis of IS in particular.

Despite the slow rate of cultural morphogenesis, by October 1995, and following cuts in funding through 1994–95 and 1995–96 and the apparent reluctance of the Chief Executive to allow the centre to maintain a policy overview and provide strategic management, what the landscape of Council X looked like from the perspective of agents at the centre was captured by one of the assistant chief executives: 'The authority used to be the traditional, centrally dominated, "Stalinist" council. Decentralisation got rid of that. But now we have lots of Stalins, each with their own empire.'[iv]

The discussion above, and the quotation in particular, provides evidence to support two analytical dimensions of this book. The first relate to Archer's meta-theoretical claims about the nature of social relations and interaction and how, for example, changes in exchange transactions and power relations led to the emergence of PEPs, which then exerted causal powers back onto social relations.

The second is that it provides evidence of the extent of structural morphogenesis within Council X: a conclusion borne out by the fact that cultural and structural *fragmentation* is the third of the three overarching themes (along with the need for change and resources, already discussed above) that emerged from the data analysis discussed in Chapter 3. In terms of the day to day activities of agents/actors within the position practice system the result – the emergence of an informal system for policy formulation and decision making at the corporate level – was summed up by a principal policy officer: 'It's all very, very informal. But that's the way the organisation operates. The lack of being able to direct and say, "that will happen"…It's all done by "let's try and get everybody behind you and go to there". And you stop, look around you and move on.'[v]

The emergence of these informal structures was further encouraged by the deliberate hands off approach of the chief executive, which led actors and agents from the centre to express frustration at their new found inability to "manage" events. While this practice may have been useful for embedding the policies of decentralisation and devolution it served to aggravate further the lack of any political leadership on policy noted above, and undermine what little impetus remained in maintaining and developing ideas and beliefs about the overarching (i.e. corporate) aims and objectives of the Council. The IS contract monitoring officer confirmed that the old top down approach to strategic management was a thing of the past when he explained that:

> …strategy really for Council X comes from the bottom up and not from the top down. It comes from departmental pressure - "we've got these systems we need to talk to you over there", and the two of us will start something up

to do that. Then other departments have come in on the back of that sort of thing.[vi]

The discussion above noted, and Chapter 2 set out in detail, how important corporate agency is in shaping the context in which all actors operate. The examples above illustrate how the removal of the material resources that had provided the corporate agents at the centre of Council X with much of their bargaining power and negotiating strength undermined their ability to control the policy process and thus their ability to shape the context of departmental actors/agents. These changes were also significant for inter-departmental initiatives. One example of organisational learning (or, as it turns out, lack of it) serves to illustrate this well.

During the early 1990s one section of the Council developed a programme to enhance service quality and effectiveness. This was highly praised and widely adopted and copied by other local authorities. As a result, staff in the new CE's office believed that within Council X the programme should be adopted widely. However, when staff from the CE's office attempted to pursue this policy they came up against an example of how the hollowing out of the centre had now shifted power to corporate agents in departments (as well as an example of the hands off approach of the CE noted above):

…we had a wonderful situation where we [the CE's office] had no money to do any publications. We wrote to departments and said, "could you let us have some money so we can try and publicise the initiative internally." And the answer was "No".

Q. So where did that expression of dissent – call it what you want – go?
It should have gone to chief officers. It should have been the CE banging heads against walls and saying, "why can't you contribute?" But that debate didn't take place. [vii]

152

Context is crucial in any critical realist analysis of structural and cultural change (Archer 1995, 1998a, Ackroyd 2004, Sayer 2004). Morphogenesis/stasis will therefore be experienced differently by agents in different contexts and according to their status as primary or corporate agents. It is unsurprising then that views and opinions differed within Council X as to whether decentralisation/devolution was "good" or "bad" (in terms of vested interests). The examples above largely reflect the views of staff working in the CE's office rather than in departments, and at the centre the consensus was largely that the structure of Council X was now such that action was conditioned and shaped to an extent where little of corporate value could be achieved.

Of course, it might be expected that these staff would be more inclined to lament the passing of the old system in which they functioned as powerful corporate agents exerting considerable influence on the policies and practices – and thus people – of the Council. However, and perhaps surprisingly, data analysis discussed later in this chapter suggests that the emergence of ad-hoc and informal systems for policy and decision making, and their impact, were also of concern to departmental actors/agents. In addition, even though departmental actors/agents had been empowered by the policies of decentralisation and devolution it was clear that there was significant variation in their commitment to, belief in, and pursuit of change. For example, corporate agents in the Education Department consistently followed a more radical path of structural reform. One result of this was that amongst UK local authorities Council X led the way in implementing the local management of schools (LMS).

An aggressive approach to decentralisation and devolution remained a feature of the Education Department throughout the period of this research, with interviewees often stating that the centre still exerted too much control. By way of an explanation the Deputy Director once commented that... 'It's because of the way in which the authority has evolved. The centre hasn't come to terms with the reality of what has evolved.' [viii] From an IS development perspective the significance of this comment is that the assistant director of education also chaired a key IS strategy group, (referred to from hereon as ISSSG): a group which prior to the privatisation of the Council's IT service had functioned as the inter departmental group responsible for allocating IT resources across Council X. Following the abolition of the IT department ISSSG became a sub group of Chief Officers' Management Group (COMG: the most senior grouping of officers in Council X) and took on the role of 'the corporate group for dealing with information issues', working to agreed terms of reference. This meant that although ISSSG members lost control of the allocation of material resources they remained an important corporate agent because they occupied a significant gate-keeping position in the structure through which IS/ICT ideas and issues were passed to COMG, as the discussion in the next chapter details and discusses.

Privatisation: increasing structural morphogenesis *and* systemic contradictions
Under the Local Government Act 1992 local authority professional 'white collar' services, such as, legal services, personnel, finance and estates were not due to be subject to CCT rules until 1996–2000. IT services were the last on the list: scheduled for 1998–2000 (Wilson and Game 1998). As we have seen however, the senior management of Council X had no intention of adopting such an incremental approach and rolled privatisation into the structural reforms of 1991. By 1995, therefore, five major areas of activity had all been privatised for a number of years: the council's catering services were outsourced; the Department of Planning and Property Services lost all property management and maintenance; the Treasurer's Department lost all payroll and exchequer services; and the County Engineers lost significant elements of highway maintenance. This, as noted above, put Council X in the forefront of local authorities that implemented the requirements of Compulsory Competitive Tendering (CCT), with the significance of this development not lost on staff:

> ...there are very few councils who have contracted out to the extent that
> we did or so long ago. The only one I can think of is Wiltshire who are

154

in a similar position...So I just get the impression that what we've done is unusual...full contracting out plus full devolution of power to departments. I think that puts us in a very unusual position. [ix]

The fact that between 1990 and 1995 the privatisation policy of Council X (as a SEP) was only contingently related to central government actions, because there was no material relationship (i.e. policy or resource) involved, failed to impress many staff. One of the most significant outcomes was that whereas for almost all councils in England contracting out was regarded as an external structural force, many of the staff of Council X saw the situation reversed, and it was regarded as of the Council's own making (i.e. the responsibility of the CE and Chief Officers). This view was reinforced by the fact that Council X had not fought against contracting out, as was the norm for most English local authorities (Wilson and Game 1998). Therefore, while criticisms of the services provided to Council X by contractors were widespread, particularly in the field of IS, actors and agents almost always regarded this as fundamentally because of the actions of the senior management of the Council, and the attitudinal effects of this amongst staff – and primary agents in particular – were particularly marked right across the Council.

Privatisation and IS development

The most far reaching "chunk" of privatisation was of the services provided by the IT department. This included contracting out to *ITC* (this is not the true acronym for this company) every function that the IT department had provided: troubleshooting and repair, training, advice and support functions, facilities management, hardware and software purchase, bespoke design services, corporate IT policy and strategy, and the operation and management of the mainframe computer. Nearly one hundred of the Council's staff transferred to *ITC* and the department was wound up.

Of course, a policy involving structural change as dramatic as this was not adopted without some dissent. Senior management in one department argued that the experience of other local authorities indicated that Council X should keep in-house IT capacity as large as possible (given the limitations that would eventually be imposed by CCT). However, these objections were overruled. As one of the department's assistant directors (and a member of the ISSSG) group explained:

> ...we were a minority on that. The whole lot, the whole central information services was externalised. There's nothing left, which is an incredible situation when you think about it.[x]

Despite the reservations of some staff the overwhelming opinion within COMG was that '*ITC* would continue to act as the [IT] department had done'. The vision was '...of a flexible arrangement which would meet our requirements and also give staff up to date skills'[xi]. The assumption was that ITC would '...provide proactive support' and that the detail of the Service Level Agreements (SLAs) would ensure that this happened. The reality was somewhat different, as another senior member of the ISSSG group noted: The contract that we had originally [with *ITC*] was a very restricted contract and it wasn't flexible enough to reflect the changes Council X was going through in terms of how it used its IT resources...[xii]

One of the main issues reflected in this quotation is that the inflexibility of the IT contract worked against the structural changes taking place as a result of decentralisation and devolution. Devolved and decentralised systems and practices required flexible IS to support them. Instead the IT contract had been drafted on the basis of historical structures, and/or estimates of what the structures of the Council might be after decentralisation and devolution. The result was that the privatisation of IT simply added further contradictions and incompatibilities, with the added complication that most of these were internal and necessary and therefore presented agents with little chance of escaping from the institutional relationship with *ITC*, or from the structural influences this created. The nature and extent of these problems led the IS contract monitoring officer to admit that: I think being wise after the event

156

we should have been more selective over the services which went and we should have retained more. This is a view that has been growing at all levels including Chief Officers since.

Given the critical role that the causal powers of reductions in human and material resources were playing in structural morphogenesis it was unsurprising that IT privatisation was affected, with the inflexibility of the contract compounded further by cut backs in staff to critical levels:

> You would probably find [in similar councils], certainly the ones that report through SOCRATES (a local authority IT personnel networking group) that it is usual to have an IT client of between six or nine people. The difficulty [for Council X] has been having a client of one and a half people, plus a student…So I don't think you'll find a smaller central client than here.[xiii]

The freedom of agency and the divergence of situational logics and forms of strategic action

The difficulties agency faces in escaping the conditioning and shaping of previous cycles of morphogenesis, particularly when situational logics and forms of strategic action are constrained by first and second order emergents, is something which the morphogenetic approach highlights (Archer 1995). In the case of Council X once the number of IT staff had been reduced the only way to increase in-house IT capacity, or the number of contract monitoring or IT related staff, under the forthcoming CCT regulations for professional services, was on the back of more IT contracts. Unfortunately, and as some senior staff had predicted, this was a very limited option because nearly everything related to IT had already been contracted out. This meant that Council X became a hostage to central government policy with senior management propagating the (highly unlikely) view that:

The pay off for this authority comes when CCT is scrapped when we can then set up the client activity properly centrally. We then save a considerable amount. But at the moment with this authority the CCT regime militates that we can't make saving on the money spent. Particularly because we have down sized so much...We are now being penalised for efficiency.[xiv]

In the meantime, however, there were several more SEPs emergent from the new system of 'governance' that privatisation had ushered in that conditioned and shaped the behaviour of actors/agents. The first, as a senior manager and member of the ISSSG explained, was complexity: ...now responsibility for IT is contracted out there are so many people involved and the lines of responsibility aren't clearly defined necessarily...what it means is that to fix a problem takes probably three times longer than it normally would.[xv]

The second was that the fragmentation of Council wide structures led to the emergence of PEPs, the defining characteristics of which, as discussed in Chapter 2, are that: '...they modify the capacities of component members (affecting their consciousness and commitments, affinities and animosities) and exert causal powers proper to their relations themselves vis-à-vis other agents or their groupings (such as association, organisation, opposition and articulation of interests).' (Archer 1995:184). The resulting fairly rapid growth of material interest groups/corporate agents whose views were that their interests were no longer served by taking a collaborative and corporate approach then led to further structural fragmentation at *intra* departmental levels. Furthermore, where devolution and the lack of corporate management and leadership combined with weak *intra departmental* management then the resulting PEPs caused the formation of ever smaller and more localised interest groups, each able to operate as their own corporate agents. This was confirmed by the manager of the Financial Planning Unit (part of the Treasurer's Department), amongst others, who explained that: 'The problem is everybody has gone their own way as far as IT is concerned across Council X and even within the Treasurer's department.'[xvi]

Significantly, however, it was empirical evidence drawn from these relatively local levels of the position-practice system that once again supports the meta-theory of critical realism that however powerful the conditioning and shaping of SEPs and CEPs might be judged to be, ultimately this judgement has to be non deterministic as agency *always* retains the power to act in a variety of ways (Archer 1995, Porpora 1998, Sayer 1998). Thus, although it was generally assumed within Council X that there was little scope for freeing IS development from the structural influences that had emerged from contracting out and decentralisation and devolution, some actors and agents never ceased in their efforts to do just that. For example, corporate agents in both the Education and Social Services departments found the means to buy back key research and intelligence staff from *ITC*. The Engineers Department also gradually built up in-house IT support staff to deliberately circumvent the need to use any of *ITC's* services (which one officer described as 'crap').

Despite repeated attempts to gain an explanation it proved impossible to find out how this was done, although clearly certain agents had been able to manipulate systems and material resources in such a way as to circumvent the contracting out policy of the Council. More significant, perhaps, was that this had usually been done without the knowledge of actors and agents elsewhere in the Council and because of the need to protect their new 'interests', a culture of secrecy developed. Furthermore, while it was obviously advantageous to particular actors/agents to circumvent the generative powers and new structural and cultural forms of contracting out it further aggravated the level of systemic contradictions within Council X.

The result was that at T1 a significant rift existed between the situational logics and forms of strategic action of those agents who had some freedom to act outside the confines of the structures of contracting out and those that could not. One of the most

159

profound ways in which this situation then played out was through the breaking down of the structural, cultural and agential mechanisms that had allowed the coordination and maintenance of common IS/ICT standards and protocols across the organisation. The overall result, as a senior manager in the Education Department remarked was that: '… most people would say that the lack of coordination [on IT systems and applications] has been a disaster and it has created all sorts of unnecessary problems'.[xvii] (This comment has added significance given the actions of agents from this department noted above). The situation was compounded further, however, because of the vacuum that had been created around political and corporate management and leadership, discussed earlier in this chapter and because of the privatisation of the IT intelligence and support functions, leaving senior managers with a lack of research data to inform IS policy development. Furthermore, senior staff resented the fact that they now had to buy this 'intelligence' back, which meant they now had to deal with ex-colleagues (who had joined *ITC*) in a formal manner, and in the knowledge that their time and advice further depleted very limited resources. This led one assistant director to remark that: 'IT was an integrated service in-house. They went out with it. I have to say it was a mistake.' [xviii]

It should now be clear that the systemic and cultural incompatibilities and contradictions brought into being through the contracting out of IS and the impact these had on the situations of both primary and corporate agents was a dominant feature of Council X at T1. Without exception staff were damning in their criticism of this situation and its impact on IS developments. Three direct quotes taken from various members of staff serve to illustrate the strength of feeling and bring the discussion of this topic to a conclusion.

There isn't a corporate policy on anything. There are corporate edicts which democratic groups will produce. Like the ISSSG will produce recommendations. But they can't actually implement them. That's not a fertile environment for fresh ideas. [xix]

The reason we haven't got networks, the reasons we haven't got standardisation, is purely because there is no real corporate knowledge about what the organisation does. [xx]

Designing a network before you actually know what the organisation does is impossible. All the [ICT] problems are not being looked into with any corporate policy.[xxi]

Interestingly, and as noted previously, a corporate agent did exist that had the responsibility for maintaining cohesion across IS/ICT developments – the ISSSG group – which, though far less significant than prior to the restructuring of Council X, did retain a formal ICT/IS overview function. However, here again the contract with *ITC* proved a significant causal mechanism, as for several years the primary activity of the ISSSG group became the renegotiation of the contract with *ITC*. When the ISSSG group did finally turn their attention to the coordination and strategic planning of IS, following the conclusion of a renegotiated contract in 1994, the group was then confronted with the structural and cultural features of the Council described above. Furthermore, the lack of political leadership and high level policy guidance also undermined the work of the group, as the chairman of the ISSSG explained: 'One of the big issues [for ISSSG] was that the authority itself didn't actually have a business strategy in terms of where the authority was actually going [and] what were its aims and objectives.[xxii]

The role and significance of the ISSSG through T2–T3 of the morphogenetic cycle is fully discussed in the next chapter, although it was appropriate to briefly note the existence of the group here so as to set it in the context of the wide range of developments that evidence suggests played a major role in the processes of structural and cultural conditioning and shaping at T1. There is however, one more feature of the environment of Council X which featured prominently at T1, as noted in Chapters 1 and 3, the Local Government Review (or LGR).

The Local Government Review as a causal process for the morphogenesis of IS

Announced in December 1991, the LGR was another example of a central government initiative aimed at affecting the structure of local government, albeit that the review process was dealt with by a (supposedly) independent Local Government Commission. As such, LGR could have featured in the section at the beginning of this chapter on the causal powers and mechanisms associated with the institutional systems and relationships between central and local government in England. For example, the generative powers emergent from the LGR impacted heavily on the institutional relationships between the different tiers of local authorities, as the agents of county, district and even town and parish councils pursued different forms of strategic action which each believed would promote their individual and/or group interests. This inevitably created conflict and hostility: in the case of Council X at T1 of this research this meant that any development that took Council X staff into contact with representatives of most district councils was regarded as anathema by the Chief Executive and many other senior officers.

Here, however, the focus will be on the ways in which the structural influences of the LGR impacted on IS developments *within* Council X. The outcome, as I will show, was that although the LGR undoubtedly acted as a powerful constraint for more than three years on the actions of agents within Council X it also created a catalyst for ideational morphogenesis through the mechanisms it created for social, socio cultural and group interaction. The generative powers of the CEPs and PEPs that were to emerge would prove highly significant to IS development, as I detail and discuss in the following two chapters. How and why this happened will now be explained.

LGR and the emergence of new situational logics and forms of strategic action

The official reason for the need for a review of the structure of local government related to the aftermath of the poll tax, and specifically to the two tier structure of much of local government. Central government argued that the two tier system was the reason the general public failed to understand why some local authorities were responsible for certain services, why there was 'overlap', and who they should hold accountable through the ballot box for poor services and/or high council tax charges. To have a single tier – 'unitary' – system of local government throughout the country would do away with this confusion, bring local government 'closer to the people', and would make it cheaper and more efficient – or so the government claimed (Young and Rao 1997, Wilson and Game 1998).

In December 1993, at the first meeting of the Council X Local Government Review Working Party, it was agreed that of the options for reform on offer Council X would support the implementation of one local authority to replace both county and district councils. By mid December councillors and senior management had agreed a draft proposal for an SCA (single countywide authority) and put this out for public consultation. In addition, a LGR 'defence group' was established consisting of a loose coalition of officers from across the Council, coordinated by a principal policy officer from the Chief Executive's Office. The group were given the ongoing task of preparing the Council's response to the LGR and, as and when necessary, taking a proactive approach to defending Council X from attacks in the media and elsewhere.

Events locally were overtaken in January 1995, however, when the High Court ruled that the revised guidance given by the Government to the Commission was illegal. This effectively changed the terms of the Review by giving the option of status quo (i.e. retaining a two tier system) equal validity with unitary solutions. The Commission put forward its three options for the area of Council X in June 1995, with a preferred option being three unitary councils. One district council rejected the Commission's view immediately, and by the end of June Council X had altered its choice to that of status quo; a position also supported by the council of the largest town in the county. The remaining councils supported the Commission's choice. Following consultation the Commission announced its final decision in October 1995: the existing two-tier system was retained.

The decision of the Commission was greeted with overwhelming relief by the vast majority of staff of Council X, and by the LGR defence group in particular. Of particular significance from an IS perspective, as well as in terms of the success of the group in defending Council X, had been that in confronting the threat of abolition, and the situations this created, the group had adopted forms of strategic action not previously deemed necessary within the Council. Crucially, this meant actors were given the freedom to think "outside the box" and it was this process, allied to the common agenda of the group, and frequent and intensive opportunities for intra organisational social interaction, that would provide the mechanisms for the emergence of new ideas and beliefs (i.e. cultural morphogenesis) concerning IS and its importance and role within the Council. A material product of this process of ideational morphogenesis for this particular corporate agent, and thus evidence of the causal powers of LGR, was the Council X Review Document, a brief review of which follows.

The Council X Review Document

Taking its starting point as the 'radical' organisational reforms of decentralisation and devolution that Council X had pursued since 1990, the report emphasised the value these policies had delivered to the authority and the benefits to consumers and citizens in terms of responsiveness and service delivery. To this the reports authors' added the service quality and effectiveness programme noted above (but which, as I also noted, had been largely ignored by departmental agents following devolution). And, by combining these with the overarching theme of community (or local) governance, discussed earlier in this chapter, the document established the principal pillars of the Council's approach to local governance:

- integrating the existing infrastructure of county, district and parish councils

    '...into a network of Service Shops and Help Points to enhance the scope for personal contact between the local authority and the public. *Combined with imaginative use of communications technology it will ensure that county X community government is truly local.*' (Emphasis added).

    community governance

- 'Local self-government is achieved by giving more powers to towns and larger parishes and also smaller ones if they wish. They could be arranging local services or specifying requirements, in various flexible permutations according to what best suited them.'

- a citizen/customer orientation

    '...services would be integrated on a geographical basis focused on the needs of the community. Citizens will therefore see the authority as a *single integrated organisation and have only one contact point* rather than having to find their way through a confusion of departmental structures.' (Emphasis added).

As previously noted a fundamental feature of the LGR defence group's approach was to highlight the ways in which ICT could be used for the delivery of public services and in driving and enabling both intra and inter organisational change. They spelt out their belief in the "revolutionary" powers of new ICTs in clear and unambiguous terms:

> Rapid changes in communications technology are transforming the way we live. Activities ranging from "armchair banking" to cable and satellite TV stations are the everyday expression of global communication networks which have "shrunk" the world in ways unimaginable only twenty years ago. It is a process that has in part been

responsible for the reassertion of a more local cultural identity exemplified in the "Europe of the Regions". Technological advances have done away with the idea that any organisation or location need be "remote". In terms of day-to day management they allow considerable potential for devolving management from the centre.

To some extent at least the defence group's references to new ICTs were inspired by an awareness of the fact that in 1992 the Chairman of the Local Government Commission announced that in his opinion the IT revolution made the geographical size of a local authority an increasingly irrelevant factor in the Review (Banham 1993). This statement prompted many English local authorities to seek to demonstrate that they were capable of exploiting ICT in such a way, with the most common result being that an increasing number of local authorities claimed to be using or developing electronic public information systems (EPIS) – a situation which favoured Council X because, as previously noted, they had been in the forefront of the development of such a system.

To demonstrate the extent to which these developments were possible, and the commitment of the Council to promoting them, the defence group went on to report two high profile ICT based initiatives which Council X was involved with. The first was a partnership project with a major telecoms provider, a major computer manufacturer, and the Rural Development Commission to establish a "Connected Community" in one of the county's towns. The project focused on training and community access to technology, including Council X's databases, and it was planned would develop to include facilities for high volume data transmission, video conferencing and electronic notice boards. The project was seen as '…a crucial catalyst in developing the social and economic infrastructure of the town and surrounding area.' The second project was the Council's own electronic public information system (EPIS). The report noted 'Council X is already a national leader in the development of its interactive videotex information system, accessible in over

166

30 libraries, leisure centres, hospitals and other public buildings throughout the county, as well as on-line in over 100 of the Council's offices, schools and social services buildings. Finally, the commitment to subsidiarity and a partnership approach to community governance provided the basis for a growing interest in experimenting with the development of one stop shops (a form of organisational development I have previously noted and that is discussed in full in Chapter 6).

It is clear that while the policies of decentralisation, devolution and privatisation feature in the Review document, some of the other ideas of the defence group run counter to the systemic and cultural contradictions and incompatibilities that had emerged as a result of these developments. Consequently some of the ideas set out in the document represent a potential challenge to corporate agents that had benefited from these developments. This was not an issue while the LGR was ongoing as the ideas of the defence group remained restricted to paper. Furthermore, it might have been assumed that this would remain the case once the Review was over, as the need for the agents of Council X to respond directly to the generative powers of the SEPs and CEPs emergent from the Review had largely disappeared. This was far from the case, however. Instead another set of situational logics, and the consequent need to adopt new and/or revised forms of strategic action to respond to these, meant the emergence of new SEPs, CEPs and PEPs, which it seemed at T1 might prove significant for the cultural and structural morphogenesis of IS.

LGR and IS development in Council X

In the process of drumming up support for Council X's preferred LGR options the impression had been given to the corporate agents of *town* and *parish* councils that should Council X survive they would benefit in some way or another. Post review this left the onus on senior managers within Council X to decide how – and just as importantly – when, they would repay their allies. There was a significant problem with delivering on this, however, because, and as discussed above, by the time the Review was over Council X had suffered considerable cuts in funding. Thus corporate agents within Council X had little to offer in the way of financial resources and had instead to offer material resources of different kinds, such as expertise and technology. This option was also far from straightforward, however. First, because those actors who had most contact with town and parish councils were from the CE's office, and as previously noted, the hollowing out of the centre of Council X meant that their standing and power as corporate agents had been substantially undermined. Consequently, their ability to make any commitment which had resource implications was extremely limited.

Second, and as noted above, many senior managers had an extremely hostile attitude to contact and collaboration with other local authorities, often appearing unwilling or unable to distinguish between allies and enemies. It was no surprise, therefore, to find the policy officer with the lead role in developing post LGR relations with towns and parishes struggling with this dilemma, as they explained: '…if this [the Partnership Initiative noted below] starts to work then it will be the first such group that has ever met to look at things like working together. He [the Chief Executive] will go up the wall, but I haven't told him.' The author asked why? To which she replied, 'Because he will think that it's a sign of weakness that we gave out to them (sic).'[xxiii]

Nevertheless, the necessity to 'be seen to be doing something' (as one senior manager put it) was a particularly powerful force, given that many of the actions of the LGR defence group had been directed at raising the profile of Council X. In fact, the group had been particularly successful at this: when MORI conducted name and service recognition polls in January 1994 and March 1995 they discovered that over this period name recognition for Council X increased from thirty six to sixty percent, and recognition of the services it provided also substantially increased. While this was crucial to Council X during LGR, unfortunately the demands and expectations it produced amongst its allies and the general public did not disappear after LGR, making it even more difficult for the Council to backtrack on its promises.

It is also crucial to note that the arguments put forward by Council X in its LGR submission clearly demonstrate that amongst the actors involved in the defence group, and other staff that assisted them with their work, the possible significance and potential of information society driven developments for supporting and enabling systems of local governance had clearly registered. As a result the group actively promoted ideas for organisational change which were impossible without IS development. Despite what was presented in their arguments to the LGR, however, the reality of the environment of Council X was that by T1 what the majority of actors/agents thought of as IS developments, and the material and technological circumstances in which actors/agents worked, was not conducive to the type of developments suggested by either local governance or information society agendas.

Despite this, and under pressure from some key actors who had been involved in the defence group – who were quick to point out the external pressures that now existed (and thus the situational logics and need for strategic action that now applied) – and with one of their number now promoted to Assistant Chief Executive, the Strategy and Resources Committee agreed to set up a 'Partnership Initiative' to explore the possibilities for moving forward on some of the key ideas that had emerged from the LGR. Importantly, but not surprisingly perhaps, many of the actors who volunteered to be members of the group set up to progress this initiative had either been members of the LGR defence group, or were strongly supportive of its work. The Partnerships Project Working Group (the PPG) had only recently come into being at T1 and for this reason their role as both an emergent corporate agent and, more importantly, because the group was to prove a crucial mechanism for social interaction, is discussed and analysed fully in the following chapter. Suffice to note that the PPG rapidly became a crucial causal mechanism in attempts to further promote the cultural morphogenesis of IS that had been initiated by the defence group, and also in following this through into the structural morphogenesis of IS. In so doing the PPG were able to exploit the low level of systemic and social integration that

169

decentralisation, devolution and privatisation had created across the Council that this chapter has explored.

Conditioning and shaping: a summary

This chapter set out to undertake two related tasks. The first was to account for the pre-distribution of systems, structures and roles and practices (SEPs); the pre-constitution of ideas, theories and beliefs (CEPs); and the pre-grouping of vested interest groups (PEPs) and the relative power and types of relationship (i.e. contingent or internal and necessary) that shaped and conditioned the interests and activities of actors and agents involved with IS development in Council X at T1. The second was to examine the level and extent of the social and systemic integration of the Council.

Archer's proposition is that analysis of the former allows us to explore why actors/agents are motivated to different courses of strategic action, and modes of interaction, between T2–T3, while analysis of the latter should provide a guide to whether morphogenesis or morphostasis (in this case of IS) is to be the likely outcome at T4. In concluding Chapter 4 the intention is to highlight some of the results of the application of the first phase of the morphogenetic approach. However, as a full discussion of the utility of the approach is the subject of the concluding chapter of this book only two brief observations are made here. The first is that the requirement to explore previous morphogenetic/static cycles, rather than simply base analysis of the activity and environment of agents on what can be observed in the present, proved extremely valuable in establishing a "base line" from which to start to construct a case for the causal processes and powers that were at work in the IS domain of Council X. Had this not been done it is likely that greater emphasis would have been placed on events observed at the time as the primary mechanisms conditioning and shaping the actions of agents (e.g. the day to day organisational politics and power relations of the place) rather than what actually lay behind these actions. The second point, which is clearly related to the previous one, is that conflation was avoided. In other words, the requirements of stage one of the morphogenetic approach directs research at exploring both structure and agency (and, in this case, culture). Consequently, from the outset it is possible to analyse the resulting interactions and begin to construct a case for the nature and outcome of these relationships.

That said, on the basis of the material presented in this chapter what are the most significant conclusions that can be drawn about conditioning and shaping? The first is that by the early 1990s Council X had become an organisation where a raft of radical policies of decentralisation, devolution and privatisation had led to the fragmentation of the organisation and the emergence of systemic incompatibilities and contradictions far beyond those produced by the 'siloisation' that is often associated with highly departmentalised organisations. In short, the structural, cultural and agential properties and powers that emerged from the policies for organisational change implemented from 1990 conditioned and shaped social practice inwards to departments and sub-units, and the high levels of systemic and social integration and compatibilities that the Council X had previously enjoyed largely disappeared.

Evidence was also presented throughout the chapter of the role of ICTs in the fragmentation of the structural and cultural domains of Council X, and how, once this had occurred technology became a powerful component in the maintenance of systemic differentiation. It is worth a reminder at this point, however, that this is as a structural *property* (or artefact) and *not* as structural systems in their own right. As such, and in *conjunction* with other structural properties such as administrative systems and practices and rules and regulations, technologies can and do play a powerful role in conditioning and shaping the actions of agents. The examples given above of *Office Power* and the divergent hardware and software applications that were adopted across Council X post 1990 clearly illustrate this.

The types of relationship that had become established between interest groups within the IS arena at T1 as a result of the conditioning and shaping of agency detailed in this chapter are illustrated in Figure 4.4. As can be seen, post LGR groups (shaded grey) enjoyed a large number of relationships that were contingent (dashed lines). That is, the existence and operation of each group was *not* dependant on the other. The only exception is with the Corporate Services Unit (CSU). As the following chapter on interaction explains, this is because most of these groups were emergent from the CSU. By contrast pre LGR groups all enjoyed internal and necessary relations (solid lines, with the nature of the relationship indicated by an arrow head or plain line). As the discussion in this chapter has shown, however, even where relationships were internal and necessary they were not unchanging over time and thus the amount of power vested in groups by those they were emergent from ebbed and flowed. Indeed, the amount of power flowing from the Corporate Services Unit to its emergent groups was significantly less than to groups shown on the left of the figure.

Figure 4.5 takes this analysis a step further and illustrates both the relative power and ideational standing of the vested interest groups of the IS environment of Council X at T1. Again, the grey shaded boxes indicate groups that were casually related to the LGR and were therefore later arrivals to the IS environment of the Council than those non shaded groups. The dominant position of departmental interest groups is clearly visible, as is the decline in the relative power of the Chief Executive's Office, represented by the CSU. The lack of high level leadership and corporate management documented earlier in this chapter is reflected in the low ideational standing of the Strategy and Resources Committee, while the impact of devolution and decentralisation is clearly reflected in the position of Departmental Chief Officer's groups and Departmental IS/IT strategy groups vis-a-vis Chief Officer's Management Group. Meanwhile the IT contractor *ITC* features prominently in terms of material resources, but, as the detailed account of the privatisation of the IT function of Council X demonstrated, their ideational standing was low and of little value.

172

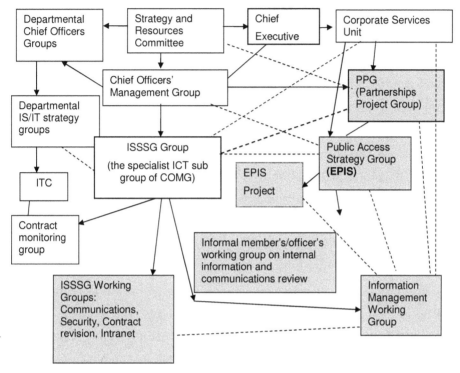

Dashed lines = contingent Solid = internal and necessary

Direction of arrows indicates the nature of an asymmetric relationship

No arrow head = symmetric or unclear internal and necessary relationship

Figure 4.4 Social interaction and IS development at Council X 1995–96:
interest group relationships by type

As discussed above, Archer argues that: '...the incidence of [systemic] complementarities serves to identify the potential loci of systemic reproduction and the occurrence of incompatibilities the potential loci of systemic transformation.' (Archer 1995:215). There is, however, a second element to this proposition, which is that the synchronicity or lack of it, of cycles of cultural and structural morphogenesis will also affect the outcome of the interplay of structure and culture. The two dimensions which the analysis undertaken in this chapter suggests were significant in the case of Council X were where structural morphogenesis had occurred but largely without cultural morphostasis. Here the results of the forced morphogenesis of structure caused by decentralisation, devolution and privatisation led to an outcome that was entirely consistent with Archer's view that there will be '...a substantial growth in material interest groups. [but that] Culture provides no spur [for] *structural change, but acts as a drag upon it.*' (Archer 1995:313. Original emphasis).

On the other hand, however, and specifically in relation to IS, the evidence presented above in respect to the LGR strongly supports Archer's proposition that where morphogenesis is occurring in the cultural domain (with structural morphostasis) this then acts as a powerful motor for more widespread change, since '...cultural change leads to the reconstitution of structural subjects (Archer 1995:317).

Again, examples given throughout this chapter, such as the (assumed) role of ICTs in systems of local governance, and how strongly ideas about the potentialities of ICTs featured in the LGR, clearly illustrate the role ICTs/IS can and do play in the cultural domain – in the realm of ideas, theories and beliefs. Thus the 'spirit' of a technology, as DeSanctis and Poole (1994) termed it, can be used to promote certain goals and values. Snellen and Donk (1996) referred to this as the 'potentialities' of new technology, and noted how important certain assumptions and beliefs about what was possible using new technology had been to the 'informatization' of government and the public sector through the 1980s and early 1990s. This is a fundamental feature of ICTs/IS that is certainly borne out by the evidence presented in this chapter.

In conclusion, the low levels of systemic and social integration that had permeated throughout Council X, taken together with the morphogenesis of the cultural domain of IS (albeit amongst a relatively small group of actors), would suggest that the possibility for the morphogenesis of ICT/IS (as a structural property) as a result of the processes of interaction between T2 and T3 was highly likely. The objective of the next chapter is therefore to analyse and evaluate how the different courses of action open to the interest groups shown in Figure 4.4 and 4.5, and their opportunity costs, were confronted and played out through socio-cultural and group interaction. The outcome – whether the morphogenesis or morphostasis of IS did occur – then becomes the focus of the penultimate chapter of this book.

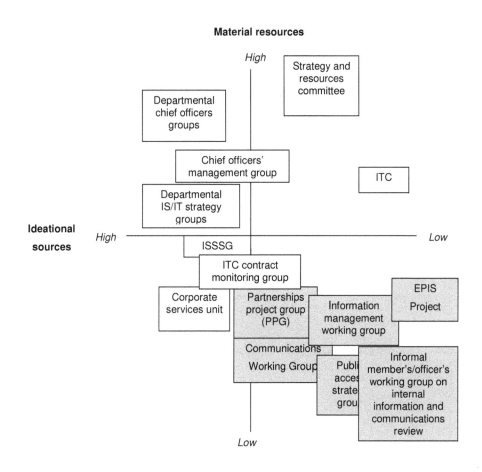

Figure 4.5 The relative power and ideational standing of interests groups within the IS domain of Council X at T1

5

ANALYSING AND EVALUATING INTERACTION

T2 – T3: Social, socio-cultural and group interaction

The grey shaded areas of Figure 5.1 illustrate the elements of the morphogenetic cycles that are the focus of this chapter. The aim is to analyse how the situational logics and opportunities for strategic action of those agents most closely associated with IS development, identified in Figures 4.4 and 4.5, such as the Partnerships Project Working Group (PPG) and the Information Systems Strategy Sub Group (ISSSG), were confronted through social, socio-cultural and group interaction. Specifically, this means:

- Identifying how interaction takes place, where, why and by which of the groups identified at T1.

- Tracking the changing resource distributions of different vested interest groups and how these influence the relations and transactions between them.

- Identifying the different forms of interaction (i.e. defensive, concessionary, competitive, and opportunistic) between different groups.

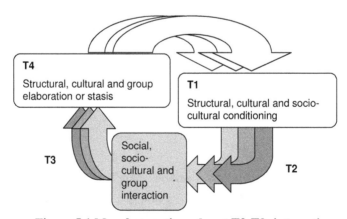

Figure 5.1 Morphogenetic cycles at T2-T3: interaction

It is worth reiterating at this point that all of these activities take place in a mediated environment for agents/actors, while agents also mediate the structured and shaped situations in which they find themselves through their reflective powers (Archer 1995, Porpora 1998). This is the double morphogenesis of agency. Crucially this means that the kinds of conditioning and shaping reported in the previous chapter are not laws or forces, as they would be presented in positivist/determinist accounts of this case study, but reasons – 'directional guidance' – that conditioning brings into being but that we are free to react to in a range of different ways because we enjoy interpretive freedom due to our reflexive powers (Archer 1995).

The timeline presented as Figure 5.2 illustrates that the origins of the PPG actually predate T1 by some months, and then continue through until April 1996. At this time a number of organisational developments that were premised on the availability and properties of ICTs began to take place, such as the launch of the OSS, which has been noted in previous chapters, and the Officers' and Members' ICT Pilot Project, also discussed previously in Chapter 3. As the discussion here demonstrates, these developments can be causally linked to the strategic actions, modes of interaction and resulting exchange transactions and power relations of agents. These are fundamental to any process of morphogenesis/stasis.

The fact that some material that predates the T2–T3 period is presented in this chapter illustrates how difficult it is to demarcate the stages of the three morphogenetic cycles, particularly when trying to maintain the interrelated nature of the structural, cultural and agential strata by presenting them in the same analysis and discussion. This issue is analysed in Chapter 7. It is sufficient to record here that the primary reason that this is problematic appears to be for the reasons discussed in Chapter 2 and at the end of Chapter 4: that the morphogenesis/stasis of the cultural, structural and agential systems may well be out of sync. For example, and as the previous chapter clearly demonstrates, within Council X the morphogenesis of the cultural system of IS began amongst a limited group of actors largely as a result of the LGR. Furthermore, as those actors/agents who had become part of the Council's response to the LGR struggled to reproduce/transform structures and cultures in response to the generative powers of the SEPs and CEPs emergent from the Review, such as the need to be more responsive to the needs of citizens/customers, so this led, in turn (and as Archer argues will be the case) to the morphogenesis of agency, because:

> ...collectivities are transformed from primary agents into promotive interest groups; social selves are re-constituted as actors personifying roles in particular ways to further their self defined ends; and corporate agency is re-defined as institutional interests promote reorganisation and re-articulation of goals in the course of strategic action for their promotion or defence. (Archer 1995:191).

In the case of Council X the outcome was the emergence of an important new corporate agent – the PPG – and the subsequent transformation of the associations, organisation and articulation of interests of other interest groups due to the generative powers of this group. There was no evidence of structural morphogenesis relevant to IS at that point, however. From April 1996 onwards examples of morphogenesis that are causally related to the social, socio-cultural and group interaction between T2–T3, such as the OSS and Officers' and Members' ICT Pilot project, did begin to emerge. These are discussed in the following chapter. The material in this chapter is ordered according to the prominence of the named groups in the causal processes that led to these developments, starting, as noted above, with the PPG.

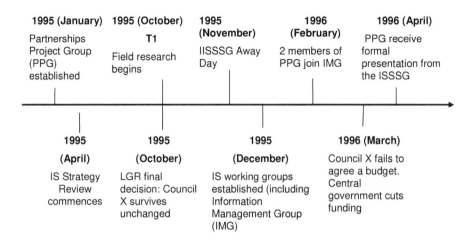

Figure 5.2 Council X: interaction and elaboration timeline 1995 - 96

Corporate and primary agents, promotive interest groups and interaction
The Partnerships Project Working Group (PPG)

Established in January 1995, as a result of the structural and cultural influences emergent from the LGR, the PPG rapidly became the most important agent for the potential morphogenesis of IS within Council X. The importance of the group comes from the fact that it actually functioned in three interrelated ways. First, as a corporate agent, because the definition of such a group is that it has the power to '…maintain/re-model the socio-cultural system and its institutional parts.' (Archer 1995: 265). The brief given to the PPG by Chief Officer's Management Group (COMG) bestowed on the group such powers, albeit that at T1 these were relatively weak when compared to other corporate agents (Figure 4.6). Second, as a promotive interest group seeking to promote many of the ideas that had emerged from the LGR. Third, as an important mechanism for intra and inter group interaction.

As a formally constituted sub group of COMG the PPG's relationship to this group was asymmetrical and internal and necessary (Figure 4.4). However, as a cross-departmental working group, it was reliant on other departments for its human resource. Initially the PPG was chaired by the Assistant Chief Executive who had been head of the LGR defence group (and had been promoted to ACE as a result of the outcome of the LGR). However, this role passed to a principal policy officer from the Chief Executives Office in early 1996. The PPG reported directly to the (COMG) and, on a quarterly basis, to the Strategy and Resources Committee (S&RC). These were the most powerful corporate agents at the Council, sitting at the apex of the hierarchy of formal committees and groups that formed the political and operational sides of the Council, as Figure 4.5 illustrates. This meant that the PPG became the primary forum for interaction and the recognised corporate agent for any matter relating to partnership working (i.e. local governance). In this capacity the objectives set for the group by COMG were to:

- identify a range of Partnership initiatives and provide a framework and guidance for implementation;
- identify and facilitate opportunities for partnership working;
- monitor and evaluate initiatives and progress;
- ensure that appropriate support mechanisms are in place to maximise the effectiveness of delivery.

How the membership of the PPG was chosen provides an interesting example of the how the unintended outcomes of past actions can become important generative mechanisms, and illustrates, therefore, why Archer and other critical realists see these as so important to the outcome of causal processes: a position which contrasts strongly with scholars of a positivist and/or determinist bent who regard these as relatively unimportant. Because of the policies of decentralisation and devolution, and the consequent loss of authority and power of actors in the CE's office, when inter departmental initiatives were established membership was dependant on the grace and favour of the chief officers of each department. As the PPG was not regarded by departments as particularly important – primarily because the LGR was over and because even if the group came up with recommendations they had no power to implement them – departments simply put a memo around to senior officers asking for expressions of interest. There wasn't a rush. After all, from the perspective of departmentally based actors there was little to be gained from involvement in corporate activities. Consequently, those people that did put their names forward were automatically co-opted on to the PPG. Because of the brief of the PPG, however, almost all of those that became members tended to have ties to the now defunct LGR defence group. Unsurprisingly therefore, this further strengthened the extent to which the ideas and beliefs of the group were informed by the Council's submission to the LG Commission. As a result a synthesis of the potentialities of new ICTs and of the emerging agenda of local governance rapidly became a hallmark of the PPG. The resulting CEPs signalled an alternative discourse of IS development: one that emphasised the networking capabilities of new ICTs, and thus not only how communities could be "connected", but how Council X could become "whole" again.

In is no surprise that such views and beliefs were regarded by many departmentally based actors and agents as primarily about rebuilding the power and influence of actors and agents of the CE's office. Such a change could potentially result in a challenge to the departmental and sub departmental 'empires' that had grown up across the Council post 1990. Consequently, the actors and agents of these 'empires' sought to resist these developments and to further condition and shape actions, ideas and discourse in such a way as to protect their interests by seeking to ensure that the courses of action open to the PPG were bounded and controlled. For example, that any attempts at IS development or organisational change were vetted by the ISSSG, hence the importance of this corporate agents, as I discuss below.

Despite the situation outlined above, and perhaps because some members of the PPG had already been involved in an enterprise that was widely expected to fail (the LGR) members of the PPG took the view that there *were* still different courses of strategic action open to them. Thus, the group set about exploring '…better ways of providing information about *services* as well as new and innovative ways of providing *services* themselves, or in partnership with other providers.' [xxiv]

The PPG: strategic action and modes of interaction

Members of the PPG were aware from the outset that to successfully promote their agenda for change they needed to develop relationships with other interests groups - and corporate agents in particular. One such group, which has been previously identified above, was the IS Strategy Sub Group (ISSSG). For reasons discussed below, and which Figure 4.5 illustrates, this corporate agent was more powerful and influential than the PPG. Nevertheless, the PPG's members realised that because their agenda for local governance was reliant on IS developments if they were to successfully promote it they would need the support of the ISSSG. Initially they accepted that even if interaction did occur it was less than certain that the ideas of the two groups would be compatible, not least because the ISSSG's interests had focused for many years on the privatisation of the ICT function of Council X and on the aftermath of this. As a result the ISSSG was regarded as integral to the post 1989 structure and culture of IS within Council X, and both its ideational and structural approach to IS development were entirely in line with this. One member of the ISSSG group illustrated the potential problem well when discussing his efforts to get his colleagues on ISSSG to think a little more progressively about ICT:

> I'd always try to argue the case of the role of IT for public use. But in the main colleagues' (on the ISSSG) perceptions was that IT was job related. Certainly some of the guys on it would get pretty antagonistic if I argued the public case. They saw it as starry eyed, utopian, the last thing to be doing. [xxv]

By early 1995, and following a limited review of IS strategy carried out by *ITC* in late 1994, members of ISSSG decided a full review of IS strategy should be carried out as this had not been updated since the privatisation of the central IT department in 1990. However, in March 1995, members of the PPG found out that an unexpected event had occurred COMG had asked the ISSSG for a revised IS strategy (information from the ISSSG was regularly passed to PPG by the head of the Corporate Services Unit [CSU] who was the CE's Office representative on the group. Minutes of the ISSSG group meetings were also publicly available within Council X, as were those of the PPG). The chairman of ISSSG explains:

> The involvement of COMG was not foreseen …It happened because the half yearly report on IT issues given to COMG on 6th March led to a request that a draft strategy should be presented to Chief Officers' away day on 27th March and that the effective delivery of services using the latest developments in IT should be explained.[xxvi]

In addition to this specific request, and following the away day on 27th March (see below), COMG also suggested that the scope of the review should be based on a composite of points made by Chief Officers and material from the limited review that had already been carried out by *ITC*. These were that…

- The review should examine the need for a framework of standards and conventions to underpin the security and integrity of the Council's information systems.
- The review should consider the need for common facilities, and the need for agreed standards to allow the common facilities to be used.
- The review should consider *whether the commitment to devolution and decentralisation may have led to the fragmentation of systems and in consequence affected the Council's ability to provide information to others*, for example towns and parishes, through and single access point. (Emphasis added).[xxvii]

As the report from which the list above is taken goes on to note: 'A request to explain the strategy a month before the terms of reference were agreed by the ISSSG posed a problem…' How the ISSSG dealt with this is discussed below. There are a number of important points to note here, however. First, what was the motive for an intervention which acted as a crucial causal mechanism in the emerging causal process for IS development that was the strategy review (directing the review into areas that it is unlikely the ISSSG would have gone)? Evidence from interviews carried out at the time suggests that when the 'half yearly report on IT issues' was given to COMG in early March 1995 a number of members were dismayed at the situation regarding the continuing problems with the services provided by *ITC* (even after the renegotiation of the contract) and their actual role in keeping the Council strategically informed. This is borne out by comments on the outcome of the strategic planning process made by the chairman of the ISSSG to COMG in a report a year later:

> The original premise that *ITC* could perform both a client and contractor role has proved to be an unrealistic assumption. Leaving aside the potential conflicts of interests in such a dual role...The idea that *ITC* would be able and willing to provide the strategic level input envisaged when the original contract was set up has not materialised in practice.[xxviii]

Evidence accumulated from a range of sources through 1995 also suggests that a number of senior officers who had been part of the LGR defence team, including the person who had subsequently become an assistant CE, lobbied sympathetic Chief Officers, such as the head of the Libraries Service, to push for inclusion of issues and ideas that had emerged during the LGR process. This was obviously successful, as the suggested scope of the review draws attention to some of the most powerful structural – both organisational and technological – and cultural features of Council X to have emerged post 1990.

As previously established, the success (in terms of morphogenesis) of any strategic course of action is not *solely* conditioned by the bargaining power and negotiating strength (i.e. relative power) of groups, however, but *also* by exchange transactions. 'Moreover, they are inextricably linked with one another and jointly account for the emergence of either reciprocity or control in the interaction between different groups.' (Archer 1995:296). Archer also maintains that *any* process of exchange and power involves the use of three specific sets of resources – political sanctions, liquid assets and expertise – with the different availability of these resources to different groups underpinning their bargaining power. The actions of the PPG certainly illustrate how this dynamic works in practice. Members of the PPG realised that although they lacked both political sanctions and liquid assets the focus of the IS review, as suggested by COMG, did mean that they possessed one valuable resource; expertise in IS and local governance, largely as a result of the LGR.

The PPG membership also knew that at that point in time the ISSSG had no terms of reference of their own and that the timetable the ISSSG group had been given for the final presentation of the revised ICT strategy was tight – April 1996. Group members therefore decided on the following approach. First, adopt what would appear to members of the ISSSG as a highly *concessionary* mode of interaction by making available their expertise (although from the perspective of the PPG this was an entirely opportunistic mode of interaction). Second, adopt a strategic course of action where their own work would 'shadow' that of ISSSG, such that they could make interventions, where necessary, with the ultimate aim being to submit their own development plan to the same COMG meeting that would receive the new IS strategy in April 1996.

The belief amongst members of the PPG was that if the ISSSG produced a conservative strategy, which downplayed or ignored the structural problems that had emerged post 1990, and of which IS was a part, then their document could be used to challenge this, albeit by putting forward alternative proposals rather than criticising the ISSSG or post 1990 policies. On the other hand, if the ISSSG actually submitted a relatively progressive document then parallels could be drawn between the two. It was then thought likely that COMG would ask the two groups to coordinate their work. Before exploring how this strategy for interaction worked in practice, and any outcomes, it is appropriate at this point to change tack slightly and undertake a more detailed discussion of the ISSSG.

Potential morphogenesis meets probable morphostasis: the IS Strategy Sub Group (ISSSG)

With decision making and resource allocation powers the ISSSG had, prior to the demise of the Council's in-house IT service, been the most powerful officer group on IS matters within Council X. After privatisation the ISSSG remained a sub group of COMG, and thus internally and necessarily related to it (Figure 4.4), but the role of the group was significantly diminished as its powers to allocate resources and make decisions on IS were transferred to departments. The role of group became simply 'the corporate group for dealing with information issues'[xxix], working to terms of reference agreed by COMG. Despite this loss of power the ISSSG remained influential because COMG formally recognised it as the corporate repository for expertise on IS matters. Consequently, and as Figure 4.5 illustrates, while the ability of the group to exert causal powers on the structural domain of Council X had diminished it still occupied a significant gate-keeping position in the cultural system through its role as a conduit for, and source of, ideas on IS development.

Membership of the ISSSG consisted of a principal officer from all departments of Council X, including the Fire Service. The IT Contract Monitoring Officer acted as co-ordinator, with junior personnel from the Contract Monitoring Unit servicing the ISSSG. The group met monthly. The Chairperson of the ISSSG was drawn from a service department because '...the perception was we need to have a service chief because there was a tension that the centre was unlikely to be sympathetic to the ways departments were wanting to move.'.[xxx] In other words, it was necessary to have actors/agents in place that would use their emergent properties (PEPs) to promote the CEPs and SEPs necessary for the process of decentralisation and devolution. As the previous chapter noted, through the course of this research the chairman of the ISSSG was the Assistant Chief Education Officer, who had held the position for three years. As has also been previously discussed the Education Department, and the ACEO specifically, were enthusiastic supporters of decentralisation, devolution and contracting out and that the interests of many of the agents and actors of that department had been well served by such policies.

As well as contributing significantly to undermining the power of the ISSSG, privatisation also presented a significant operational challenge. Problems with the detail and application of the contract soon emerged, as a number of the themes discussed towards the end of the previous chapter indicate. Indeed, it was these concerns that drove COMG's intervention into the IS strategy process. The underlying problem was that there had been an assumption that the privatised service Council X received would duplicate the service previously provided in-house. In other words, that the structure of the contract and the emergent properties, causal powers and agential interactions brought into being by it, would replicate past SEPs, CEPs, and PEPs. This belief soon proved to be wrong, with the result that: '...the Council's requirements and the service started to diverge'[xxxi]. As a consequence the role of the ISSSG for the period 1991–93 became: '...coming to terms with the *ITC* contract and trying to sort that out.'[xxxii] The result was a full review of the contract with a renegotiated deal in place from 1994. However, this did not resolve every problem, with some aspects of the contractual relationship (such as, advice and support to users, training, and strategic information on IT development) continuing to have 'quite severe consequences'[xxxiii].

By late 1994, and in the face of growing concern with the "health" of the Council's data network, following a report by *ITC* that had confirmed that the network was in urgent need of modernisation, the ISSSG began to take a more proactive interest in IS developments. Nevertheless, these were firmly conditioned by the structural and cultural features of Council X, and of IS specifically, that were set out in the previous chapter. Then, in early 1995, came the 'surprise' request from COMG for a revised IS strategy. Despite their 'guidance', which clearly posed questions about the impact that decentralisation and devolution had had on IS, in his report to COMG in May 1995 the chairman of the ISSSG reported that:

> The Sub Group propose that the Review should be built up from an analysis of departmental plans plus consideration of the information needs of members, communities, clients, and other agencies.[xxxiv]

Here is a clear indication that although the ISSSG could not avoid the post LGR environment in which Council X now had to operate, they did not intend to forget that the interests of most members of the group were best served by the existing structure and culture of the Council and of the direction that IS developments had taken since 1990. Consequently, and despite its stated role to take an organisation wide (i.e. corporate) view of IS developments the group primarily functioned as a corporate agent promoting the interests of departments. Nevertheless, given the groups relationship with COMG they could not ignore its wishes as the opportunity costs to the ISSSG, and likely to its members individually, of a schism with COMG were potentially high (e.g. a loss of influence to other groups such as the PPG). Thus, the final terms of reference for the strategic review became:

- To agree an appropriate model for co-ordination of Departmental ISSSG plans, information access and provision.
- To agree a framework for guiding departments on attaining and demonstrating benefits from IT investment.
- To agree a framework of standards and protocols aimed at achieving systems compatibility and connectivity.
- To agree a framework of standards/protocols aimed at ensuring that access to systems is properly controlled and is secure.[xxxv]

While accepting the need for standards and protocols and compatibility and connectivity, the ISSSG were quick to add caveats which steered both the control and focus of the review back towards departments. Thus, the 22nd May report states that the review should be a 'bottom up departmentally led process where the potential to meet common needs is the emphasis rather than the imposition of corporate conformity.'. The ISSSG concluded by drawing attention to a series of points of concern which had apparently been raised by departments, one of which was the value of the ISSSG as a forum for '...creating a corporate context...' for IS developments. Thus, despite the groups loss of the power as a result of the removal of their resource allocation function it is clear that they had no intention of weakening their powerful gate-keeping role and intended to adopt a highly defensive mode of interaction to protect this.

Tension between the structure and culture of departmentalism, and the resulting SEPs and CEPs, and their causal powers, and the need for some form of corporate approach to IS developments was a consistent theme for the ISSSG throughout the period of my research, as it was for the PPG. However, whereas the PPG accepted from the outset that more often than not the low levels of systemic integration within Council X worked against the development and implementation of policies for IS development that could enable effective examples of local governance, the ISSSG did not. Consequently, despite agreeing the terms of reference for the Strategy Review in May, by November 1995 actual work had progressed at a very slow pace despite the stated objective that: 'In the initial period of three months, all departments will be asked to prepare IS&T plans on a three and five year timescale.'[xxxvi]. This lack of progress was largely due to stonewalling while departmental corporate agents considered what the opportunity costs of the various courses of action might be and what modes of interaction to employ.

There was, however, another unexpected outcome of these processes of formal and informal interaction and negotiation within and between departments. During their regular exchanges with primary agents (i.e. ordinary members of staff) members of the ISSSG increasingly came to realise that the levels of dissatisfaction with IS developments post 1990 were far higher than they had assumed (this situation was borne out by the responses to the survey of officers and members attitudes to ICT carried out by PSTAG in early 1996 and reported in Chapter 3). Of course, much of this was due to privatisation. Nevertheless, it was clear that corporate agents would have to act on this dissatisfaction before long, as a failure to do so might well result in primary agency unleashing '...a stream of aggregate environmental pressures and problems which affect the attainment [of the formers] promotive interests (Archer 1995:260). As things turned out, however, in early November 1995 an event took place which provided the opportunity for intense group interaction for the ISSSG's members and, as such, proved significant for cultural morphogenesis and thus ideational and discursive reshaping. Meanwhile, the resulting PEPs modified the powers of the members of the ISSSG in exactly the way Archer predicts: '...affecting their consciousness and commitments, affinities and animosities, while exerting causal powers on agents and groupings.' (Archer 1995: 182). The result, as we shall see, was a change in the mode of interaction employed by the group from largely defensive to largely concessionary.

The ICT Away Day

'...that Away Day was a landmark.'[xxxvii]

Although the ICT Away Day of November 1995 was internally and necessarily related to the ISSSG the impetus for the event was clearly the intervention of COMG in the IS strategy and the resulting need to get the strategy process moving. The aim of the day was, therefore, to identify the steps which needed to be taken to create an 'effective ICT process and developing [sic] appropriate ICT thinking for the future [strategy]'. And, in particular, address the conundrum that: One of the problems with any statement of strategy in relation to IS&T is that it is out of date no sooner than it is written.[xxxviii]

The ISSSG commissioned an external consultant to organise and facilitate the event. His brief included discussing the nature and function of the ISSSG itself, as well as the operation of the wider organisation. Participants took part in a wide ranging group discussion and each person completed a questionnaire before the day ended. The consultant the produced a report based on this material. The report makes interesting reading, not least because the results replicate many of the findings of the research reported here, and that of PSTAG. For example, 80% of the participants in the away day thought that the ISSSG was falling well short of fulfilling its role. The tension between the corporate and departmental dimensions of the organisation were also clearly evident, with 50% agreeing that 'a department/service focused basis for ICT development hampers thinking /development at a corporate/council wide level' and the other 50% disagreeing. There was a similar divide in the responses to a question on how departments could improve their contribution to council wide ICT thinking.

The second part of the report was based on the group discussion and is extensive in scope. It ranges over group dynamics and interpersonal skills, a new role and philosophy for the ISSSG, the IT contractor's role and the relationship between the two organisations – in particular, the strengthening of the 'corporate client' and priorities for the future. Considerable attention is given to some of the major issues which constrain and shape the actions of Council X, such as whether decentralisation and devolution had undermined the Council's ability to provide information to other organisations in a planned, coordinated and effective manner. Also whether, as a result of LGR, Council X should project itself as an 'entity' and, in so doing, make more and better use of information, regardless of where, or who, in the organisation has it. In other words, recognition that the authority had to consider the wider information needs of 'members, communities, clients and other agencies' and how it could provide this information, preferably in a holistic way. Finally, and unsurprisingly, the underlying issue – fragmentation and the resulting tension between corporate and decentralised and devolved modes of operation – is identified. The consultant's comments are worth quoting in full here as they are a powerful indictment of the policies for organisational change, and thus IS development, that Council X had followed since 1990:

> I am very much in favour of the devolvement of budgets to departments...this should release the requisite diversity and creative thinking at those levels. However, from the Survey, and from the above [the consultants final report] it is clear there needs to be funds available at the centre to fund county wide, non-departmental, corporate/client IS/IT initiatives/thinking. To rely on subventions from departments on a bidding or as and when basis is to misunderstand the nature, extent, complexity and importance of the processes involved. Without adequate budgets for pump priming, stimulating research, commissioning pilot work, provision of workshops, seminars and training much of the work of the ISSSG group, as proposed, may fail, or, even worse, fail to "get off the ground". This would have direct implications for the ISSSG, progressing the wider IS/IT initiatives, and the long term work of the Council.[xxxix]

Amongst members of the ISSSG opinions of the Away Day were unanimously positive, regardless of whether, following the event, members emerged as "reformers" or not (see below). For example, the sentiments of the Assistant Director of Education (who could not be regarded as a reformer) cited at the head of this section, were echoed by the Assistant Director of Library Services (who was a reformer), who remarked: '...we had quite an Away Day and the thing [ISSSG] has changed out of all recognition.'[xl]

The involvement of the consultant was also important. Taken together, the event itself and the content of his subsequent report gave legitimacy to ideas and beliefs, and/or confirmed doubts, that some members of the ISSSG had about the nature and direction of IS developments. The result was the emergence of what might best be called a reformist wing of the ISSSG. As events discussed later in this chapter illustrate, this became visible within a short space of time and demonstrated that despite the fact that the membership of the ISSSG and the PPG were different, the sentiments of at least half of the ISSSG were now broadly in line with those of the PPG. However, the strategic options and tactics available to members of the PPG for any further ideational shift within the ISSSG were constrained because the ISSSG's members did not want to be seen to be 'taking on' COMG. This issue was rooted in the discussion in the previous chapter of the fact that a combination of the 'hung' nature of the council, central government policy and the low levels of systemic integration of Council X had created what numerous staff referred to a 'corporate vacuum' in policy and decision making.

From a morphogenetic perspective this represents the causal powers of a range of SEPs (sets of internal and necessary relations which entail material resources, whether physical or human) impacting on the position practice system of the Council. The outcome – a breakdown in political and managerial leadership – was felt throughout the Council. However, because of the radical policy of contracting out imposed on the ICT environment of Council X, it was here that it hit hardest as there were very few of the historical SEPs left to fill the vacuum. The situations this created mean that actors and corporate agents, such as the ISSSG, were forced into ad-hoc courses of strategic action, as the Chairperson of the group, explained:

> [The lack of overall strategy was] one of the issues for the away day. What came out of that was the view that we couldn't go back and tell them [Chief Officers] that. You've got to be joking. If you think I'm going to the Chief Officers and the Chief Executive particularly, and tell them what your bloody business strategy is, and I can't do an IT strategy, I'm going to get booted into touch. It might be right basically, but it's another thing saying it. What we came up with was "there's no point in going into conflict. Better to go along and say, in the absence of you coming up with a business structure, this is what we are actually

going to do in terms of what we perceive to be the business needs and therefore what we are going to do as ISSSG strategy to accord with that". You've got the opportunity – which was the unwritten message – to tell us something different...We didn't get that. So basically, by default we actually got an endorsement of the business needs of the authority which is largely enshrined in the way the ISSSG works.[xli]

The reluctance of the ISSSG to put forward proposals which might appear critical of the past actions of COMG is understandable given that the group's authority/power and existence depended on COMG, as established above, and Figure 4.4 illustrates. Therefore, no individual or group interest would be served by such a confrontational relationship. Nevertheless, the consequence of the 'corporate vacuum' in policy and decision making was that the power and influence of the ISSSG increased as its newly inherited role as *the* ideational source for the definition of the business needs of the Council became apparent to other corporate agents. From the perspective of the PPG this was a mixed blessing, although it did mean that if their concessionary approach to interaction were successful it was more likely that the IS and local governance agenda would be incorporated into Council wide policy.

Within a month of the away day, however, the causal powers of that event were responsible for the emergence of further SEPs, in the form of formally constituted specialist working groups. As the discussion that follows explains, although internally and necessarily related to the ISSSG these groups were to largely militate against the increased power and influence of that group through the increased opportunities for socio-cultural interaction they provided. They also proved crucial to the emergence of further CEPs and PEPS, and thus the eventual morphogenesis of the cultural and structural systems of IS. It is also worth noting at this point that the classification of these groups as SEPs is not straightforward and is therefore an issue for discussion in the broader debate on the utility of Archer's definitions of emergent properties in Chapter 7.

194

Opportunities for interaction, bargaining and negotiation increase

In his report to COMG on the ICT Away Day, approximately one month after the event, the chairman of the ISSSG noted that: 'There was dissatisfaction with the output from the ISSSG, and the feeling that more could be done.'[xlii] In an attempt to address this issue the ISSSG accepted the consultant's suggestion that they set up a range of working groups tasked with analysing and evaluating many of the practical issues which it was assumed would emerge from the full strategy review. The four areas identified for special attention were: structure and process of the ISSSG; IS/IT contract 1998 (both these areas were identified as in need of further review); communications and information management; and network and data security. The ISSSG decided that given the specialist focus and probable workload of these groups it did not posses the necessary manpower or expertise to adequately resource them. Consequently when the working groups were formally constituted, with terms of reference and a specified membership, the latter was not restricted to actors from the ISSSG but widened to include experts from across the Council.

This was a highly significant move for three related reasons. First, it diluted the internal and necessary relationship between the working groups and the group they were emergent from, the ISSSG, as the groups developed necessary relations – via human resources – with other corporate agents. Second, because of the needs of the ISSSG for expertise it altered the balance of negotiating strength and power relations between it and the working groups in favour of both the non ISSSG actors and the groups they were drawn from. Combined, these two factors meant that each working group had the potential to take a far more autonomous approach to its task, in terms of both remit and mode of interaction, than the ISSSG's members might have expected. Third, it presented certain actors and/or vested interest groups with an opportunity to participate in decision making processes that had previously been closed to them.

It was unsurprising therefore, that the PPG and the Corporate Services Unit (CSU), a unit closely associated with the PPG and other IS and local governance groups (Figures 4.4 and 5.3) were quick to volunteer people for the working groups. Their success at getting people on to these was at least in part aided by the fact that the culture of devolution meant that once again these groups were generally perceived by departmental staff as likely to be nothing more than 'talking shops' and therefore of little importance. Members of PPG took a different view, however, seeing 'capture' of the groups as a means to move from concessionary to opportunistic interaction, both with the ISSSG and with other actors/agents via the working groups. In practice, however, the success of this tactic, as well as the degree to which groups became autonomous, actually depended on how many actors on a working group came from the reformist wing of the ISSSG. That is, where actors from the CSU/PPG joined working groups that contained a predominance of reformers from the ISSSG then that group tended to adopt an autonomous and opportunistic mode of interaction, and a far more open and radical approach to the ideational reshaping that interaction allowed. This was, in turn, reflected in the proposals the groups came forward with, as we shall see below.

In practice, the CPU and the PPG only 'captured' one working group: the Communications and Information Management Group (or CWG). While there is little doubt that the capture of other groups would have been beneficial to the advancement of their interests it is clear that of the four working groups the CWG offered the most potential for progressing the interests of the PPG. In fact, an undated paper headed *The ISSSG: Issues for the PPG*, sets out in note form a range of issues concerning the ICT strategy process. Only one working group – communications – is singled out for attention in the paper, which goes on to list an 'agenda' of things the working group could look at, and, importantly, the date by which it has to produce recommendations to the ISSSG – March 1996. Clearly, therefore, this document must have been put together well in advance of that date otherwise it had no use. Whether or not it was drafted before or after membership of the working groups was decided cannot be verified, however.

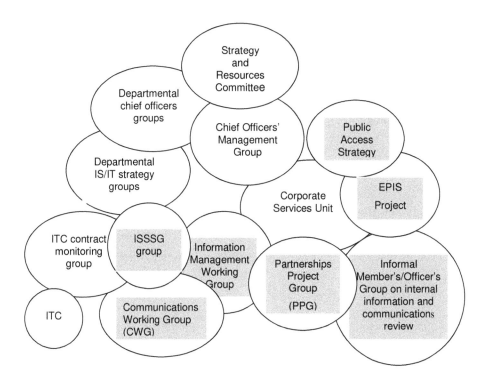

Figure 5.3 The overlap of membership between interest groups/corporate agents of the IS domain of Council X at T3

Whether deliberate or otherwise, and despite the outright capture of only one of the four working groups, by the time membership for all groups had been agreed actors from either the PPG or CSU had joined all of the groups. This effectively created a network of pro IS and local governance actors, and thus a mechanism for coordinated interaction across all of the relevant interest groups (Figure 5.3). The discussion that follows briefly outlines the work of the CWG and the Security and Networks Working Group (SNWG) as, of the four working groups, these are the only two of significance to the causal process of post LGR IS development.

The Communications Working Group (CWG)

In their first report to the ISSSG the CWG notes that:

> At the Away Day communication issues were identified as an important
> area for corporate development work. The Communications Working
> Group was asked to clarify departments' needs and priorities within this
> broad heading.[xliii]

The CWG pursued this task on two major fronts, both of which focused on the
information and systems dimensions of IS development rather than the technology.
Importantly, the group also brought the community governance agenda into play by
arguing that it was no longer sufficient to concentrate on internal information flows
and systems. This was ground breaking stuff, as a senior member of the ISSSG
explained:

> ...the communication strategy [from the Communications Working
> Group], that really encapsulates the information flows within the
> organisation and also outside to the public. It's been a tremendous
> integrating experience [devising the strategy]. We'd never had anything
> like it in all the time I've been in the county.
>
> Q.   Why the sudden change?
>
> Everyone has got to be aware of these issues themselves these days so it is
> not us trying to guess what priorities are...I've got to say for the first time
> ever, to my recollection, when we [the ISSSG group] started to decide
> which were priorities and how they would be funded, people were prepared
> to put their own money back into the central corporate pot.[xliv]

The second way in which the CWG made a significant impression on the ISSSG was
by identifying a series of key short term initiatives in the management and the

communication of information. Projects fell into three categories: exploiting and sharing existing information resources; developing electronic methods of communication with the public, members and between departments; and improving the security of IT systems. A major advance was quickly made on the first of these tasks, with the production of a data map for Council X. The data map showed each department's IS and the interrelationship with other IS within the same department and elsewhere. Keeping this up to date was subsequently adopted as a priority by the ISSSG.

Developing a computer database of new ICT applications and a register of new IS requirements were also regarded as important and complimentary activities. Of course, these steps were primarily directed at internal system users. But the development of electronic information services for external users was also recognised as crucial, although it was accepted that this was dependant in large part on the provision of a secure communications infrastructure, hence the CWG's interest in the IS security and the work of the SNWG.

In summary, CWG's ability to quickly put forward proposals that addressed a range of communications issues opened the door to ideas and actions that had previously been regarded by members of the ISSSG, and other actors and agents, as unwarranted or unwanted, or both. In particular, much of the impetus for making sure that coordination between the requirements of community governance and IS development became a reality came from CWG. Because of the perceived value of its work the ideational significance of CWG also increased significantly over a relatively short period of time, as comparison of Figures 4.5 and 5.5 illustrates. This subsequently influenced relations and transactions between other interest groups, and particularly between the PPG and the ISSSG. In short, the CWG had been the advance guard for ideas that emanated from the PPG and CSU. For example, by gaining acceptance that: 'The transfer of the Council's own electronic information system to Univision software opens up new opportunities for departments.'[xlv], where previously the electronic public information system (EPIS), which was, as noted in the previous chapter, one of the best local authority systems in Britain, had been largely ignored by departments.

Ultimately the approach employed by CWG, and the recommendations that came from their work, proved instrumental in the development of a strategic view of communication and information management, and, more surprisingly still, funding being voluntarily brought forward from departmental budgets to support key elements of the group's recommendations. The outcome of the strategic actions and interaction of CWG, in terms of structural, cultural and group elaboration and IS development will be dealt with in the next chapter. But first the morphogenetic significance of a second working group requires a brief review.

The Security and Networks Working Group (SNWG)

While the CWG pursued a broad range of communication issues and ideas, work also progressed well for the groups reviewing the nature and role of the ISSSG group and the drafting of the new IT contract. However, as nothing of significance to the structural and cultural elaboration of IS at T4 emerged from either group between T2 and T3 that then it is not relevant to discuss their work here.

Not everything went so smoothly with the SNWG. Network security soon proved a very live issue of considerable importance to certain departments. Social Services, for example, with the child protection register, and Treasurer's, both had strong objections to the development of internal networks which incorporated gateways to allow external access. In particular they feared links to the Internet would open up their systems to possible hacking.

Although assurances were given by *ITC* that internal networks could be made secure, because decision making within Council X depended entirely on a consensus being reached between departmental agents then as long as these fears persisted amongst some actors/agents, as they did for several months, no consensus could be reached and therefore network development stalled. The situation was aggravated further because the spending cuts that had been forced on Council X meant the supporters of network development, and particularly wide scale internet access for staff across the organisation, (i.e. the PPG, and the CSU) were not in a position to buy in a sufficiently robust fire wall. Here again, then, we have a clear example of the emergent properties of one strata conditioning the actions of the agents of another strata, as Archer (1995) argues will be the case. In this specific case, the causal powers of the institutional system playing key role in the causal processes of IS development within the position practice system of Council X.

The impact of the actions and interactions of the CWG and SNWG on the morphogenesis, or otherwise, of IS will be dealt with fully in the next chapter. But before moving on to the final section of this chapter a brief review and discussion of other relevant mechanisms for social interaction shown on Figure 5.3 is in order. Although these groups did enjoy internal and necessary relations with multiple groups, via human resources, due to the lack of any formally agreed remit for these groups they have not been defined as SEPs, as the working groups were. They were, nevertheless, important agential mechanisms for interaction, although, as I explain in Chapter 7, only contingently influential on IS development.

Supplementary interest groups and networks for interaction
The Information Management Group (IMG)
The IMG was established by the Communications Working Group shortly after it came into being in December 1995, following a series of meetings between its members and both primary and corporate agents dealing with communications issues from across the Council. The IMG was an 'informal' working group in that it had no written remit. Nevertheless, it brought together actors from the electronic public information system (EPIS – part of the CSU), from the PPG and from the ISSSG. In a relatively short period of time (i.e. December 1995 to April 1996) the IMG became

crucially important to all that has been discussed in this chapter, for two reasons. First, because members of the group were all IS reformers. Second, because, despite the status of the group, it actually functioned as a bridging mechanism between the PPG, the ISSSG *and* the CSU (Figure 5.3). The later point is significant because members of CSU had only limited representation in the 'official' IS arena (i.e. through the ISSSG), although they were strong reformists and committed promoters of the link between community governance and IS, via their membership of the PPG and involvement with the groups shown linking to CSU in Figure 5.3.

Within a short time of its emergence the IMG set about exploring the extent to which developments in all three areas from which the groups members were drawn 'overlap and reinforce' each other. The conclusion was:

> ...that, as well as looking at the technical "how" (the initial scope of most communications projects), there is an urgent need to plan corporately the information which would flow across any communications links and how it could be managed.[xlvi]

Once again this statement reflects a concern with the corporate-ness of IS, as might be expected from a group dominated by actors with those views. In isolation this would have meant little, but in reality yet another group adding their voice to this view was a useful and timely move for influencing the ISSSG and IS Strategy Review. This was not a one way exchange transaction, however, because the value of the expertise that the IMG brought to the IS strategy process meant that the ideational standing of the group increased significantly over the period of this research (Figures 4.5 and 5.4).

Another important feature of the IMG was that it served as very useful forum for intelligence gathering for both the CSU and the PPG. Consequently, between February and April 1996 information was fed back to the CSU initiated groups working on the Officer's and Member's Pilot Project (OMPP) and the One Stop Shop (OSS) initiative through the Public Access Strategy Group (see below), where it was used to shape both projects in such as way that they could then be used to further promote the ideas of IS reformers, and thus hopefully influence the wider IS agenda of Council X. A discussion of the early – interactional – stages of the OSS concludes this chapter, with further details of both projects held over until the next chapter as they are clearly examples of morphogenesis.

The Public Access Strategy Group (PASG)

The PASG was established shortly after the conclusion of the LGR in October 1995. By January 1996 the specific focus of coordination was either the OSS initiative, and an 'output' of the PPG, or the OMPP, which was largely an 'output' of the IMG. The reason for this was that it was planned that the EPIS project would be a key feature of both the OSS and OMPP. Its significance as far as morphogenetic cycles are concerned is that it provided opportunities for interaction and information exchange between key reformist actors from the IMG, the OSS, the OMPP and the EPIS project. This was possible because a member of CSU staff was a member of both the IMG and PASG, while also being involved in the management of the EPIS project.

Despite its small membership, actors from the PASG were able to seed ideas into the discussions and debates that were taking place in the multiple groups they were involved with. Thus, they were extremely active and effective at promoting the EPIS project, which by definition meant promoting intra organisational information sharing and systems. Furthermore, there was a consistency to their approach, regardless of which group outside of the PASG they were involved with, because they had been able to coordinate their actions and ideas. It is for this reason that comparison of Figures 4.5 and 5.4 indicates a significant increase in the ideational standing of this group within the IS arena. Consequently group members, both individually and collectively, played an important role in the causal processes of the morphogenesis of IS reported in the next chapter, in particularly in extending the use (and thus importance) of the EPIS.

The Informal Officers' and Members' Group on Information and Communication Review (IOMG)

The IOMG was set up as part of the Internal Information and Communications Review that took place in mid 1994 and which had been one of the drivers behind the launch of the IS Strategy Review. This group convened as a when deemed appropriate (by officers in consultation with members). The group met in October 1995 to discuss progress made on information management in the previous year and the forthcoming OMPP project. Present at this meeting were seven councillors, from the three main political parties, and six officers, representing departments, the CSU and the IS contract monitoring unit. The group had previously met in September 1994 to consider the findings of a report from consultants on information management within Council X.

The official purpose of the group was to provide a forum through which officers could report to members on progress made on IS and hear the views and concerns of members. However, evidence collected from a number of officers involved with the group suggests that IOMG was a device to enable the interaction through which reformers hoped ideational and discursive reshaping around IS could be promoted. By the October 1995 meeting there was a more specific ideational agenda, which was to promote the idea that 'the centre' (i.e. the Chief Executive's Office, and therefore the CSU) needed to be strengthened to combat the increase in the relative power of departmental actors and agents due to decentralisation and devolution, and how this process might be enabled using new IS.

The actual extent to which this course of action was successful was difficult to ascertain from the data collected. Nevertheless, it is clear that officers from CSU believed that the existence of the IOMG was valuable, albeit that it had only met once in a year. The timing of the October 1995 meeting was certainly significant in that it corresponded with the announcement of the final result of the LGR and thus signalled an ideal point at which to present the proposal to undertake the Officers' and Members' ICT pilot project to members (since the Council X was no longer under threat of abolition). Interestingly, the meeting was also used to bring the problems experienced by the e-telephone directory team to the notice of Members.[xlvii].

Overall, the IOMG can be judged as both materially and ideationally useful to IS reformers because through the IOMG Members were informed of proposals and ideas and then fed these back to other Members, and thus into the political side of Council X. It was assumed (by officers) that were then more likely to support requests for resources for projects such as the OMP, the OSS, the EPIS and so on. It is for these reasons that comparison of Figures 4.5 and 5.4 shows a move, albeit small, in both the ideational and material standing of the IOMG.

Approaching T4: the possible outcomes of social, socio-cultural and group interaction

The activities of the two most causally significant corporate agents to IS development within Council X, and a range of less influential interest groups, have now analysed. However, one final feature of the second stage of the morphogenetic cycle requires analysis before bringing this chapter to a conclusion: how effective were the strategies and interactions of the actors and agents identified above at influencing the ISSSG into different modes of interaction?

Signs of morphogenesis: the ISSSG moves from defensive to concessionary interaction

Earlier in this chapter it was noted that in the early days of the PPG the group had planned to submit their own development plan to the same COMG meeting to which the ISSSG were due to submit their IS Strategy Review. This tactic was designed to counteract what the PPG suspected would happen if their actions and interactions, and those of their allied groups, discussed above, had failed to achieve an acceptable degree of ideational shift amongst the ISSSG members. The result, it was assumed, would be that the ISSSG would submit a Review based firmly on maintaining the post 1990 structural and cultural status quo of IS within Council. This tactic was not needed, however, and as discussed above, because of the intervention of COMG and the subsequent ICT Away Day. This caused a substantial shift in the attitudes and ideas of members of the ISSSG and a general shift to a concessionary mode of interaction with the PPG. The outcome of this was felt in three related ways. First, in early March 1996 the ISSSG requested they make a formal presentation of their work to the PPG. Second, they alerted the PPG to the fact that due to the slow progress of the early stages of the strategy review and the outcomes of the Away Day they would not be submitting a fully revised IS strategy to COMG in April but a report on the process and principles that would underpin the review. Third, that to take into account the new process and principles the terms of reference for the ISSSG would be revised.

A detailed discussion of the Strategy Process Report from ISSSG to COMG is held over to the following chapter as it represents an outcome of interaction at T4. Suffice to note here that individually all of these actions were significant, with the first and third representing clear evidence that the supporters of IS reform within the ISSSG had made significant headway in influencing the strategic actions and mode of interaction of the ISSSG generally. Additionally, notice of the delay in the presentation of a new IS strategy also bought time for the PPG, which, as the discussion in the following chapter illustrates, was highly advantageous for the PPG Development Plan (another outcome).

The presentation by the ISSSG took place on the morning of 15 April 1996 (the COMG meeting took place in the afternoon) and from this point on updates of the ISSSG's work appeared as a regular PPG agenda item. The presentation centred on two short, related, papers. The first was a summary of the ISSSG's work since 1992.

Of particular importance was the fact that the paper made it plain that part of ISSSG's new strategic approach was to 'formalise links with other [internal] groups'[xlviii] which had an interest in new technology. The paper went on to highlight the key initiatives where there was likely to be considerable overlap between the work and interests of the ISSSG and the PPG. As might be expected given the actions and interactions of the CWG discussed above, information management and internal and external communications were leading examples.

The second paper dealt with a range of technologies which could be used to support PPG initiatives. The objective being: '...service availability, accessibility and quality *gain*. Cost, time, and environmental *savings*.'[xlix]. What is interesting is that the paper starts by recognising that the telephone is 'the first choice for local councils [to communicate with Council X]' because it is 'Cheap, ubiquitous and fully accepted...' The 'options for development' suggested in the paper were, therefore, all based on telephone technology. They included: virtual meetings, video conferencing, voice mail, call forwarding (e.g. to allow staff to telework from home), links to external organisations (e.g. a 'virtual private network'), an automated reception service, a 'pool' of mobile phones for staff to allow calls to be diverted from desk phones, and pagers for peripatetic staff.

While the tone and content of this paper epitomises the incremental approach to change, which, as we have seen in this chapter, was a hallmark of the ISSSG group, the presentation itself clearly signals the move to a concessionary mode of interaction by the group previously discussed. Furthermore, as a result of the ISSSG presentation it was agreed that although the PPG would continue work on their development plan, with a completion date of October 1996, the ISSSG and the PPG would also aim for a joint presentation to COMG at that time.

Interaction: a summary

This chapter set out to identify how, and in what form, interaction took place between those actors and agents causally associated with IS development (where, why and by which of the groups identified at T1), and track the changing resource distributions of these interest groups and how these influenced the relations and transactions between them. As discussed in Chapter 2, Archer (1995) argues that this represents an analysis of the connection between stage one and two of the morphogenetic cycle (i.e. the distribution of vested interests and different situations that confront agents when they try to attain these) and stages two and three (i.e. exchange transactions and power relations) leading to morphogenesis/morphostasis as outcomes at T4. As with the previous chapter, it is appropriate at this point to make some brief comments on the application of the second stage of the morphogenetic approach (Figure 5.1) before concluding this chapter. A fuller discussion of the utility of the approach and issues that arose, such as defining generative mechanisms and emergent properties and the nature of relationships between entities that I have previously noted, is reserved for Chapter 7.

The first comment to make, and something which emerges from this chapter very clearly, is that the actors and agents of Council X exhibited exactly the complexity of systems of human relationships amongst social positions that Porpora (1998), Archer (1988, 1995, 1998), and critical realists in general, argue it is necessary to analyse if we are to understand what causal powers are active in any given situation. From within this 'nexus of connections between human actors', as Porpora (1998:344) succinctly puts it, the morphogenetic approach directed attention at constructing a detailed narrative of the history, membership, role, and bargaining power and negotiating strength (i.e. relative power) of the actors and agents of the position practice system of IS, and of the courses of action, and modes of interaction, they employed in pursuit of their interests. What emerged was evidence of different interest groups being causally influential in ongoing causal processes at different times and for different reasons. However, due to the distributions of the structural and cultural properties of the Council, and thus their position as corporate agents, two collectivities of actors – the PPG and the ISSSG – clearly emerged as the most significant groups in the IS domain.

At T2 the ISSSG was relatively more powerful than the PPG, enjoying a superior ideational and material standing in the period to November 1995 (Figure 4.5). By April 1996, however, the ideational standing of the PPG had increased significantly (Figure 5.4) for two reasons – one planned, one unplanned. The planned reason has two related dimensions. First, members of the PPG and their allies cleverly and effectively used the one resource they had at their disposal – expertise – to influence the relations and transactions between IS interest groups. Second, the group employed increasingly opportunistic forms of interaction to spread their ideas to and through other subsidiary fora for interaction, such as the CWG, the PASG and the IMG. The ideational standing of all of these interest groups then increased (Figure 5.4), further strengthening the causal significance of the PPG.

However, the context in which the PPG and its allied groups had to operate, and the extent of the success of their actions, was undoubtedly affected by an unplanned event – the intervention of COMG in the IS strategy process. There is no doubt that this action was causally significant for another event – the ICT Away Day – and that this was, in turn, causally significant to the ideational and discursive reshaping of members of the ISSSG. In other words, the resulting PEPs '…modified the consciousness and commitment and affinities and animosities' of actors, as Archer puts it (1995:184). The ISSSG's mode of interaction shifted from defensive to concessionary as a result, while the ideational standing of the group within the IS domain declined compared to the PPG (Figure 5.4). The outcome was that the ISSSG became more open and supportive of a 'reformist' IS agenda, and, over a relatively short period of time, as the nature of the exchange transactions and power relations between the groups altered, both groups and their actions and agendas became interlinked and interdependent.

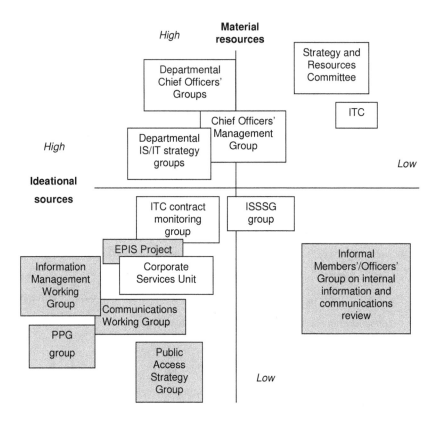

Figure 5.4 The relative power and ideational standing of corporate agents and interest groups within the IS domain of Council X at T3

The second comment to make in concluding this chapter is to draw attention, once again, to the nature and importance of the unintended consequences of past actions to causal processes. Although it is easy to read negative connotations into this term, in reality this is often not the outcome, or, as the following examples illustrate, not for some actors and agents. The first example relates to COMG, the most significant corporate agent within Council X. The intervention into IS strategy of this group was caused by an unintended consequence of the privatisation of IT, namely the failure of the IT contract/contractor to deliver an IT service on a par with the previous in-house service. The significance of this event to interaction has already been discussed. Its significance to the eventual morphogenesis of IS will be made apparent in the next chapter.

The second example of an unintended consequence of past actions concerns the involvement of the PPG in IS policy and practice. As Chapter 4 established, the formal brief of the PPG was not IS development, it was promoting and enabling community governance through partnerships with other agencies in the emerging systems of local governance in Council X's geographical area. However, an unintended consequence of the causal powers of the SEPs and CEPs of the LGR, which were about joining up organisations (i.e. *inter* organisational relationships), was to expose the fragmented nature of Council X, while at the same time highlighting the possibilities that the morphogenesis of ICTs/IS offered to join up the Council (i.e. *intra* organisational relationships). This then caused the PPG's involvement in the IS arena.

While it is impossible to be unequivocal in stating that ideas and beliefs about the potential for ICTs to 'join up' an organisation would not have entered the position practice system of Council X via another ideational route, it is, nevertheless, clear that without the LGR they would not have become as clearly articulated and logically related (such that they can be defined as CEPs) at that particular point in time without the LGR. The question that remains is to what extent did this, and the other strategic actions and modes of interaction reported in this chapter, lead to the morphogenesis of IS (as the material presented in Chapter 4 suggested would be the case) or morphostasis? Answering that question is the aim of the next chapter.

6

OUTCOME: MORPHOGENESIS OR MORPHOSTASIS?

The outcome of interaction at T4

At the end of Chapter 4 I noted that the low levels of systemic and social integration within Council X taken together with the beginnings of a limited *cultural* morphogenesis in the IS arena, signalled that the conditions existed for morphogenesis of IS (as a structural property) at T4 (Figure 6.1). The actual outcome would, however, be dependant on the 'success' of agential action and interaction to promote and support these developments between T2 and T3. As the previous chapter confirmed this was largely the outcome.

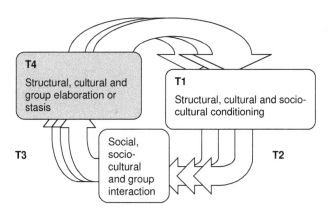

Figure 6.1 Morphogenetic cycles at T4: morphogenesis or stasis?

It is also clear from the material on the LGR at the end of Chapter 4, and the examples of ideational and discursive change amongst actors/agents presented in the previous chapter, that the limited but increasingly widespread cultural morphogenesis within the IS arena noted above was happening considerably before T4 (i.e. April 1996: a date chosen for reasons set out below (see Figure 6.3). This supports Archer's (1995) view that change in the structural and cultural domains of any social setting is just as likely to be unsynchronised as synchronised. It also illustrates, once

212

again, how difficult it is to order material in a consistent manner on the T1 to T4 continuum when detailing and discussing the causal processes that are associated with all three morphogenetic cycles simultaneously in dynamic contexts, rather than focusing on only one (i.e. the structural, cultural and/or agential).

A full discussion of this and other issues that emerge from the application of Archer's morphogenetic approach to the case study of Council X is held over until Chapter 7, as was made clear in the previous two chapters. It is sufficient to note here, therefore, that for the reasons discussed in Chapter 1, throughout this book the aim has been to continue to apply a set T1–T4 demarcation to all three cycles. Not withstanding the comments above about cultural morphogenesis, April 1996 was chosen as T4 as this represents the point at which real and actual outcomes emerged (i.e. at the level of structures and causal powers and at the level of events) from *significant phases* in a number of causal processes (Figure 6.2). The first task of this chapter is, therefore, to provide an account of these examples of the cultural and structural morphogenesis of IS. Accompanying this discussion, and the second task of this chapter, is an analysis of the contradictions and/or complementarities brought into being by these developments. That is, the degree to which morphogenesis added to, or subtracted from, the low levels of systemic integration within the position-practice system of Council X.

The chapter closes with an assessment of the possibilities for the "future" morphogenesis/stasis of IS within Council X. These can be taken as examples of the kind of 'tendential prediction' proposed by Fleetwood and Hesketh (2006) discussed in the early chapters of this book. Of course, given the time that has elapsed since the case study ended in 1996 any developments that took place after that date are now clearly matters of history. Nevertheless, as Archer (1995) suggests that an assessment of the future likelihood of either morphogenesis or morphostasis beyond T4 allows the formal completion of the morphogenetic approach then this is deemed necessary. Furthermore, as my involvement with, and knowledge of, Council X ceased in early

1997 any conclusions drawn are based entirely on the data presented in this book and are not, therefore, written with the benefit of hindsight. This situation does, of course, signal an opportunity for some potentially interesting follow up research should resources and permissions allow, as well as providing an obvious point from which to move to the concluding chapter of this book: an evaluation of the utility of morphogenetic approach as a methodology for exploring and explaining the complexity of the information polity, and therefore of the role of IS/ICTs in public administration.

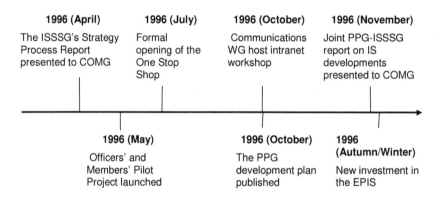

Figure 6.2 Council X - timeline 1996: primary examples of the cultural

and

structural morphogenesis of IS

Cultural elaboration: examples, causal powers and contradictions and complementarities

Given that the ideas and discourse of an increasing number of actors/agents associated with the ISSSG and the PPG underwent cultural morphogenesis before T4 an obvious starting point for any analysis of whether, and how, this situation played out at the level of events (the actual) and the real (the level of structures and causal powers), is to look for documented examples of this elaboration, and the impact these published ideas and beliefs then had more widely within the IS arena of Council X.

From April 1996 (T4) three reports emerged from the interaction documented through Chapter 5. Each can be regarded as both the distillation of the cultural morphogenesis of specific agents/actors *and* as signalling significant end points in a series of causal processes. In chronological order, the reports to be evaluated are: the ISSSG's Strategy Process Report; the PPG's Development Plan; and the joint report on IS development from the ISSSG and the PPG to COMG (Figure 6.2). A brief discussion of the Intranet Workshop, which occurred between publication of the Development Plan and joint report, is also included for the reasons set out in that section.

The IS Strategy Process Report: signalling acceptance of structural and cultural elaboration

While the ICT Away Day provided the ISSSG with an opportunity for intense social interaction, and thus acted as a catalyst for ideational and discursive reshaping and new PEPs, as discussed in the previous chapter, it also provided the impetus to push on with the Strategy Review. It was not the results of the Review that were presented to COMG in April 1996, however, but a report by the chairman of the ISSSG on the *process* to be adopted and on the progress of the process to date. In addition to making a number of proposals the Process Report highlighted a range of IS issues, the most fundamental of which was 'what does a strategy mean.' Rather than attempting to document at any given time a view of the world of ICTs, which the group argued was out of date before it was even published, the ISSSG asked COMG to recognise the importance of focusing on the process by which an IS strategy would be formulated and how future IS developments would be evaluated. The ISSSG saw the key to this process approach being:

> [acceptance] of the view of most (if not all) departments that the decentralisation of ISSSG has been a positive development and should be built on and that the focus should now be on how to get all departments working together on issues of joint benefit. Whilst departments will be free

in theory to develop their own information systems to meet particular business needs, the ISSSG group will monitor any such initiatives to identify whether there is scope for wider application for other departments or for the corporate information needs of the Council as a whole.[l]

While this quotation clearly illustrates the rather defensive mode of interaction that the ISSSG employed when dealing with COMG (for the reasons discussed in Chapter 5) it also illustrates that by April 1996 the reformist wing of the group, aided by outside influences such as the PPG, were sufficiently influential to manoeuvre the ISSSG into emphasising the need to join up the structures of IS that had become fragmented post 1990. Also of significance is that many of the proposals in the report imply a more proactive role for the ISSSG. Consequently, it was unsurprising that the final recommendation of the report was that COMG accept new terms of reference for the ISSSG. Both the Process Report and terms of reference were approved by COMG. There were three significant revisions:

- that the responsibility of the group changed from ensuring '…the production of departmental IT plans and [provision of an] IS and T strategy for the Council.' To, '…creating and managing [a] framework for information management and a process for monitoring the development of IS and IT issues and initiatives within the Council.'
- that instead of the group advising '…on common standards and ensuring these are continually reviewed…' they would '…set common standards to be applied to IS and T…'
- that instead of simply 'promoting and sponsoring' new IS and T initiatives '…and areas of common development.', they would, '…identify issues and initiatives…promote and sponsor [and] encourage and foster a vision and an innovative approach towards IT development by extending and challenging departmental approaches as part of a mechanism for support.'[li]

Causal powers

The IS Strategy Process Report was a highly significant document because it clearly illustrates the extent to which the ideational position of the ISSSG had changed and the emergence of a discourse that reflects this. In practical terms, therefore, the ISSSG was now prepared to accept that their primary concern for the future would not be departmental IS development, but rather the links between the information requirements *of the Council* and the systems which could support these. The group would become proactive in promoting the process by which *shared areas of activity* could be developed. Where wider applications could be identified then other agents and actors, such as the PPG (who, as we saw in the previous chapter, the ISSSG had already approached to partner their work), and working groups, would be involved *in setting standards to allow the sharing of systems and data*. The Report, and the activities that surrounded its production, were therefore causally significant to IS, both culturally and agentially, as the examples of the joint presentation to COMG, and support for the Intranet Workshop discussed below, illustrate.

Data gathered during late 1995, early 1996, also strongly suggests that the *anticipated outcomes* of the Report also proved *structurally* significant for IS. The most significant of these anticipated outcomes was the proposed new terms of reference for the ISSSG. When allied to the increased significance of the ISSSG with respect to Council's strategic management, discussed above, departmentally based corporate agents increasingly came to realise that the opportunity costs of pursuing new spending on IS project were low if these had the support of the ISSSG. In other words, it was unlikely that COMG would impose political sanctions on departments that would be damaging to their broader interests. Consequently departments came forward with a range of IS developments before publication of the Report. These included a new Fire Service Command and Control System, a computerised loan and classification system for the Libraries Service, updating of the EPIS public information system and a new financial management system for the Treasurer's. At the same time the ICL based equipment configuration introduced in the 1980's was largely replaced by industry standard equipment based on open systems. Each of these represents an example of the morphogenesis of IS, although the detail of these developments falls outside of the scope of this book. What was also notable was that these developments also signalled a move from a defensive to an opportunistic mode of interaction on the part of a number of corporate agents. However, as awareness of the unifying features of the new terms of reference for the ISSSG increased so interaction became more concessionary.

Potential contradictions and/or complementarities

The ISSSG's embracing of the need for new IS that could 'join up' Council X and of the cultural and agential mechanisms that would underpin it, clearly went some way to addressing the low levels of IS specific systemic and social integration within Council X. Furthermore, the group's role in defining the 'missing' business case for Council X, combined with the importance of IS as a structural property, meant their decisions and recommendations were highly likely to have a similar effect on the underlying direction of general structural change and therefore back onto IS development via the generative powers of the SEPs produced.

For example, as well as altering the relationship between agents, as discussed above, the generative powers of the new terms of reference (as a SEP), also altered the relationship between the ISSSG and actual IS developments at departmental level. With the formal role of the ISSSG broadened and the increased influence of the reformist wing of the group these would no longer be allowed to be as contingent (i.e. autonomous) as they had been prior to the revised terms. This would place the ISSSG in a stronger position to take action to ameliorate IS developments that threatened to add further to IS contradictions of the Council. This was a small but not insignificant change in such a systemically and socially weak environment.

The PPG's Development Plan

The PPG's Development Plan was published in October 1996, some six months after the publication of the ISSSG's Strategy Process Report. This is important because with the Process Report in the public domain, and the ISSSG enjoying concessionary interaction with the PPG following the formal exchange of views between the two groups in April 1996, the PPG had been able to adapt the plan to take account of the reaction to the ISSSG's Report. A significant result was that the Plan explicitly specified examples of the structural elaboration of IS, whereas any suggestions of this in the ISSSG report had been largely implicit.

The tone and content of the Plan reflects the confidence of the PPG's members that given the reformist stance now being adopted by the ISSSG the time was right to go public with their progressive views of IS, and of the relationship between IS and partnership working/local governance. In particular, it clearly signalled the belief of the group that a significant number of members of COMG would have been influenced by the Strategy Process report, and therefore be open to ideas that IS could be used to address some specific elements of the low level of systemic integration that now affected the Council. Thus, the report begins:

> The purpose of the Plan is to identify a coherent and consistent way forward, to maximise resources and build on opportunities for internal and external co-operation and collaboration. Its overall aim is to ensure that the potential benefits of partnership working are realised...[lii]

The body of the Plan was devoted to setting out a range of issues and proposals under four 'categories for action'. By far the biggest section was devoted to 'improving information services'; seven of the plan's 20 pages were devoted solely to elements of this topic, while the remaining three categories were dealt with in two and a half pages. The information services section started by posing three straight-forward questions: 'What information is required? Where can it be accessed? And how can it be accessed?' The conclusion was that: '...based on the principle of maximising use of resources, there is significant scope for improving access to information within current Council resources and premises[liii]

Causal powers

The significance of the Development Plan as an example of the actual distillation of the cultural morphogenesis of IS amongst actors/agents, and the 'capture' of the resulting CEPs, cannot be overstated. It was causally significant for both the Intranet Workshop and the joint PPG and ISSSG report and presentation to COMG in early November 1996, both discussed below. Furthermore, the ideas and proposals contained in the plan were presented in such a way as to accessible and understandable to primary and corporate agents alike. Consequently, they were easily spread through the cultural system of Council X, and therefore served as a significant aid to the ongoing process of socio-cultural interaction that members of both the PPG and the ISSSG were involved in.

Structurally, for both IS and local governance, the Plan proved an invaluable mechanism for bringing to the attention of actors/agents the true nature of local governance. That this was not simply about the external environment – the institutional strata beyond Council X – and therefore CEPs and SEPs, and their causal powers, that could largely be ignored by the majority of agents whose work seldom if ever stretched beyond the boundaries of the Council's procedures and practices.

It is important to recognise that without an appropriate supporting infrastructure, the potential impact of the Partnership initiative may not be realised. Although the initiative's primary focus is external - looking at partnerships and ways of getting closer to the public - its ability to deliver its promises will depend upon the effectiveness of its internal systems.

220

Internal cohesiveness and coordination is essential to ensure seamless delivery of information and services.[liv]

This emphasis on the need for the *internal* cohesiveness and coordination of systems to support external partnerships became central to the structural elaboration of the OSS specifically, as we shall see. Crucially, however, the Plan was explicit about how this form of local governance could be enabled. Six means of communication were highlighted. The first five (mail, telephone, meetings, members and publications) had all emerged as important from a survey of town and parish council communication and access needs carried out on behalf of the PPG in July 1996. The last – ICT – was added by the PPG and had considerably more coverage than the other five. It is important to emphasise, however, as I did in Chapter 5, that the capabilities of new ICTs being quoted by the group were, more often than not, reference to the *potentialities* of new ICTs, rather than actual capabilities that had been witnessed by members of the PPG. That said a number of the PPG's members had been either directly or indirectly involved in a range of ground breaking examples of ICT projects, as discussed in full in Chapter 4. The Council's EPIS was a particularly important example of why the potentialities of IS featured so prominently in the Plan, not least because of the belief amongst some of the IS reformers that this system could be used as a Trojan horse for IS change. This is an issue discussed under the section on the EPIS, below.

As Chapter 4 explained, within local government circles in Britain Council X was recognised as one of the pioneers of EPIS developments, having had a system in place since the early 1990s. The EPIS had been developed almost single-handedly by a member of staff from the CSU, and consistently championed by a senior member of that Unit. Although the EPIS was severely under resourced, and as a result often suffered technical problems, it nevertheless served as both a real and ideational template for many of the ideas and proposals for ICT developments of the PPG. The full significance of this is discussed below. For now it is sufficient to note that the provision of EPIS terminals that could be used to network remote locations into an effective and comprehensive information system became a central feature of the PPG's proposals for IS to support local governance, and subsequently, as is also detailed below, the joint ISSSG/PPG presentation to COMG.

The Development Plan went further, however, arguing that a comprehensive corporate information database and communications system should be accessible by members and officers regardless of their location. There should also be a public database, accessible by citizens, businesses and voluntary organisations, via OSS, libraries, Citizen's Advice Bureaux, and so on. The basis for this proposal was that as the number of organisations providing out of hours services increased and this mode of operation became the accepted norm so the expectation that local authorities should follow suit would increase. A computerised information system which would allow "armchair" telephone information/enquiry services, supported by trained helpline staff was an obvious solution. The suggestion was that with appropriate ICTs this service could be provided by staff working from home from 8.00 am to 8.00pm, seven days a week. This, it was noted, would be a significant development in improving accessibility to the Council. The proposal had the added advantage of building on the strengths and strategic nature of Council X: 'whilst adopting a business-led approach, focusing on working in partnership without blurring the role and identity of Council services and providing an effective and radical approach to the challenges ahead, in the most cost effective way.' The conclusion was that:

The importance of appropriate IT systems cannot be over-emphasised. Without a comprehensive information infrastructure, the Council will not be able to respond to many of the demands for information. It is essential that work focuses on the provision of appropriate IT support, and developments in this area should be given a high priority.[lv]

Potential contradictions and/or complementarities

The PPG Development Plan clearly employed a more direct approach to confronting the low levels of systemic integration within Council X than did the ISSSG's report. Consequently, the ideas and proposals it contained for IS developments, and therefore its cultural and structural significance, were entirely *complementary* to any moves towards higher levels of systemic and social integration.

Mindful that their ideas sat awkwardly with the structural and cultural systems that had emerged from the policies for organisational change of the early 1990s, and thus the vested interests of actors and agents whose power and influence had grown as a result, the PPG put considerable effort into presenting their proposals in a neutral manner. For example, a significant feature of the Plan was recognition that the OSS initiative (discussed below), was not a panacea for the provision of information and services to the public: '…given the nature of Council X's services and for reasons of efficiency and effectiveness, the Council is offering a "first stop" rather than "one stop" shop service.' Additionally, a range of alternatives to one stop/first stop shops were proposed, as the telephone based services discussed above demonstrate. This all looked highly non prescriptive, although in reality the PPG knew that for any of these developments to be effective a comprehensive and organisation wide IS would be required, which was, in turn, consistent with their goal of improving systemic integration.

The Intranet Workshop

The Workshop took place on the afternoon of Wednesday 9th October 1996. Analysis of the preparation for the meeting is interesting. Background papers on intranets were circulated: a magazine article ('Thin Clients and Hot Java', *Local Government Executive*, July/August 1996); an 'academic' style paper from a senior officer from Social Services (*Intranet: the silent revolution*); and a document outlining potential applications for an intranet within Council X (on which participants were asked to '…scribble on your own ideas and return…'). Additionally, participants were encouraged to attend a demonstration of the latest developments with the Council's EPIS and of an intranet.

The basis of the Intranet Workshop was a report from the Communications Working Group (CWG) which detailed a number of 'communications' and 'information management' projects that would or could be pursued during 1996/97, such as the One Stop Shop (OSS) and Officers' and Members' Pilot Project (OMPP), discussed below. Of most significance, however, was evidence from the group of the need for an intranet initiative. Apart from providing another example of the influence and ideational standing of the CWG, as reported in the previous chapter, the report provides clear evidence of how interaction between members of the CWG and the ISSSG was generating PEPs, leading to further examples of group elaboration, thus:

> ...broader information management issues should be dealt with alongside technical issues, and *the working group should become an Information Management and Communications Working Group*, with membership extended to include a principal policy officer from the Chief Executive's Office. In addition, an *Intranet Implementation project group would be created*, chaired by the head of the CSU and reporting to the working group.[lvi] (emphasis added)

Causal powers

Although clearly providing an important forum for interaction the Intranet Workshop also represents a real example of agential and cultural elaboration, hence its inclusion in this chapter. First, it represents an attempt by actors with a reformist IS agenda to spread ideational and discursive reshaping to and through other agents and actors beyond the socio-cultural interaction of the groups discussed in the previous chapter. Second, the scale and scope of the event is significant: bringing together 26 senior officers (and this researcher) from every department of Council X, plus the CE's Office, Fire Service and Contract Monitoring Unit, was no easy exercise and would almost certainly not have been possible prior to April 1996. Third, the Workshop was jointly organised by the Education Department and CSU on behalf of the ISSSG and hosted by a senior officer from both. This is significant because the views of the Education Department and CSU often diverged on the outcome of post 1990 organisational change and its impact on IS, as I established in Chapter. Finally, the event was specifically targeted at one development – an intranet – that had significant potential for the structural elaboration (morphogenesis) of IS, and to gain support for that course of strategic action from key actors/agents.

Potential contradictions and/or complementarities

As with each of the examples of elaboration noted above, the ultimate aim of the Intranet Workshop was to promote an IS agenda that would help address the structural and cultural contradictions that had arisen because of the policies of organisational change implemented from 1990. Consequently, both the event itself, and the proposal that the Council needed to develop an intranet, were aimed at encouraging systemic and social integration. Therefore they complement the other examples of cultural and structural elaboration reported in this chapter.

The Joint ISSSG and PPG report on IS Development

This report was presented to COMG on 11th November 1996 and represents the actual, physical, manifestation of the drawing together of the ideational agendas of both the PPG and the ISSSG. The presentation set out clearly the interrelationship between the two groups and their respective initiatives and agendas. Consequently, and importantly, the presentation signals the success, in the cultural system in particular, of the courses of strategic action that the members of the PPG had embarked upon early in 1995, allied with the results of the intervention of COMG into the IS policy area, as I detailed earlier in this chapter.

Having outlined how the two groups had started to work collaboratively the proposal that was forthcoming was for the development of an intranet for Council X. The fact

225

that this proposal, rather than any other, was presented was in large part due to the success (in terms of the positive and/or neutral responses of the participating actors) of the Intranet Workshop. Furthermore, the presentation also drew on the responses of the Workshop's participants to being asked for suggestions about the potential applications of an intranet. As a result, the plan was to open the intranet to elected members, town and parish councils, other Council establishments such as schools, and other local organisations, school governors and staff in area offices. Clearly, the reality of the 'complex systems of local governance' that Council X was increasingly becoming part of were beginning to register with actors, although, as the discussion of the OSS below illustrates, this was almost solely amongst actors whose positions/roles meant they were members of corporate agents.

The Joint Report stated that if 'commitment at senior levels' (i.e. COMG) was forthcoming the proposals for an intranet would create: 'A *connected* county; *communicating creatively* and effectively; changing the information *culture*; and enhancing *citizenship*.' (original emphasis)[lvii]. The potential benefits would be: 'Improved communications within and beyond the organisation, information sharing, improved efficiency, opportunities to offer new services and work differently [and] improved understanding of the potential of IT and the value of timely, accurate information.'[lviii] The intranet was costed at £65k for 1996/97 for the 'investigative stage', to be met by departments; £85k for 1997/98 for the 'initial implementation phase', to be met from departments and the PPG's budget; and £65–100k in 1998/99 'to be met as a first call on any sums becoming available after recontracting IS&T...'[lix]

Causal powers

The response from COMG to the proposal for an intranet was positive, thus serving to cement the joint agendas of the PPG and the ISSSG and add impetus to their ICT based community governance initiatives. For the ISSSG, in particular, it reinforced its new 'proactive' role as the major forum for social interaction and strategic thinking on IS. Furthermore, the ICT contract was about to be put out to tender, with a new contract effective from May 1998. It was planned that at that point the direction of ICT developments would largely transfer back to Council X. With the rejuvenated strategic role of the ISSSG, and a range of initiatives (noted here) being taken to restore some degree of systemic integration of IS the potential for change was regarded as substantial. As a result several of the ISSSG's members that the author spoke to at that time were genuinely excited at the potential for 'rewriting' the rules of IS within Council X. In short, the role that IS had played, and was playing (as a fundamental structural property), in creating and/or maintaining the contradictions and incompatibilities inherent in the structural morphogenesis of Council X from 1990, which led, in turn, to the systemic weaknesses experienced by actors/agents at T1, were about to be challenged.

There were, however, other structural conditions pertaining to IS over which the ISSSG remained largely powerless. Funding, which had been identified as a major issue at the ICT Away Day, was the most important example. In the Strategy Process Report it was noted that in an ideal world there would be adequate funding available corporately to fund countywide, non-departmental initiatives - pump priming, research and so on. The reality was different, however. There was little chance of a central budget being recreated, either by growth money being made available, or by some form of subvention on departmental budgets. The scope for taking forward the key initiatives adopted by the ISSSG would therefore be dependant on funding being identified on a scheme by scheme basis. Two options were suggested by the ISSSG/PPG:

- If the benefits of an initiative were clear to all departments, collaboration could lead to a joint funding proposal from existing departmental funds which could then be agreed at the ISSSG.

- If the benefits to departments were less obvious, or overall costs too high, a bid for Policy and Budget Plan approval could be prepared for the ISSSG and submitted to COMG for endorsement.

These options were not seen as mutually exclusive, although both required a cost/benefit analysis before submission. It was accepted, however, that money was so short that the re-tendering of the ICT contract offered the only reasonable opportunity for the Council to reconfigure ICT funding in any major way. This makes COMG's support for the intranet proposal all the more significant, albeit that in the third year it to would become dependant on monies from the renegotiated ICT contract (largely due to come from savings in the Council's mainframe costs). Ultimately therefore the belief that dominated IS circles was that the structural elaboration of IS on any significant scale was dependant on the SEPs – resources, both material and human – that would emerge from the new ICT contract. However, in the light of the actions of one corporate agent over the OSS, discussed below, and the fact that the same corporate agent, and others, came forward with costly IS projects during preparation of the IS Strategy Process Report, as discussed above, it may be that there were more resources available for IS in certain parts of the Council than was widely known.

Potential contradictions/complementarities

Both the form and content of the joint presentation and report of the PPG/ISSSG represent a clear agenda to address both specific and general examples of the role IS played in creating and maintaining the systemic and social weaknesses of Council X. On the one hand, therefore, they were entirely complementary to systemic and social integration but, potentially ran counter to the structural forms and cultural systems, and thus the interests of numerous actors/agents, that had emerged from the post 1990 organisational reforms. Whether or not the increase in the relative power of the ISSSG, combined with the ideational standing and strategic actions of the PPG and other reformist IS groups, would be causally sufficient to create the CEPs, SEPs and PEPs necessary for more widespread structural morphogenesis of IS is a matter for later in this chapter. What is clear is that both the timing of events and the role of primary agency would prove significant to this question, as the discussion of both the OMPP and OSS, below, illustrates.

Structural elaboration: examples, causal powers and contradictions and complementarities

The Electronic Public Information System (EPIS)

On the strength of the positive feedback and (what appeared to be) high level of departmental support for the intranet initiative, and with reformist IS actors taking majority membership of the IMCWG (the Information Management *and* Communications Working Group, which, as noted above, emerged from the elaboration of the Communications Working Group and Information Management Group), IS reformers launched a number of initiatives designed to raise the profile of new developments in IS. These developments took three separate forms. The first was to push forward with further development of the Council's EPIS and the external promotion of the system via the OSS. Ideationally this example of structural morphogenesis was emergent from the actions and interactions reported in chapter 5, allied with the increasing ideational and structural significance of the EPIS project. The result is reflected in a comparison of Figures 4.5 and 5.4. Furthermore, one of the primary reasons for investing in an existing project rather than something new was the belief of several key actors that the EPIS could be used '…as a Trojan Horse of change, taking the agenda away from technology to information management.'[lx] Interestingly, it was clear that the project had been used for the same purpose in the past:

> [the development of the system had] been done really by adopting emerging technologies externally and then taking them on internally, whether people like it or not. The internal structure (of the Council) has had a bit of a shock. There was a ban on Internet connections. It was lifted

because of our work (and) ...our experience has put us in a position to advise on what corporate policy should be.[lxi]

The second development was the Officers' and Members' ICT Pilot Project (OMPP), first mentioned in Chapter 3, and discussed further below. Ideationally this development can be seen as emergent from the concerns of the ISSSG, expressed explicitly in a statement in the Strategy Process Report outlining 'the information needs' of members, communities and the general public: '...which can be set alongside departmental plans and the subsequent analysis'.[lxii] In actual fact this statement reflects the influence of actors from the CSU and the PPG, who the ISSSG had turned to for their expertise in this area when preparing this element of their statement to COMG.

The third project, the One Stop Shop (OSS), mentioned on several occasions in this and previous chapters, was the most difficult to plan and execute, as the discussion below makes clear. The OSS was primarily structurally emergent from the actions and interactions of the PPG. However, because of the projects importance for promoting the EPIS, and relationship with the LGR, discussed below, actors from the CE's office took a direct, although low key, interest. For this reason the internal and necessary relations that the OSS had with the PPG also extend back to the CE's Office. The project also attracted support generally from reformist IS agents/actors, although this transpired to be not as clear cut as was assumed, as discussed below. It is also worth noting that as with many of the examples of *cultural* morphogenesis of IS reported in this book the causal process from which the OSS emerged can be traced back, through various actors, to the LGR defence group and, ultimately, to the causal powers of the LGR. Hence it is unsurprising that it was the example of morphogenesis most explicitly concerned with promoting IS and local governance.

230

The Officers' and Members' ICT Pilot Project (OMPP)

The OMPP launched in May 1996. Although ideationally broadly emergent from the causal powers of reformist IS agents, actors from the Information Management Group (IMG) and CSU had been particularly important in taking the project from idea to actual structural morphogenesis. Consequently, it was unsurprising that the OMPP had internal and necessary relations with the CSU, being dependant on the Unit for both material and human resources.

It was planned that the OMPP would run for six months, although start up delays meant the project continued for an extra month. The OMPP was designed around two small groups of officers and members, 12 of each from different departments and political parties, with different levels of expertise in the use of ICTs. Each person was provided with a package of off-line and on-line PC based applications – specifically, email, file transfer, access to the internet, and remote access to a database of council papers, such as reports, committee papers and minutes. The aims of the pilot were:

- to allow the Council to learn from the experience of participants;
- assess whether and to what extent ICT awareness was raised by the pilot;
- and assess the cost and benefits

To underpin the independence and objective credibility of the project, researchers from the Programme for the Study of Telematics and Governance (PSTAG) at Nottingham Trent University were recruited to undertake a programme of evaluative research (as one part of a broader project – the Information Management Programme – which included evaluation of the OSS). One of the interesting results to emerge from early survey work was that the vast majority of respondents (both officers and councillors) had an extremely positive attitude towards new technology, appreciated its importance as an organisational tool, and would welcome further developments. [10]

---

[10] The survey achieved very high response rates of 78.5% from councillors (55 from 70) and 78.8% (197 from 250) of our sample of senior officers scale 2 and above (Horrocks and Hambley 1996).

Thus, it appeared from the outset that the conditions existed on both sides of the Council to embrace new ICTs, although to what extent this translated into support for renewed IS development, and thus spending, was not clear at that stage.

Causal powers

By the time the OMMP came to an end in late 1996 there was no doubt that it was widely regarded by both officers and members as a pioneering attempt to explore the opportunities inherent in new ICTs and the organisational, managerial and political issues associated with these. Analysis of usage data confirmed that despite initial problems with hardware and software (discussed below) by the end of the pilot the full range of features of the technologies available were being used by participants. When the pilot came to an end all participants reported being reluctant to hand back their OMMP packages. In fact, on returning to Council X in January 1997 to give a presentation on the results of the OMMP, PSTAG researchers found that four of the (member) participants had been so forthright in their complaints about returning to their pre OMMP way of working that they had been allowed to continue using the packages, regardless of the financial costs this created for the CSU. Despite this development, and for the reasons discussed below, in the short term the emergence of more widespread structural change of IS that could be related back to the OMMP appeared very limited.

One area in which the OMMP was seen as highly instrumental, however, was in continuing to raise awareness of the possibilities of networked ICTs within the Council. As awareness was already at high levels the sponsors and supporters of the OMMP hoped that further efforts would have two outcomes. First, provide a renewed push for cultural morphogenesis amongst agents outside of the immediate socio-cultural networks of IS. If successful, it was hoped this would result in more widespread ideational and discursive reshaping and CEPs, and thus the promotion of the reformist IS agenda more and more widely across the Council. Second, and more importantly, once councillors became more aware of the potential of new ICTs this should provide the impetus for party political actors/agents to put pressure on chief officers to allocate resources to such developments. As discussed above, by November 1996 this did appear to have been a successful strategy in respect to the intranet and EPIS, where COMG agreed further investment. Unfortunately, and as we shall see, this shift in COMG's position occurred too late for both the OMMP and, more significantly, the OSS.

Potential contradictions/complementarities

The OMMP, as with all of the examples of cultural and structural elaboration discussed in this chapter, was conceived by reformist IS actors/agents as a means to challenge the low levels of systemic and social integration that had increasingly become symptomatic of Council X from 1990. That is, actors and agents believed that the use of specific ICTs could act as an ideational and structural stimulus that might promote an increase in both structural and social complementarities within the organisation. In practice, a combination of limited resources, the adequacy of hardware and software, and a lack of sufficient technical support and training, undermined the effectiveness of the OMPP, particularly on the members' side. Furthermore, the PSTAG researchers concluded that this situation:

> …was undoubtedly aggravated, and resolving such problems made more difficult, when combined with other factors…in particular, individual/departmental/party reluctance to commit to the project.[lxiii]

The overall conclusion that can be drawn, therefore, is that a range of agents did not regard the OMMP as being in their best interests and therefore sought to obstruct its operation. Interestingly there is no evidence to suggest that this was done aggressively: that actors and agents actively sought to undermine the project. Instead, what they were able to rely on was that the generative powers of existing systemic and cultural properties would be sufficiently powerful to stop, or severely limit, the morphogenetic potential of the OMMP. Indeed, other related projects suffered the

233

same fate, such as the development and implementation of the electronic phone book discussed in Chapter 4. Ultimately, the significant factor here seems to be timing. The e-phone book, OMMP and the OSS, all emerged in early to mid 1996, with the majority of their development obviously preceding that date. It seems safe to conclude, therefore, that the limited but growing morphogenesis of the cultural and agential realms of IS that had been occurring through 1995, was, by early to mid 1996, still too limited/weak to be a significant force for structural morphogenesis, whether of IS specifically or more generally. Interestingly, the view of key reformist actors in the IS domain was that the lack of the structural impact of the OMMP was unfortunate but that further awareness raising/cultural morphogenesis had been a valuable outcome.

The 'partnership approach' and interaction with external agents: the OSS
The One Stop Shop concept – an overview
During the early to mid 1990s OSS became an increasingly common term used in government and the public sector for describing a multitude of initiatives designed to provide a broad range of services to the public from one location. It was not a form of structural change that was restricted to the UK, however, as across most of the developed world interest in the concept grew as governments and public service organisations sought to develop alternatives to traditional systems of departmentalised, functionally specific, and often distant, public services[11]. The causal processes and mechanisms behind OSS were very much as discussed in Chapter 4: the emergence of a set of closely related, largely neo-liberal ideas, concerning governance and the privatisation of government activities and public services, the advent of a so-called new public management, and the belief that organisations could be 're-engineered' to make them more efficient, effective and customer focused.

---

[11] From 1993 to 1997 the author was a member of the Nordic Network for One Stop Shops. This group served as a forum for academics and practitioners from countries in North Western Europe who were involved with one stop shop development. The background information in this section is based on information and knowledge acquired through that involvement.

Chapters 4 and 1 both documented how ICTs were deeply implicated in these ideas, as the views/beliefs of supporters of this reform agenda were that new technologies could provide the structural mechanisms and transformational powers to enable new economic and social relations. What this actually meant was that the dominant set of ideas and beliefs in the cultural system of many developed countries was that organisations would be more efficient, with higher levels of productivity delivered by less staff, by investing heavily in new ICTs. This mindset was particularly prominent amongst the group of countries that were in the forefront of promoting a neo-liberal political agenda, such as the UK, USA and Australia. Thus, OSS development in these countries, and the closely related First Stop Shop (FSS), are examples of SEPs at the strata of local institutions that are causally related to the generative powers of the CEPs and SEPs resulting from the causal powers of these ideas in the strata above. This contrasts with evidence from the Nordic Network for One Stop Shops, and other studies of developments in public administration of that time (e.g. Kooiman 1993, Lane 1995), which demonstrate that in continental Europe similar developments were generally much less driven by a neo-liberal agenda.

The term one stop shop actually masks some subtle and not so subtle differences between variants of OSS that actually developed during the 1990s. In the UK very few OSS were anywhere near the 'ideal type': facilities which offered a comprehensive range of services to 'whole person' customers, where the exchange of information between customer and agency led to a completed transaction, without any direct contact between the customer and the back office, or production unit, of the bureaucracy. This situation was largely due to the difference in the constitutional status of local government in the UK and the constraints this places on the range of responsibilities, powers and resources available to it. Most OSS at local government level in the UK therefore took one of two structural forms:

- service specific. Offering a holistic service but primarily within the confines of a specific 'client/customer' area (e.g. housing, youth services, elderly, etc.). This type of OSS was associated with models of service decentralisation common throughout the 1980s and 1990s.
- multi/cross service. In which case (and for a multitude of organisational, political and legal reasons) the OSS acts as a signpost for users, providing basic information and advice, and/or directing them to the place where their query can be dealt with fully.

The second variant of OSS, above, should more appropriately be described as FSS and was, in almost all cases, the SEP that became a feature of British local government, due to the generative powers noted above. In practice many FSS employed staff who were sufficiently skilled and knowledgeable to be able to provide solutions to quite complex problems/queries without having to refer users to third parties, or call on the support of the 'back office'. In other words, the reflexive freedom and agential powers of the staff were such that they could escape from, and therefore compensate for, the conditioning of the structural forms and systemic properties of the FSS and thus produce a service closer to that of an OSS. Furthermore, and again as discussed in Chapter 4, the emergence of OSS/FSS, gained further momentum from the causal powers of the LGR, and the commitment to 'community' government given by many county and district councils. In many cases this then required them to work with town/parish councils to deliver on this commitment at the level of communities.

The development of the Council X OSS was on exactly this basis: it was emergent from ideas for partnership working and community governance developed by the LGR defence group, and subsequently adopted by the PPG (it was also an FSS, although OSS has been used through this book as this was the term used within Council X and between the partner councils). However, and as has also been discussed previously, the LGR created the paradoxical position of providing a catalyst for ideational change while at the same time putting a brake on structural change, at least for the duration of the Review. The required conditions for the structural elaboration of the OSS did not exist until after the Review ended in October 1995, therefore. Consequently, shortly after being formally established in January 1995 the PPG became the mechanism through which Council X's involvement in the structural elaboration of the OSS, in partnership with Councils Y and Z, would occur.

The Council X One Stop Shop

By the time the conditions existed to allow the agents of Councils X, Y, and Z to move to commence the structural development of an OSS the agenda for community governance and a partnership approach *within* Council X had been largely supplanted by a belief amongst the reformist IS groups that an OSS might be better used to promote other interests. Specifically, this was that IS development could be used to surreptitiously challenge some of the systemic and social contradictions and weaknesses within Council X. Furthermore, the same actors believed that there were other mechanisms allied to the specific OSS proposal under consideration that might also advance this agenda. The first was that Council Z was keen to take on new roles and responsibilities, thus requiring a more extensive package of IS support from Council X. The second was that Council Z was in a position to provide the majority of material resources: the buildings, staff and the majority of funding for ICTs. In return Council X would provide expertise, political support for the project, and access to the information sources judged vital to the effective operation of the OSS via a connection to the EPIS.

Given the powerful role that cuts in funding played in conditioning and shaping the actions of agents within Council X, then the exchange transactions on which the OSS partnership was to be based were obviously an extremely attractive and opportunistic basis for interaction for actors from Council X. It did mean, however, that the relationship between Council X and the OSS project was almost entirely contingent, altering the basis of the institutional relationship between Councils X and Z and consequently the relative power of the respective agents/actors. Council Y, meanwhile, had no plans to expand on the service it had traditionally provided through the offices of Council Z and therefore the cultural and structural significance of this agent on OSS development seemed likely to be limited.

The OSS had the following aims agreed between the partners:

- provide a facility managed by receptionist staff [from Council Z] with skills and knowledge across a range of local authority services.
- provide a necessary and appropriate focal point for members of the public.
- provide a two way communication and information/feedback process to assist Council X and Council Y to improve services.
- improve access to all council services.

An officers' steering group provided the official mechanism for interaction between the partner councils. Initially, at least, interaction was largely concessionary. There was also direct contact between individual steering group members as and when the situation required. Importantly, officers from Council X made special efforts to meet OSS staff, and the manager in particular. In fact, actors from Council X invited the OSS manager to occasional meetings of the PPG, as well as other meetings and events within Council X that they deemed relevant. This was significant because it represents efforts to expose the OSS manager to the cultural system of Council X, and thus the ideas and beliefs actors had concerning how IS could be used to underpin the development of the OSS. The objective was to influence what the agent/actors of Council Z might then ask for from Council X in the way of IS.

The OSS was formally opened in July 1996, although in practice it had been open to the public on a limited basis since May. With newly refurbished offices in a prime high street location, material on a wide range of services offered by a range of public

238

and voluntary bodies, an EPIS terminal, and full time staff, it was no surprise that the OSS was soon well used by the public. According to data from the PSTAG evaluation, between the first and second month of operation enquiries increased from 479 to 683 and remained at 600 plus for the six month period of the evaluations study. Furthermore, these figures are more than double those for the same period in 1995. From the perspective of Council X, enquiries averaged 76 per month, which compared to an average of 34 per month received via the offices of Council Z before the OSS opened. This means that enquiries for Council X average nine percent of the total (approximately 50% were for Council Y). Interestingly, the vast majority of these related to three specific areas: highways and street lighting, public transport and social services. Nearly 60% of enquiries were by phone, approximately 2% by letter and the remainder 'drop ins'.[lxiv]

Causal powers

Despite the relatively limited scale and scope of activity relating to Council X at the OSS, the PPG regarded the doubling in enquiries as significant. It therefore became the basis for a push to further expand this type of cultural and structural morphogenesis, as well as ideational and discursive reshaping around the concept of ICT enabled community governance, which the PPG argued the OSS encapsulated. Consequently, the PPG's members began to plan for an expansion in the number of OSS. Their belief was that this was course of action was strengthened because, on the basis of the success of the original OSS, several other councils had approached members of the PPG with proposals for OSS. Clearly, the original OSS was acting as a generative mechanism within the emerging system of local governance for that area, affecting the ideas and actions of actors/agents beyond the position-practice system of Council X.

Indeed, evidence collected from the officers' steering group confirmed that within a couple of months of the opening of the OSS its generative powers were so great that they began to influence council to council relations. Thus, while the mode of interaction between actors from all three councils had been concessionary during the development period, actors from Council Y soon switched to a defensive/competitive position once the OSS was launched. This occurred because of the belief that the clear plan of action for OSS development that the PPG was promoting was an attempt by Council X to impose its ideas on other councils. As this was perceived by the actors and agents of Council Y as altering the situational logic that had initially applied between the partners away from serving their interests they set about adopting courses of action that they believed would counter this, both in the eyes of actors from Council Z, and with the actors and agents of other councils. One such strategy was to exploit the fact that Council X had very limited financial resources to put into OSS developments. By highlighting this Council Y hoped to undermine the benefits of any partnership with Council X.

Interestingly, this led to yet another example of the unintended consequences of action; in this instance having a positive outcome for the PPG. Councillors who twin tracked (i.e. held seats on the both Council X and Council Y, as did the leader of Council Y) but were members of the political party out of power in Council X, used Council Xs inability/unwillingness to provide financial backing to the OSS as ammunition to attack the Council. Eventually this pressure began to tell, becoming a factor in COMG agreeing to additional financial support to the EPIS (as a feature of the OSS) following the joint ISSSG and PPG presentation to COMG in November 1996. This served to progress the IS agenda of the supporters of IS reform further, while enabling the PPG to offer EPIS terminals to other councils who had expressed an interest in an OSS, thus increasing the positive aspects of a partnership with Council X.

While the causal powers of the OSS seemed to have had a powerful impact on actors and agents beyond the confines of Council X, internally it became increasingly clear that this was far from the case. The PPG's aim had been to use the emergence of the OSS, and the role of IS as a fundamental property of that structure, to further highlight the need for increased systemic integration within Council X. That is, internally, the OSS project required collaboration, coordination and the development of common standards and protocols to allow the management and exchange of the information necessary to enable the OSS to function effectively, and thus deliver on the Council's resource obligations to the project.

Unfortunately, the limited morphogenesis of the cultural system of IS that had taken place by July–August 1996 was not sufficient to provide the basis for structural morphogenesis on this scale. Consequently, although the OSS initiative did provide the PPG and supporters of IS reform with an opportunity to expand the EPIS, they were not able to gain the support of departmental corporate agents for a broader agenda for IS developments that focused on the wider issue of what information was required to support OSS developments generally, and how this information could be managed and made to move through the Council to whichever organisation, agent or actor might require it. Furthermore, and of crucial importance to the outcome just discussed, was that once the OSS became an actual structural form the generative powers of the emergent cultural, structural and agential properties rapidly caused one interest group/corporate agent, the Libraries Service, to adopt an overtly competitive mode of interaction with regard to the PPG, the OSS, and actors associated with it. This issue, and its implications, are discussed fully in the next section.

Potential contradictions/complementarities

The case for the OSS creating complementarities is similar to the other examples of cultural and structural elaboration cited in this chapter. It is sufficient to add, therefore, that with the OSS up and running, additional investment in the EPIS, and the intranet development, reformist IS actors/agents believed that sufficient mechanisms might now have been created for their generative powers to cause a more widespread structural morphogenesis of IS. It is also worth emphasising that the OSS development was also significant externally, because it created a mechanism that offered the potential to repair the council to council relations which the LGR had undermined. As we have seen, however, in some cases at least, the PEPs created served to reinforce existing structural and cultural divisions, as was the case with the actors and agents of Council Y.

In the short term, and despite the increasing degree of cultural morphogenesis that the advocates of IS reform had been able to engender within Council X, the elaboration of the OSS acted as a trigger for a significant *challenge* to the ideas and actions of the PPG. Seeing a potential threat to their interests, the Libraries Service launched an alternative policy of OSS/FSS development – referred to as information points. Of course, culturally, structurally and agentially, the libraries service provided an ideal basis for a whole range of informational services that could deliver on the policy commitment of Council X to raise its visibility/accessibility to the public. This had been well recognised within Council X since the LGR. However, although information points could provide a wide range of information from a range of sources on activities in a particular geographical area, and often beyond, they were solely the domain of Council X. Consequently, they failed to address the post LGR policy objective to pursue a *multi agency* partnership approach to local governance.

On the basis of pre and post LGR statements from actors from the Libraries Service, as well as the endorsement of COMG, the vast majority of the members of the PPG believed Libraries had signed up to this view. Ultimately, however, members of the PPG had underestimated the causal power of another situational logic: that when the Libraries Service looked vulnerable to cuts in its funding information points became a very useful mechanism, and visible structure, to promote libraries, especially externally to the public (as voters). In other words, although senior actors from Libraries recognised the need for internal structural change to combat the systemic weaknesses that had arisen post 1990, and had been vocal in speaking out against these and in favour of developments such as the OSS through their membership of the PPG and ISSSG, ultimately they judged that their interests were better served by unilateral action. Furthermore, they judged that their bargaining power and

242

negotiating strength was sufficient to overcome any negative opportunity costs arising from their actions, at least in the short term.

Coincidentally (or not) the action of the Libraries Service actually reflected an option that the PPG had explored as a weaker version of the structural elaboration of OSS/FSS. This involved exploiting the decentralised nature of Council X and thus that certain services had offices located in communities around the county. These were service specific, but the PPG had realised that there was considerable potential to re-orientate these offices to incorporate other services and uses by other organisations. In other words, turn these offices from a specialist to a generalist function along the lines of an OSS. Of course, actors from the Libraries Service were well aware that once they adopted an option for structural elaboration that was similar to one that had been seriously considered by the PPG this made any attempt to criticise information points more difficult.

Following the launch of the OSS two other areas of tension began to emerge within Council X. Both had implications for IS reform as promoted by the PPG and the ISSSG. Firstly, there appeared to be confusion in the minds of many *primary agents* over which of two courses of strategic action should be paramount to the Council: developing partnerships with other organisations as the means by which a range of services could be delivered to citizens; or, continuing to mount a rearguard action based on the historic role of Council X as the major provider of public services in the county. If the latter was paramount it had a significant bearing on the whole ethos and operation of a partnership approach. More importantly, it raised fundamental questions concerning the degree to which many of the Council's staff recognised, and were committed to, developing new roles and relationships within an emerging system of local governance. On this occasion the morphogenesis of the cultural system had yet to create the conditions for the social integration of corporate and primary agents that was necessary to enable the wider acceptance of the need for local governance and related structural change.

The second area of tension concerned what might appropriately be called 'demand management'. That is, balancing the pursuit of a policy objective of 'improving the public's access to services' (which emerged from the LGR and subsequently underpinned much of the work of the PPG) which explicitly involved increasing demand for services, while at the same time suffering significant cuts in funding. Promoting the OSS (via publicity campaigns etc.) might well increase the number of users rapidly, putting pressure on resources. Taking a more low key approach would lead to a slower increase in use, but one which would be more easily managed and resourced. However, from the perspective of the PPG the concern was that the latter would not raise the profile of, and necessity for, IS development sufficiently to act as a mechanism for triggering more widespread IS development within Council X. On the other hand, however, members of the PPG were also conscious that if demand increased, such that it led to a sudden and/or substantial increase in the workload of agents within Council X, this would reflect badly on the project. Furthermore, the expressed wish of Council Z to adopt a wider range of services and responsibilities also had to be handled in such a way as not to be seen to threaten existing providers/interest groups within Council X.

Seven examples of morphogenesis relating to IS – four cultural (the Strategy Process Report, the PPG Development Plan, the Intranet Workshop, and the joint PPG/ISSSG presentation to COMG) and three structural (EPIS expansion, the OMPP and the OSS) – have now been examined, and their causal powers, and incompatibilities or compatibilities with the systemic and social integration of Council X, analysed. The morphogenesis of agency was also highlighted, were appropriate, such as the elaboration of the CWG and IMG into the combined IMCWG, and the emergence of an intranet implementation group, and an OSS steering group.

The majority of cases of PEPs and agential morphogenesis, such as the elaboration of the ISSSG working groups, were discussed in the previous chapter, given that their emergence was fairly seamless from the ongoing process of interaction documented in that chapter. Indeed, and as was discussed at the outset of this chapter, examples, and/or properties, of both cultural and structural elaboration also emerged before the date taken as signifying T4 – April 1996, and therefore also appeared as material in Chapter 5. A discussion of the difficulties associated with ordering material from three simultaneous morphogenetic cycles of emergence-interplay-outcome into specified time periods of a complex and dynamic case study such as Council X, have been noted previously and will be an issue for detailed discussion in the following chapter. Regardless of this 'untidiness', what the examples of morphogenesis at T4 presented in this chapter represent are real and actual outcomes from significant phases in a number of interrelated causal processes. It is appropriate, therefore, to draw some general conclusions from the material presented above before moving to a discussion of the possibilities (i.e. tendential predictions) for future morphogenesis that concludes the chapter.

Cultural and structural morphogenesis: general conclusions

It is clear from the process of retroduction undertaken in the previous two chapters, allied with the material presented above, that all of the examples of structural and cultural morphogenesis featured in this book are emergent from a range of *interrelated* causal processes, powers and mechanisms. Some were unexpected, such as the causal powers that emerged following a fourth political party (the Green Party) taking a seat on the Council. Others were more predictable, such as the effects of central government imposed cuts in funding.

The most significant causal process was the Local Government Review (LGR). The generative powers of the CEPs, SEPs and PEPs to emerge from the LGR created the situational logics for a limited number of actors and agents at the position-practice level of Council X to begin to merge ideas and beliefs about the potential of new ICT with ideas and beliefs about emerging systems of local governance. The CEPs associated with this proposed model of local governance proved instrumental in two ways. First, in Council X emerging from the LGR unchanged. Second, in exposing the extent to which the IS, and the social and systemic structures more generally, of Council X had fragmented as a result of the structural morphogenesis emergent from the far reaching policies of decentralisation, devolution and privatisation implemented in 1990. The structural properties and causal powers of these developments had undermined the high levels of *systemic* integration of the Council, generating, in turn, PEPs and the rapid emergence of new interests groups who no longer perceived that their interests were best served by maintaining high levels of *social* integration.

Following the conclusion of the LGR the ideas for ICT enabled community governance, and of the discourse that now accompanied it, became the cultural 'property' of the PPG. This corporate agent, and the actors associated with it, collectively and individually, set about adopting a strategic course of action, and modes of interaction, that led to further CEPs. The causal powers of these then proved instrumental in generating PEPs within another corporate agent – the ISSSG – leading to a change in the ideas and commitments of a substantial number of its members. As the ideational significance, and thus influence, of both the PPG and the ISSSG grew (Figures 4.5 and 5.4), and other actors signed up to a reformist IS agenda, so the extent of the morphogenesis of the cultural system of IS continued to increase (Figure 6.3). The IS Strategy Process Report of April 1996 reflects this. However, in praising the benefits of decentralisation, devolution and privatisation the language of the Report also reflects the pressures towards morphostasis, and thus the relative power of departmental agents/actors, when compared to the PPG and the ISSSG.

By October 1996 there is little doubt that the cultural morphogenesis of IS had increased further amongst actors involved in corporate agency (Figure 6.3). The assumption of these actors was generally that it was also spreading amongst primary agents, with more and more people appreciating the significance of IS enabled local

246

governance to the structures and systems and roles and practices of Council X. The content and language of the PPG's Development Plan, the Intranet Workshop (and its supporting documentation) and the joint presentation and report on IS development by the PPG and the ISSSG to COMG all reflect this belief. COMG, or, at the least, the majority of its members, certainly appear to have become increasingly influenced by the power of the reformist IS CEPs. Even allowing for the political pressure COMG was receiving from the few twin track councillors, discussed above, the material resources for the intranet and EPIS, following the joint presentation of November 1996, clearly demonstrate COMG's support for reformist IS objectives. In fact it was COMG's awareness of, or suspicions about, the systemic outcomes of the privatisation of IT and their increasing awareness of the argument that new IS could reverse this process that was causally significant in the ideational shift of the ISSSG. However, the actions taken by the Libraries Service in setting up information points throws into question the real level of commitment to, and motivation behind, the cultural morphogenesis of at least some corporate agents. Similarly assumptions about the extent and depth of cultural morphogenesis amongst primary agents, and about their commitment to ideas about local governance, also need to be treated with caution.

Figure 6.3 summaries in a graphical way the situation regarding the social and systemic integration and cultural and structural morphogenesis of Council X from January 1995 to the end of 1996. The systemic integration of IS was low, which is unsurprising given that the systemic integration of the structures of Council X generally had declined post 1990 and continued to decline. As IS are *properties* of these structures we might expect to see a strong relationship. However, due to the privatisation of IS systemic integration had been undermined more rapidly and more extensively than systemic integration generally, although by April 1996 evidence suggests it was increasing, albeit slowly.

The social integration of non IS primary agents declined steadily from 1990. However, due to the extent of the outsourcing of IS *amongst primary agents in the IS domain* social integration was considerably weaker here than generally within the Council. Although not illustrated in Figure 6.3 it is important to note that the social integration of IS actors involved in *corporate* agency never declined as much as for primary agents and was increasing more rapidly by May 1996.

Amongst corporate actors in the IS domain cultural morphogenesis that centred on ideas and beliefs about IS and local governance increased steadily from November 1995, having previously risen slowly with the increasing acceptance of the ideas and beliefs on which the policies of organisational reform of the early 1990s were based. Structurally IS had actually gone into morphostasis following a burst of activity that is accounted for by the privatisation of IS, but by early 1996 limited morphogenesis had begun again and was continuing at November 1996.

Tendential prediction: possibilities for the morphogenesis of IS within Council X
On the basis of the process of retroduction that underpins the material presented in this and the two previous chapters it possible to make a number of tendential predictions as to where, when and with whom transformational versus reproductive power lies and the conditions for future morphogenesis? Chapter 2 discussed Archer's proposition that where '...the overall state of systemic integration' is coherent this '...serves to contain the transformative potential of agency.', while incompatibilities '...foster actualisation.' (Archer 1995:191). However, and as has previously been explained, the levels of systemic and social integration differ *between* corporate agency and primary agency *and* between actors/agents within the IS domain and external to it, with systemic and social integration within the IS domain declining more rapidly and deeply than generally. Consequently, and as the morphogenetic approach would suggest, the transformative potential of the actors and agents of the IS realm has been actualised significantly more than for the actors and agents of Council X generally.

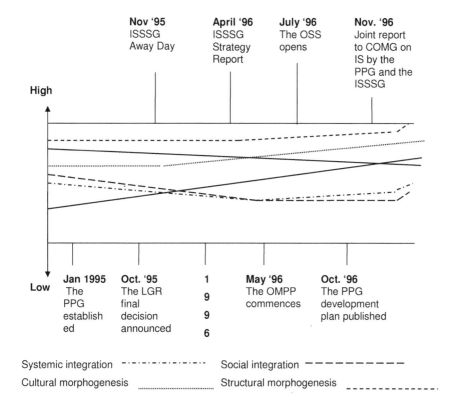

Nov '95
ISSSG
Away Day

April '96
ISSSG
Strategy
Report

July '96
The OSS
opens

Nov. '96
Joint report
to COMG on
IS by the
PPG and the
ISSSG

High

Low

Jan 1995
The
PPG
establish
ed

Oct. '95
The LGR
final
decision
announced

1
9
9
6

May '96
The OMPP
commences

Oct. '96
The PPG
development
plan published

Systemic integration ‐ ‐ ‐ ‐ ‐ ‐ ‐ ‐   Social integration ‐ ‐ ‐ ‐ ‐ ‐ ‐ ‐

Cultural morphogenesis ....   Structural morphogenesis ‐ ‐ ‐ ‐ ‐ ‐ ‐

Note: Dashed lines for social integration and cultural morphogenesis apply to corporate
agents, solid lines to primary agents.

Figure 6.3 Systemic and social integration and cultural and structural

morphogenesis in the IS domain of Council X 1995–96

The second element of the morphogenetic approach that has to be taken into account
at this point is the reciprocal influences of the cycles of structural and cultural
morphogenesis/stasis. Chapter 2 also noted that Archer's proposition is that:

…when there are discontinuities between morphostatic/morphogenetic
sequences in the structural and cultural domains that one of these is found
to be *more consequential* for the other, temporally and temporarily.

> Correspondingly, conjunction between the two cycles coincides with *reciprocal influences* between structure and culture.
>
> (Archer 1995:308 Original emphasis)

Again a differentiated approach has to be employed when considering Council X because cultural morphogenesis has not been uniform. It has been most pronounced amongst IS corporate agents, with the likelihood that IS primary agents were also being more heavily influenced by the cultural morphogenesis of IS than were primary agents generally. Furthermore, structural morphogenesis, both generally and specific to IS, had been out of sync with cultural morphogenesis since the early 1990s. Ironically it would appear that amongst primary agents, both in IS and generally, acceptance of decentralisation, devolution and privatisation had begun to increase by 1995. Consequently, cultural morphogenesis which had, as I noted in Chapter 4, lagged substantially behind the forced morphogenesis of structure, began to align. However, from late 1995, and significantly before this date for some actors/corporate agents in the IS domain, cultural morphogenesis was increasingly centred on a different set of ideas – IS and local governance – rather than decentralisation and devolution. Structural morphogenesis was being shaped accordingly. Consequently the reality within Council X was that the cultural and structural morphogenesis of IS was following two trajectories, *with each being out of sync internally and with the other*.

On the basis of this analysis of CEPs and SEPs it is possible to make the tendential prediction that post November 1996 both cultural and structural morphogenesis to promote IS and local governance would continue. Indeed, the ideational and material support of such an important corporate agent as COMG should lead to speedier developments for a number of reasons. First, and most obviously, because resources were made available for the development of actual examples of structural elaboration, such as the EPIS and intranet. Second, because COMG's support should act as a mechanism to further increase the relative power (ideationally and materially) of the

250

PPG, the ISSSG and reformist IS actors/agents generally vis a vis other agents and actors. This ought to alter the situational logics of those who choose not to voluntarily sign up to the IS and local governance agenda, causing them to reconsider the opportunity costs of not following the ideational lead set by the IS reformists. Because IS are such a fundamental structural property, and IS reformists increasingly controlled access to IS resources, as corporate agents across the Council reviewed the strategic courses of action in which IS were implicated (which is almost any example of organisational development) they would have perceived that increasingly their interests were best served by adopting modes of interaction with the ISSSG and its supporters that were concessionary, or, at the least, opportunistic, rather than, for example, the defensive and competitive mode that had been adopted by the Libraries Service.

The significance of the temporal dimension of the relationship between structural and cultural morphogenesis that Archer highlights would also have been likely to feature prominently in future IS development in Council X. Specifically, this means that unless over time the cultural morphogenesis of IS amongst the general population of primary agents becomes more closely aligned with the ideas and discourse of the IS domain it is unlikely that wider scale structural morphogenesis of IS would be possible. The examples of the OMPP and the OSS, discussed above, illustrate this clearly. This is an issue that is not restricted to primary agents, however, as the example of the Libraries Service demonstrates. Nevertheless, from the perspective of the morphogenetic approach it is primary agents who hold the key to successfully implementing widespread structural morphogenesis, as the discussion in Chapter 2 explained, due to the fact that while corporate agents – in this case primarily the PPG, the ISSSG, the CSU and COMG – have the power to shape the context in which primary agents operate, ultimately, as Archer (1995) argues, corporate agents are dependant on primary agents for the attainment of their interests.

Powerful corporate agents clearly have the resources to impose structural morphogenesis, as the examples of the power relations between central and local government and of the policies for organisational restructuring undertaken by the senior management of Council X discussed in this book demonstrate. On the evidence presented here it seems highly unlikely that reformist IS agents would gain sufficient bargaining power and negotiating strength to pursue this course of action within Council X, however. Furthermore, even if this course of action became possible it would almost certainly lead to the creation of further contradictions and incompatibilities within Council X. These would then further undermine the systemic integration of the Council. As has been highlighted throughout this and the previous two chapters, for members of the PPG, their predecessors from the LGR defence group, and a growing group of IS reformists, this outcome would have fundamentally contradicted one of the overarching aims of one of the most important courses of strategic action to emerge from the Local Government Review – the use of new IS to 'join up' Council X once again.

Recognising the interrelationship of the strata of society

Further reference to the fundamental role that the LGR played in the causal processes that led to the morphogenesis of IS within Council X also provides an ideal opportunity to briefly revisit the importance of the relationship between the causal processes of one strata and those of other strata. Chapter 2 discussed the relationship between strata – systems, institutions, and positions and practices – and causal process and mechanisms, while Chapter 4 explored their relevance to Council X under the heading of inter governmental relations and local governance. The argument put was that the SEPs and CEPs produced by the social relations (of the causal processes) of the institutional strata, in the form of policies from central government (such as CCT and the Rates Act of 1984) impacted on the causal processes of the position-practice strata of local authorities such as Council X. The generative powers of these SEPs led, in turn, to the emergence of systemic contradictions and incompatibilities – tensions between central and local government

– which then became part of the situational and ideational logics that confronted the actors and agents of Council X (Figure 2.5). The LGR, and the necessary and contingent incompatibilities and complementarities it created, was just another example of the outcome of social relations from the institutional strata of the late 1980s early 1990s to impact on English local government.

As a review of the literature on local government referenced for this book will confirm (e.g. Leach, Stewart and Walsh 1994, Young and Rao 1997, Wilson and Game 1998), for scholars of British local government the LGR was, and remains, largely regarded as less of a threat, and therefore of less significance to local government, than CCT and the plethora of policies concerned with restructuring and reengineering local government. Certainly its significance was relatively short term, although as noted in Chapter 1, local government reform appears to remain an open issue in central government circles. Be that as it may, for Council X it was the generative powers of the LGR that *proved fundamental* in creating the ideational and agential mechanisms that allowed actors to use the structural properties of IS to challenge the systemic and social disintegration of the Council. Somewhat ironically this situation was emergent from the actions and interactions of corporate agents (i.e. senior managers) as they sought to respond – far too rapidly perhaps – to the emergent properties and causal powers of previous cycles of structural and cultural morphogenesis at the level of central government.

The importance of the 'spirit' and 'possibilities' of technology for morphogenesis or morphostasis
The final element of significance to the morphogenesis of IS within Council X returns us to Snellen's and Donk's insight, cited in Chapter 1, that: 'ICTs do not *cause* developments in public administration…The possibilities of technology function as *attractors* for aspirations that are already (or always were) existent in public administration, or are aroused by them.' (1998: 9, Original emphasis). De Sanctis and Poole (1994) refer to this cultural dimension of technology as the 'spirit':

what a technology promotes, in terms of goals and values, rather than what it *actually* consists of or can do (as discussed in Chapter 2). Regardless of the terminology used, what is clear, is that Snellen's and Donk's proposition is entirely borne out by this book, with the case study graphically illustrating that at every stage of the morphogenetic cycles under review one of the most significant features was the key role that the 'possibilities' of IS/ICTs played as 'attractors' for the wider aspirations of interest groups. So fundamental is this dimension of the case study to the outcomes that the probability is that the concept of ICTs as 'attractors' is likely to be significant in *any* social context. Indeed, this is reflected either implicitly or explicitly in much of the literature on organisational, economic and social change cited in Chapter 1, and particularly in government reports, such as Gershon (2004) and Lyons (2004).

A strength of the morphogenetic approach is that it allowed a fine grained account to be given of the ability of reformist IS actors and agents to work with and through the cultural dimension of new IS/ICTs. The picture that emerged was of a lengthy process of socio-cultural interaction, that started with the LGR defence group and was then pursued by a small but steadily growing number of actors, who formulated ideas based on the potential of new IS/ICTs, logically related these to other ideas about organisational change (and to local governance in particular) and used the resulting CEPs as 'attractors' for different forms of strategic action. In short, what was observed was exactly the type of morphogenetic cycle that Archer claims should occur: ideas, theories, beliefs and values about IS/ICTs (which constitute part of the cultural system of any organisation) that are, at any point in time a product of previous socio-cultural interaction, then becoming the subject of morphogenesis through the emergence of new cultural properties (CEPs).

Finally, it is worth pointing out that IT professionals played only a minor role in these causal processes, which is unsurprising given the extent of the privatisation of the IS functions of Council X in 1991. Had the Council not followed this course of action, and the vast majority of councils did not, both the context and the outcome of

254

the case study would undoubtedly have been very different. Indeed, based on the material presented in Chapter 4, it is clear that in those parts of Council X where small pockets of IT professionals 'survived' privatisation IS became a more powerful property of the structures that emerged as the organisation fragmented than where there were no IT specialists. Consequently, it is not difficult to conclude, for example, that the situational logics that would have been created by the existence of such actors and agents would have undermined the relative power of the PPG. Indeed, as the source of this power was very largely ideational and came from the group being able to trade on their 'expertise' in IS and local governance it is likely that their claim to this expertise may well have been significantly undermined had 'real' ICT experts existed. This would have made tying together the two cultural agendas of IS and local governance difficult, as well as undermining the ability of the PPG to launch and maintain these ideas as 'attractors' for the aspiration of other IS interest groups.

The fundamental point here is that without the integration of the two ideational agendas of IS and local governance, and of the discourse associated with the CEPs that emerged, it is doubtful that the underlying project of the PPG and its allies – the development of new structures, systems and roles and responsibilities that would promote systemic integration - would have proved possible. The value of the 'possibilities' and causal powers of local governance were that they allowed the systemic and social contradictions and incompatibilities that had emerged from the organisational reforms of the early 1990s to be exposed, albeit often implicitly. The value of the 'possibilities' and causal powers of IS are perhaps best summed up in a one line quotation from an interview with an actor who played a key role in the complex interplay of structure and agency that this book documents:

IT was an acceptable issue, one that most people could see needed looking at.[lxv]

Information Systems Development and the Morphogenetic Approach: an assessment

Why the morphogenetic approach?

The overarching aim of this book was to examine the complex relationship between agency, structure and culture in the context of cycles of information systems (IS) development and organisational change in English local government through a longitudinal case study of a specific local authority – Council X. This was to be done through the use of a methodology for the non conflationary analysis of the agency/structure dynamic was: Margaret Archer's morphogenetic approach (1988, 1995, 1998b, 1998c, 2002, Figure 1.2). As discussed in Chapter 1, the application of Archer's approach to empirical research remains limited, and there is certainly no published evidence of its application to a largely micro level case study of IS development in the public sector. The aim of this chapter is, therefore, to reflect back on this exercise and assess the utility of Archer's approach when applied to the type of case study research reported here. First however, and by way of restating the strengths of the approach, it is worth recapping the core features (as detailed and discussed in Chapter 2) by citing the following quotation:

...the objective [of the morphogenetic approach] is to set out as clearly as possible the conditions under which morphogenesis versus morphostasis ensues from particular chains of socio-cultural interaction, as conditioned in a prior social context. Obviously given the nature of society as an open system, these will only be tendential conditions which will have to be complemented by an analysis of the concrete contingencies in every research undertaking. Nevertheless, this seems to be of considerably more use than either deterministic prophecies (upward and downward conflation) or indeterminate assertions of central conflation...the second aim is even more precise, namely to account for the form (though not the substantive content) of social elaboration to take place…Since what eventually transpires at the level of events is a combination of the tendential and the contingent, the aim cannot be to furnish a predictive formulae but rather an explanatory methodology for the researcher to employ, namely the analytical history of emergence.

(Archer 1995:294).

Instrumental in directing the research on which this book is based towards non conflationary theoretical and methodological approaches, such as Archer's, were Snellen and Donk (1998), two scholars from the European 'informatization' research community of the 1990s. To recap the discussion in Chapter 1, by the early 1990s it was clear that IS/ICT were playing an increasingly powerful role in broad ranging initiatives aimed at organisational change in the public domain. This was a trend that was unlikely to diminish given that a core function of public administration is: '…information acquisition, storage, handling, diffusion and communication…' (Snellen and Donk 1998:34). Consequently, many scholars of IS and public administration (including the author) supported Snellen's and Donk's view that the ongoing development of theories of 'informatization' was a priority for the advancement of this field of research.

Snellen and Donk argued that one way to attempt to capture the complexity of informatization was by applying a model that combined causal and functional reasoning. Causal reasoning explained later occurrences by reference to former ones, and functional reasoning explained former occurrences by reference to later ones. Chapter 1 argued that there are distinct parallels between Snellen's and Donk's proposed model (which they never associate with critical realism) and that of the morphogenetic approach of Archer, as well as with the process of retroduction (i.e. identifying what causal mechanisms and powers are active in any given situation) that is central to critical realist explanations of social structures, institutional systems and positions and practices (Figure 1.1). Consequently, it is true to say that it was their arguments that inspired the exploration and subsequent adoption of a critical realist/morphogenetic approach for this book.

Applying the morphogenetic approach involved the detailed documentation and analysis of the causal processes of the IS domain of Council X. Chapters 4 to 6 represent the 'analytical narrative' (Archer 1995:343) this produced of the emergence, interplay and outcome of structure, culture and agency and the subsequent morphogenesis and/or morphostasis of IS. This represents the type of wide ranging and intensive research endeavour that Figure 1.4 illustrates. Given the limited extent to which the potential of the morphogenetic approach for empirical research has been realised to date, the aim of this chapter is to reflect on the lessons that can be learned from its application to a micro level case study such as Council X and thus provide an assessment of its utility to the is type of social science research.

Applying the morphogenetic approach
Strengths
On the basis of the material presented in the three analytical chapters of this book Archer's claims for the analytical strengths of the morphogenetic approach are very largely borne out. Certainly there is little doubt that as an explanatory methodology the approach allowed an extremely detailed account to be given of the history of the emergence (and interplay and outcome) of IS as a structural property and of the complexity of the (inter) relationship between the structure(s), culture(s) and agents of the IS environment of the position-practice system of the case study organisation. It is possible to claim, therefore, that the central aim of this book has been fulfilled: that the critical and revelatory nature of the case study provides valuable insights into the complexity of IS development, and of organisational change more generally, in English local government.

The key to capturing this complexity has undoubtedly been constructing the 'analytical history/narrative' of the case study, with the morphogenetic approach providing the tools and techniques necessary for this exercise. However, and as might be expected, utilising such an approach is not without issues. Archer, for example, notes that: 'The whole notion of analytical histories of emergence has to transcend a fairly common tendency to regard the narrative and the analytical as standing in opposition to one another, which is exactly the opposite of what is proposed here.' (Archer 1995:343). This is an epistemological issue of the type discussed in Chapters 1 and 2 and requires no further discussion here. Instead the discussion which follows focuses on issues that emerged during the *application* of the morphogenetic approach. In some cases these arose for conceptual reasons – as is the case with emergent properties/generative mechanisms. In other cases, such as when demarcating stages and cycles, the application of Archer's methods proved problematic precisely because of its application to a micro level case study of the position-practice system of an organisation rather than, for example, constructing a case from entirely historical data, or working at a higher level of abstraction/strata. In a few cases, such as with unintended outcomes and aggregate effects, issues arose because of both. In addition, some issues relate to some of the core concepts of critical realism rather than the morphogenetic approach specifically, one of the most fundamental being that: '…emergent properties and the causal mechanisms in which they are implicated are *not directly available to observation* but can be apprehended indirectly.' (Ackroyd 2004:155 Emphasis added).

Two further points also need emphasising. First, there is no case where an issue negates the extra analytical value that the morphogenetic approach brings to the type of social research reported in this book. Second, regardless of the source(s) of the highlighted issues my conclusion would be that ultimately, and as noted above, they represent the inevitable flip side of a philosophy of social science (critical realism), and its methodological complement, which, precisely because of their complexity enable a detailed exploration of the stratified and interrelated causes behind specific outcomes and events. As Archer (1995) claims, this then allows something of practical (i.e. applied) value to be said as to the possibilities for change and/or stasis in any social setting. The scope and depth of the analytical history set out in this book is an example in itself of the numerous strengths of the morphogenetic approach. However, before embarking on the penultimate section of this chapter and book by examining these "problem" issues it would be inappropriate not to highlight the remaining aspects of the morphogenetic methodology that proved particularly insightful when researching Council X but which have not previously been discussed in Chapter 6 or the concluding sections of Chapters 5 and 4.

Strata

Accepting the stratified ontology of critical realism, and subsequently adopting a methodology based on this view, certainly played a crucial role in the process of causal analysis. For example, it signalled the importance of the relationship between first and second order emergents in the context of English (British) local government and thus exploration of the nature of the institutional relationships that were causally efficacious in the late 1980s and early to mid 1990s. Thus, Chapter 4 set out the stratified nature and causal significance of the internal and necessary relations between central and local government and how through the 1980s the necessary complementarities that had largely marked out post war inter governmental relationships were rapidly replaced by necessary incompatibilities. The result was the emergence of social and systemic 'fault lines', as Archer refers to them, manifest in such events as the poll tax rebellions and riots of 1990, and the refusal of a variety of councils to conform to central government imposed spending limits, as weak social and systemic integration became the norm for the polity of England.

Actors and corporate and primary agents

Another area of analysis where a stratified approach was particular insightful was in maintaining a distinction between humans as individuals, as people with roles and positions and as groups and collectivities. As the case study of Council X focused on the position-practice system the appropriate differentiation was between actors and agents – both corporate and primary. The distinctions were set out in the relevant sections of Chapter 2, where the point was also made that a standard practice in IS research, as in social science generally, is to dispense with differentiation. The result is that the terms actor/agent are used interchangeably and the value of maintaining a distinction as an analytical device, as well as in recognition of the reality of the differential powers and positions of different people in different context and at different times, is thus undermined.

In the ICT/IS research community, as with consultants and other "experts" in this field, an example of the tendency to ignore the stratified nature of people is reflected in the very common practice of referring to 'champions' and/or 'project champions' without any indication as to whether this refers to a person or group of people. Indeed, there is often little attempt to define project champion(s), except implicitly – i.e. that they are senior managers/management. The author admits to being guilty of such a tendency at one time, along with numerous colleagues and associates from PSTAG (e.g. Bellamy, Horrocks and Webb 1995), EGPA (e.g. Horrocks 1997) and the GaDIA project (e.g. Hoff, Horrocks and Tops 2000). Furthermore, evidence that this trend continues, and of the significant role it almost certainly plays in masking the real and actual causal positions and powers of projects champions is powerfully illustrated by reference to the recent government reports and statements on ICT/IS and organisational change cited in Chapter 1 (e.g. Gershon 2004, Lyons 2004, Cabinet Office 2005).

As the account of IS development set out in this book demonstrates, and as Archer argues, this is surely a mistake. For example, defining all groups as agents, without distinguishing between corporate agents (those who have a say in '...structural and cultural modelling [and who] organise for their strategic pursuit.' and primary agents – who don't, but who, nonetheless, have ultimate influence over the 'promotive interests' of the former (Archer 1995:259) would not have allowed the key role of and relationship between the PPG and the ISSSG to be identified and analysed vis a vis other interest groups. Nor would a full account have been possible of the causal significance (for IS development) of the largely morphostatic environment that both groups experienced through their interactions with primary agents. Furthermore, maintaining a distinction between actors/corporate/primary agents allowed analysis of how, why and when the interests of people as actors ran counter to their interests as members of collectivities, and/or between their membership of different collectivities.

When combined with Archer's proposition that the 'interpretive freedom' and 'reflexive powers' that humans enjoy in any given situation is influenced by vested interest and opportunity costs, and framed by processes of exchange and power, stratification becomes an even more powerful analytical tool. The latter point was graphically illustrated by the outcome of the interaction between members of the PPG and the Libraries Service, both as corporate agents and actors, over the structural morphogenesis of the one stop shop. In common with the majority of the material in Chapter 5, this demonstrated that it is the emergent properties/generative mechanisms of systemic interaction – social, socio-cultural and group – which ultimately produce the causal powers for structural, cultural and/or agential morphogenesis. Consequently, the analysis of the causal processes behind the one stop shop and other examples of structural and cultural morphogenesis reported in this book demonstrate the strength of Archer's proposition that: 'All generative mechanisms are only influential through people...' But also and crucially, that this actually involves '...the confluence of three sets of emergent properties...' (ibid:193) – cultural, structural and agential.

From the perspective of an IS/organisational change consultant and/or advisor to government, or indeed, most organisations, it is easy to see why such an account of project champions, whether defined as groups or individuals, is unattractive. For example, it requires accepting that simply because a project champion is more powerful than other actors/agents – in terms of bargaining power and negotiating strength – this is only half the story. Exchange transactions, such as the trade of expertise that was so important to the PPG and the ISSSG, are as important to social elaboration. It requires accepting that while 'directional guidance' can be applied to actors and agents via policies, strategies, and management decisions – which condition and shape culture, structure and agency – ultimately any outcome is mediated by people. *However,* the different forms of strategic action and modes of interaction they choose to pursue in advancing or protecting their interests are difficult to predict and even more difficult to control. In short, it requires full recognition that the complexity of the nexus of connections that make up social structures and systems cannot be reduced to, or understood via, positivistic and deterministic models and flow diagrams.

Issues

Some of the key features of the morphogenetic approach which allow a realist analysis and interpretation of social systems to be constructed, and thus something of practical use to be said about IS development and organisational change in general, have now been reviewed. It is now appropriate to move on to a review of some of the features that proved problematic during the application of Archer's approach to the specific empirical study of Council X. The starting point for this exercise is, as briefly outlined in Chapter 2, the interchangeability of the terminology of emergent properties/generative mechanisms.

Causal mechanisms and powers

One of the most time consuming features of both the morphogenetic approach and critical realism to become fully conversant with, and one of the most difficult to apply, is the concept of mechanisms. The reasons for this all in one way or another relate to the less than clear cut nature of mechanisms. Leaving aside the fact that, as noted above, they are not observable, there are several closely related issues that arise concerning terminology and definitions. These regularly proved problematic during the writing up of this book. Consequently, it is important to explore the range of views on offer before discussing the specific difficulties that emerged from adopting Archer's approach.

First, the terms causal powers/causal mechanisms and causal mechanisms/generative mechanisms are often used interchangeably in the literature. In the case of the former (and as I discussed in Chapter 2) Sayer (2004) helpfully suggests that a mechanism indicates the *way* in which a causal power might work, rather than what the power actually is. In the context of Council X this is taken to mean, for example, the reports, meetings, workshops, etc (the ways) through which members of the PPG, both as actors and corporate agent, used their expertise (a causal power emergent from the social interaction of the group) to influence other actors and agents, such as the ISSSG. In the case of causal versus generative mechanisms as there appears to be no substantive difference between them this book has adopted the critical realist convention and tended to use the terms interchangeably, although usually representing this as: causal/generative.

Second, are emergent properties and causal/generative mechanisms one and the same or different? Thus, when reporting on one of the ESRC funded seminars on *Social Realism and Empirical Research* (a series of events which brought together many of the leading lights of critical realism), Caroline New notes that:

> There followed, yet again, a lengthy discussion into the status of mechanisms. Are they emergent properties of certain relationships or social practices? Soon we had left the contextual features of tertiary education providers behind and were discussing the causal powers of the seminar, considered as a generative mechanism.' (New 2001:45).

As the quotation above from New illustrates, it is clear that one viewpoint – the one shared by Archer – is: a/ that generative mechanisms are not simply 'social practices' (e.g. Archer 1995:174); and, b/ that a causal/generative mechanism *is* an emergent property. Thus, for example, Archer variously discusses '...the *generative mechanisms* potentially emanating from structures (and cultures) *as emergent properties* (Archer 1995:175 Emphasis added); and that: '...all generative mechanisms are only influential through people...what is involved is the confluence of *three sets of emergent properties...*' (ibid: 193 Original emphasis). Archer's 'structural influences' therefore become the generative powers (i.e. causal powers) of cultural and structural emergent properties.

A second school of thought clearly regards mechanisms and emergent properties as separate. Ackroyd, for example, states that groups: '...have properties that emerge from interaction and are *often involved in the causal mechanisms* affecting people.' He continues: 'These emergent properties *and* the causal mechanisms in which they are implicated...'(Ackroyd 2004:155, emphasis added). On this reading it is clear that emergent properties are *usually* a feature of causal/generative mechanisms but they are certainly not one and the same.

Sidestepping whether or not a distinction between an emergent property and a mechanism exists, C and P Kennedy take the view that: 'Mechanisms, meanwhile, unlike objects, are not things in themselves, but moments of the structure/object that generate the link between structural power and the events and perceptions held by agents located at the less ontologically significant levels.' (C and P Kennedy 2004:333). Interestingly, in taking this view it could be interpreted that the authors are favouring an argument and terminology very close to that of structuration theory, which, as was demonstrated in Chapter 1, would be anathema to critical realists such as Archer. This is reinforced by Moren and Blom (2003:48), who also question whether mechanisms are simply 'moments' and/or analytical constructs, concluding that if they are accepted as such then this view: '...is obviously not in accordance with critical realism.'

Ackroyd (2004) meanwhile, seems to concur. He states that: '...emergent properties and the causal mechanisms in which they are implicated are not directly available to observation but can be apprehended indirectly...' (Ackroyd 2004:155). Here he is drawing on the critical realist view of a stratified ontology, of the empirical – the level of experiences; the actual – the level of events; and the real – the level of structures and causal powers. Thus although mechanisms may or may not be experienced, depending on the phenomenon in question, they are, nonetheless, more than 'analytical constructs', as the quotation from Sayer (1998) at the beginning of this chapter makes clear. Ackroyd continues by explaining that: '...causal processes are constituted by chains of causal mechanisms interacting to produce the events we observe [thus] The specific mechanisms in which realist social researchers are interested typically involve the interaction between individuals and groups considered as agents and their interaction with other groups in the context of larger collectivities.' (ibid:153–154). Ackroyd concludes by noting that: '...in order to clarify the nature of a mechanism, it has to be examined in a context. [while recognising also that] The capacity to formulate and express reasons is a human power, and potentially, therefore, may feature as a link in a generative mechanism.' (ibid:157).

Finally, in his more recent work Fleetwood argues for moving away from using mechanism as 'a generalising term' for sets of causal factors to a specific: '...a mechanism as one [causal] component alongside several others.' (Fleetwood 2004:47). Thus a mechanism consist of 'structures and relations' and represents *a component* in a causal configuration. That is, an entity in '...clusters of causal factors and components'. (ibid:47). Interestingly, by also arguing that: 'Configurations, then, are emergent from, but irreducible to, the cluster of components that constitute them.' (ibid:48), Fleetwood's configurations exhibit strong similarities with Archer's generative mechanisms/emergent properties. Ultimately however, they diverge over the relationship/nature of a causal mechanism and emergent property, with, as noted above, Archer considering them one and the same while Fleetwood clearly does not;

266

and Archer's view that only entities that are internally and necessarily related give rise to emergent properties. In this respect Fleetwood's position seems to be on a par with the position taken by Elder-Vass (2005) on emergence, noted in Chapter 2.

Another equally important definitional issue is that there is disagreement over exactly what the *status* of a mechanism is. Again the quotation from New (2001:45), cited above, illustrates the issue: 'Are they emergent properties of certain social relationships or social practices.'. Archer's view is clearly that they are the former, with 'certain' referring to the proposition that emergent properties are *only* emergent from internal and necessary relations: 'Fundamentally, what distinguishes an "emergent property" is its real homogeneity, namely that the relations between its components are internal and necessary ones rather than seemingly regular concatenations of heterogeneous features...' (Archer 1995:173). Of course, this contrasts fairly starkly with the view that they are 'social practices' (i.e. a seminar, meeting, etc), or indeed, that they are simply 'appropriate ideas and opportunities'. Both would be anathema to Archer, who clearly states that while emergent properties and powers come into being through 'social combination' not all relationships give rise to them.

As the concept of a causal/generative mechanism is so central to realist analysis clearly the definition of what a mechanism *is* and *how it comes into being* that is adopted by a researcher will have a profound effect on the outcome of their research. Chapter 2 made clear that the intention for this book was to hold to Archer's definition of a generative/causal mechanism, accepting therefore that: i/ generative/causal mechanisms and emergent properties are one and the same; and, ii/ that they are only emergent from internal and necessary social relations. As the material presented in Chapters 4, 5 and 6 confirmed, this required working with three types of emergent property – structural, cultural and peoples' (SEPs, CEPs and PEPs in Archer's shorthand) – and therefore three types of generative/causal mechanism as well as three types of causal powers. Furthermore, it also required working with Archer's definitions of the characteristics of each. For example, that SEPs '...are specifically defined as those internal and necessary relationships which entail material resources, whether physical or human, and which generate causal powers proper to the relations itself.' (Archer 1995:177). SEPs are, therefore, '...distributions [of resources], roles, institutional structures, social systems...' (Archer 1995:176). Applying Sayer's distinction between a mechanism and a power to Archer's combined emergent property/mechanism formulation seems to produce the same result, with SEPs, CEPs and PEPs relating to the *way* in which causal/generative powers (Archer's 'structural influences') work, while structural influence(s) describe *what* the power actually is.

Internal and necessary versus contingent relationships

While the detailed descriptions of the defining characteristics of SEPs, CEPs and PEPs, and the detailed discussion and examples of emergence that Archer provides in *Realist Social Theory: The Morphogenetic Approach* (1995), proved invaluable to understanding and interpreting the concept theoretically, when applied to an empirical case study the matter was not so straightforward. Two related activities proved particularly problematic on a regular basis during data analysis and writing up this book. The first was identifying whether internal and necessary relations did exist and, if they did, whether they were reciprocal or asymmetrical (i.e. two way or one way). If internal and necessary relations could be identified then a generative mechanism (with causal powers) had been identified. If there were no internal and necessary relations then the entity was simply a '...contingent combinations of disparate elements from different strata which happen to co-manifest themselves at a given time.' (Archer 1995:173).

This is not to deny that contingently related entities can exert influence: 'To state that the relationship between two entities is contingent is not to assert that the one exerts no influence upon the other (reciprocally or asymmetrically): it is merely to maintain that the two can exist on their own for they are existentially independent.' (Archer 1995:174). In terms of exploring causal processes the significance of the distinction

268

has to be, therefore, that contingent relations between entities *may* be causally efficacious, but internal and necessary relations (where exercised) *will* be. However, this raises a fundamental question, and one that Archer poses herself: are people, whether as actors and/or agents, consciously aware of the existence of internal/necessary and contingent relations *given these are not observable*, and therefore of the significance of this distinction? If they are then they should be able to recognise that influence based on contingent relationships between entities can ultimately be ignored, whereas the causal powers – where exercised – of the emergent properties of internal and necessary relationships cannot.

On the evidence presented in this book the argument has been that in the case of IS development in Council X one corporate agent – the PPG – and the actors involved in it, pursued a strategic course of action, and modes of interaction, that were consciously directed at influencing the behaviour of other actors and agents within and related to the IS domain. Cultural, structural and agential properties all emerged from the actions and interactions of that group and the causal powers of these were instrumental in the cultural and structural morphogenesis related to IS development. Clearly members of the PPG, collectively and individually, and at least some of their supporters (the head of the CSU would be one obvious example), were aware that in pursuing their agenda for IS development their relationships with some agents/actors were more significant than with others. The ISSSG and its members were clearly identified as such an example.

However, and to complicate matters further, another conclusion was that these relationships and transactions were not static. Archer fully recognises this, hence one of the tasks when applying the morphogenetic approach to interaction (T2–T3) is to track these changes. As I established in Chapter 5, the outcome of this exercise demonstrates how the relationship between the ISSSG and the PPG changed over time. Initially (i.e. from January 1995) this was not internal and necessary. However, evidence was presented in Chapter 5 of the actions the PPG took to develop an internal and necessary relationship with the ISSSG: for example, the *human* resource supplied by the PPG (and its allied interest groups) to the ISSSG working groups. This does not represent a direct internal and necessary relationship with the ISSSG, of course (see the discussion below), but there is little doubt that without this resource the working groups could not have functioned (although they would still have existed) and the authority and standing of the ISSSG would have therefore been undermined, particularly relative to COMG and departmental corporate agents.

Interestingly, the PPG's increasing need for *physical* resources to enable it to develop new IS for community governance, which it became clear the ISSSG might be able to provide after COMG handed it a revised remit in April 1996, meant an increasingly *reciprocal* example of internal and necessary relations began to develop. It is possible to conclude, therefore, that members of the PPG, collectively and individually, and at least some of their supporters, were conscious that certain types of relationship were more causally significant than others, although whether they would have used the terminology of critical realism is doubtful.

In the context of Council X there is no doubt that establishing a distinction between internal and necessary and contingent relationships between the collectivities and other entities of the position-practice system of Council X added analytical purchase, exposing the comprehensive *range* of causal relationships behind IS development, the *basis* of these, and their dynamic nature (i.e. how they *changed over time*). For example, both the ISSSG and the PPG were internally and necessarily related to COMG (as the latter was to the Council's strategy and resources committee). As SEPs (i.e. institutional structures) they were emergent from COMG and reliant on COMG for the material (physical) resources which would generate the causal powers proper to the relation itself. The stratified nature of causal relationship was also exposed. Thus, relationships occurred at the level of structures and causal powers (the real); at the level of events (the actual); and at the level of experiences (the empirical). However, and this is where things become complex and thus analytically

270

messy (which is unsurprising given the openness of all social systems): all of the entities noted above, including COMG, were reliant on other entities – departments specifically – for other (mainly human) resources that were essential to their operation and from which they also drew causal powers. In other words, there seems to be a range of internal and necessary relations between entities, some weaker, some stronger, and some more clear-cut than others. In practice separating the latter from what might best be described as strong contingent relations on the basis of the data available was no easy exercise.

Unintended outcomes and aggregate effects

One of the underlying principles of Archer's work is that 'Society is that which nobody wants, in the form in which they encounter it, for it is an unintended consequence.' (Archer 1995:165). In similar vein Archer also states that social change 'does not approximate to what anyone wants' being the result of the aggregate effects of the actions of primary and corporate agents (ibid:265). However, having reached what would appear to some to be rather disturbing conclusions verging on chaos theory Archer is quick to point out that to argue that society '...is an unintended consequence is not the same as to assert that all things social are a matter of contingency.' (ibid:166). This is the most fundamental reason why maintaining a distinction between internal and necessary and contingent relations is crucial to the morphogenetic approach, for it allows '...the essential transcendental commitment to society not being wholly contingent...' ibid:167) that sits at the core of critical realism. Specifically, this is done by arguing that SEPs are a *sub-class* of unintended consequences and can therefore be differentiated from 'the totality of unintended consequences' because not all unintended consequences are '...irreducible, enduring, involved in internal and necessary relations with others and *because* of this possessing determinate causal powers. (ibid:177. Original emphasis).

It is worth emphasising again here, as with contingent entities, above, that Archer fully accepts that contingent unintended consequences *can have important causal effects*. Nevertheless she argues that '...they can always be disaggregated into the sum of individual actions, that is they are reducible.' (ibid 177). As discussed above with regard to emergent properties, while in theory this kind of exercise is no doubt do-able, in an applied situation and when based on empirical data that may well be less than perfect, it is not such an easy task, as discussed below. The suspicion has to be, therefore, that faced with the resource constraints that confront many scholars the question that inevitably arises is whether the outcome, in terms of value added to the results of research, justifies the means! This would almost certainly be the case to anyone unconvinced by the core arguments of, and for, critical realism. It is unsurprising therefore that there is bound to be a certain attraction in not distinguishing between aggregate unintended consequences. In fact, this is a point Archer seems to accept when she states that there is '...a general difficulty in practical social analysis, namely the frequent tendency of those working exclusively at the level of events, to *treat* emergent properties as mere aggregate consequences.' (ibid: 178. Original emphasis).

As previously noted, for this book the extensive period of field research and the wealth of data collected from different sources, the lengthy period over which data analysis and re-analysis took place, and the growth in extant literature on critical realism over the period of writing up , have all contributed to a situation where it has been possible here to try to work fully to the detail of the morphogenetic approach. Consequently, and not withstanding the remarks above on definitions, wherever possible SEPs have been separated from the aggregate of unintended consequences, as have CEPs and PEPs.

A number of further issues concerning unintended consequences also deserve mention before concluding this section. The most fundamental picks up on the quotations from Archer at the head of this section, and returns us to the stratified nature of society and the level at which social analysis takes place. It can most easily be posed as a question: Does the claim that *society* is an unintended consequence of past actions and that *social change* does not approximate to what anyone wants hold at the level of a position-practice system (of an organisation)? In other words, and to be specific, were all situations that people encountered, whether as actors or corporate/primary agents within Council X, the unintended consequences of past actions? And did the results of the actions of corporate and primary agents that were observed and/or recorded *never* approximate to what *anyone* wants?

On the evidence of the material presented in this book the answer would have to be no. For example, the material presented in Chapter 4 strongly indicates that the fragmentation of IS and the systemic contradictions from which this resulted, were, in large part, the *unintended* consequences (of the causal powers of the generative mechanisms) emergent from the policies of decentralisation, devolution and privatisation. In other words, there is no evidence from any of the agents/actors involved in the formulation and implementation of these policies that they intended they should fragment the organisation – structurally, culturally and socially – to the extent that occurred. Contrast this, however, with the example of the electronic phone book, also discussed in Chapter 4. Clearly the team who developed the e-phonebook (and the corporate agent that backed the development) intended that it should be implemented Council wide. The fact that its implementation was blocked by a range of corporate agents was clearly an unintended consequence as far as the development team (and their sponsoring corporate agent) were concerned. However, blocking the implementation of the e-phonebook, as opposed to suggesting some alternative course of action, was certainly an *intended* consequence of the actions of the other corporate agents. In short, the outcome was not an approximation, it was exactly what these corporate agents (and we can therefore assume, a good number of the relevant actors) wanted.

Similar examples of unintended and intended consequences can be regularly identified throughout chapters 4, 5 and 6 (e.g. and also discussed in Chapter 4 – the election of a Green Party councillor was an intended consequence of the actions of

273

the Green Party but the impact this subsequently had on certain structures, (IS) system and actors/agents of Council X was certainly unintended as far as many staff were concerned). Two conclusions can be drawn from this. First, at the level of experiences and events (the empirical and the actual) the position-practice system of Council X consists of *both* intended and unintended consequences/outcomes. This runs counter to Archer's arguments. There is agreement here that some of these consequences will be contingent and some internal and necessary (i.e. emergent) and that all *may* be causally significant in certain contexts at certain times.

As society is an open system and Council X is a part of that social system then what occurs there cannot be an isolated case. Consequently it is difficult to conclude that at the level of higher strata there are no examples of intended outcomes, although it is accepted that the aggregating effect of ever larger populations of primary and corporate agents at the strata of institutional and social systems makes this less and less likely. Second, unintended consequences may be negative or positive in terms of causal processes. That is, they may unintentionally serve the interests of some agents while acting against the interests of others, as occurred on a number of occasions with the PPG and the ISSSG reported in Chapter 5. Taken together with the argument for unintended consequences this is, of course, what makes emergence such a powerful and dynamic concept.

Defining emergent properties: SEPs, CEPs and PEPs

This highlights the second activity that proved problematic – identifying from the data available *all* of the features of SEPs, CEPs and PEPs that Archer stipulates – and thus the *mechanisms* that were likely to be causally efficacious to the case study. Archer's definition of a SEP was noted above. Following this rubric this book classed COMG, the ISSSG, the PPG as institutional structures and roles and hence SEPs. However, Archer also states that as well as '…entailing material resources, whether physical or human…' SEPs are '…irreducible to people and relatively enduring…' (ibid:177). With respect to the first three of the groups noted above my judgement

274

would be that they clearly fulfil this criterion: they were all *formally* recognised structures within an institutional system, with *published terms of reference* and *a specified membership* that was constituted as independent of any particular individual person. Here this is taken to signify that they were not reducible to people and are also relatively enduring. Indeed, it is clear from Chapters 4 and 5 that both COMG and the ISSSG had existed as structures (i.e. as the outcome of morphogenetic cycles somewhere in the past) irrespective of their membership at that time for a considerable period prior to this case study.

Defining SEPs became less clear cut, however, when considering the ISSSG working groups, and the groups identified as 'supplementary interest groups' in Chapter 5. This is unsurprising perhaps, when one considers that it was and is a convention in English local government, and Council X was no exception, that all but the most ad hoc/one off groups have published terms of reference, formally constituted memberships and, crucially, usually enjoy internal and necessary relations with at least one 'sponsor' department. In short, social relations are almost always formalised in a governmental context. The result is often that these become structures that are irreducible to people and relatively enduring, hence the oft criticised tendency of bureaucracies to self propagate. Hence in a government/public administration context this element of Archer's definition of a SEP may well be distorted when compared to similar types of social relations in other organisational settings.

In the specific case of the ISSSG's working groups they enjoyed asymmetrical internal and necessary relationship with the ISSSG, being dependant on it for material resource (as well as being dependant on other entities for specifically human resources). They also had published terms of reference with a formally constituted membership. However, how 'irreducible to people and relatively enduring' the working groups were was difficult to define at that time as they had only just come into being when fieldwork for this book was being carried out. On balance however, the conclusion drawn here was that the working groups *were* SEPs. The remaining groups which, as can be seen from the analysis in Chapter 5, all exhibit some but not all of the features of SEPs that have been classified here simply as interest groups active in the IS domain. It is crucial to note, however, as discussed above, that although *only* classified as 'contingently influential' the material presented in Chapters 5 and 6 makes clear that these groups did exhibit strong causal influences that were in many cases significant to the morphogenesis of the structures, cultures and agents of IS.

Although what has been highlighted here are primarily issues that arose when identifying the defining characteristic of SEPs similar problems did apply to CEPs. Archer's theory of a CEP, as Chapter 2 explained, is that they are properties of the cultural system: 'relations between the components of culture' (i.e. ideas/theories/values/beliefs) and independent of the socio-cultural: 'relations between cultural agents'. Furthermore, she also argues that: '…in asserting the existence of a CEP, we never need and never should descend from the logical to the causal.' (Archer 1995:182–183). However, based on the author's knowledge of the other case studies to which the morphogenetic approach has been applied (see below and Chapter 1) the contention is that maintaining this example of analytical dualism is much more difficult when analysing contemporary or near contemporary data from the position-practice system of an organisation than it is with historical and/or when investigating higher strata such as institutional and social systems. Thus, for example, establishing the CEPs relevant to the intergovernmental systems of English central and local government between 1945 and the 1980s, or the neo liberal economic theories and beliefs that increasingly dominated the social systems of the developed world through the 1980s, both detailed in Chapter 4, was far more straightforward than defining contemporary (at that time) CEPs within either English local government in general or the position-practice system of Council X specifically.

That said, I have argued that the data presented in this book suggests that a range of ideas, theories and beliefs about IS that were contemporary to that time did enter the cultural system of Council X as CEPs during the period covered by this research. For example, that the properties of new ICTs rendered geographical location relatively meaningless (which became a feature of the LGR), and that ICTs were fundamental to organisational 'reengineering' (which was a separate idea/belief). These ideas/theories/beliefs escaped their makers, as Archer puts it, and became staples of the cultural systems of government and public administration across the developed world generally, and, in variant, context specific forms, in English local government specifically. The extent to which the generative/causal powers of these CEPs impacted on the cultural system of Council X was reflected most noticeably in the discourse of actors and agents, as numerous quotations in this book illustrate.

There is a wealth of literature on the importance of culture to organisations and organisational change, some of which was referenced in the earlier chapters of this book (e.g. Margulies and Raia 1978, Morgan 1997, Bartol and Martin 1998). Indeed, the reports into the reform of government by Lyons (2004) and Gershon (2004) noted above and discussed in Chapter 1 also give prominence to organisational culture in their analysis and recommendations. Consequently it is unsurprising that a methodology such as Archer's, that explicitly incorporates the cultural realm of social systems and society in its analysis, should produce findings which further emphasise the fundamental role culture plays in social, and thus structural, change.

There are, however, two features of the morphogenetic approach which require highlighting as adding analytical depth to cultural analysis. Both were discussed in Chapter 2. The first is to clearly establish that the cultural, the structural and the agential are all *equally* implicated – although in different ways and, more than likely, at different times – in cycles of change/reproduction. The second is to provide the means, and the reasons for, not conflating the cultural system and cultural agents. While it is acknowledged above that maintaining this example of analytical dualism was difficult in the context of this case study it did, nevertheless, allow clear distinctions to be drawn on numerous occasions across Chapters 4 to 6 between the causal relations of cultural agents (i.e. actors and agents) and the logical relations between the items of the cultural system (i.e. ideas, theories, beliefs and values). Examples of the outcome of this approach have already been noted above.

The final category of emergent property is a PEP. Interestingly this was the least problematic to deal with. Identifying the defining features: '...they modify the capacities of component members (affecting their consciousness and commitments, affinities and animosities) and exert causal powers proper to their relations vis a vis other agents or groupings...' (Archer 1995:184) across a range of situations relevant to IS within Council X was relatively straightforward. Examples of interaction leading to the emergence of PEPs were provided throughout Chapters, 4, 5 and 6, such as the LGR defence group, ISSSG Away Day, the working groups, and the Intranet workshop. All of these modified the capacities of participating actors and led them to exert causal powers on other agents/actors. So too did interaction within and between a wide range of agents, such as the PPG and ISSSG, as the detailed analysis and discussion presented in Chapter 5 demonstrates.

Working across morphogenetic cycles and stages

The final aspect of the morphogenetic approach that requires comment, as noted at the outset of Chapter 6, concerns difficulties with analysing and ordering material on the causal processes associated with three simultaneous morphogenetic cycles across the T1 to T4 periodisation. In other words, presenting the analytical narrative that Archer's approach produces in a consistent and understandable manner when analysing the interaction between structure, culture and agency from an extensive and dynamic case study such as Council X.

As Chapter 2 established, the three stages of the morphogenetic/static cycle cover structure, culture and agency '...each of which has relative autonomy and yet interacts with the others.' (ibid: 193). This certainly comes across as a relatively straightforward dynamic to work with from the (relevant) examples of the application

278

of the morphogenetic approach that noted in Chapter 1, such as Archer's (1995) and Skinningsrud's (2005) study of the elaboration of state education systems; Moren and Blom's (2003) evaluation of social work practice; Thursfield's and Hamblett's (2004) study of human resource management at a major chemical processing plant; and Kowalczyk's (2004) study of hospital mergers. In common with this book these authors document the use of the morphogenetic approach to analyse their research data. In each case the application of Archer's methods appear unproblematic in terms of both the temporal dimensions and definable outcomes of the research. However, as has been noted at various points in the previous three chapters, and earlier in this chapter, applying the morphogenetic approach to all three strata of Council X has *not* been unproblematic. Specifically, the stages of the morphogenetic cycles were often *not* easily definable, making construction of a narrative which adequately and consistently explored and explained the causal processes, mechanisms and powers at work difficult and extremely time consuming.

The reasons for what appear to be a divergence between my experience and that of others becomes clear when a comparison is made of how we have used the approach. The first concerns one of its key foci, namely temporality. In other words, the time period over which the stages of morphogenetic cycles occur. As noted above, Archer argues that the cycles should be delineated 'according to the scope of the problem in hand.' Archer then introduces the T1–T4 periodisation to represent the stages of emergence-interplay-outcome that constitute the morphogenetic cycle(s) of the 'problem', and it is here – the use of the T1–T4 periodisation – that my application differs from others. First, some use it and some do not, and where it is used it is often used loosely. Second, with the exception of Archer and Skinningsrud the time period over which the reported cycles of transformation or reproduction occur do not feature prominently, if at all. Thus, Moren and Blom make no mention of the time period covered by their cycles. Thursfield and Hamblett give a brief mention to the period covered by their research but are not very specific (it is approximately a decade). While Kowalczyk makes no mention of the period of her case study, although it is possible to deduce from the data she cites that it is approximately three years. Third, and as the discussion above illustrates, none of the examples currently available of the application of the morphogenetic approach are bounded by a fixed period of empirical research. Consequently the start and end point (i.e. T1 to T4) can be moved to allow the inclusion of data that can then be used to construct a more comprehensive and consistent narrative of cycles of morphogenesis or morphostasis than is possible with a bounded study such as Council X.

I suggest that two conclusions can be drawn from these areas of divergence. First, in almost all cases applying the morphogenetic approach to case studies over longer periods of time and/or to historical data, allows many more "problems", to be identified. This creates a similar situation to the one noted above, in that a bigger sample of "problems" may well provide more scope to identify cases where the stages and multiple strata of morphogenetic cycles, and the relationship between them, can be more clearly defined, thus emphasising this dimension of the morphogenetic approach. Secondly, by not attaching specific dates/times to the T1–T4 labels, the actual and empirically messy nature of identifying and demarcating between the stages of emergence-interplay-outcome of three simultaneous morphogenetic cycles can be downplayed or ignored. Furthermore, the temporal features of the "problem" under investigation can also be blurred by not seeking to establish whether there was an identifiable start and end point (to the problem) and if and to what these were causally related.

There is little doubt that it is the features of the application of Archer's methodology set out above that are central to explaining my experience of dealing with the stages and cycles of morphogenesis. However, the most noticeable contrasts, and therefore the ones judged most significant, concern the level/strata or context (i.e. social structures, institutional systems, position-practice system) and scope (i.e. one, two or all three of the morphogenetic cycles) of the research to which the morphogenetic methodology is applied. Choice of strata and of scope has important implications for the degree to which a researcher needs to engage with the complexity of the *interaction* within and between strata and cycles. Interestingly, Skinningsrud's application of the morphogenetic approach to the Norwegian state education system and her comparison of this with Archer's studies of education systems illustrate these tensions and complexities well, and thus supports the argument set out hear.

Conclusion: the morphogenesis of the morphogenetic approach?

The two related definitional issues discussed in the section on causal mechanisms and powers, above, raised a number of questions, the most significant of which is returned to here. Is it not the case that by conflating emergent properties and causal/generative mechanisms, as Archer does and has been adopted here, that we underplay the real *causal powers* of entities that are not emergent properties, replacing these instead with the less significant label of causal *influences*, because only causal/generative mechanisms can have causal/generative powers and only emergent properties can be mechanisms? An alternative approach, presumably along the lines that would be advocated by those who do not consider an emergent property and a generative mechanism to be one and the same, would be that a causal/generative mechanism can consist of emergent properties *and* other, non emergent, entities. What Fleetwood (2004:47) refers to as '...an ensemble of structures and relations...'. It is then for the researcher to identify these and evaluate the relative causal powers of each in a particular context.

From a morphogenetic perspective, however, this suggestion would almost certainly be regarded as conflationary: conflating contingent entities with emergent entities, thus undermining the exploratory power of analytical dualism. Nevertheless, Fleetwood's recent work does appear to offer a way out of this conflationary quandary. As discussed in Chapter 2, having reappraised his use of the term mechanism, and as a result moved away from using this as 'a generalising term' for sets of causal factors, Fleetwood adopts a specific definition, that a mechanism is '...one [causal] component alongside several others.' (ibid:47). In addition,

Fleetwood regards the *status* of a mechanism in a looser way than Archer, seeing them simply as 'structures and relations'. Building on from this he then proposes the concept of *causal configurations*: 'clusters of causal factors or components' which in an organisational context would typically be: '...social structures, positioned practices, relations, rules, resources and so on.' (ibid:47–48). At this point emergence is brought back into the equation: 'Causal configurations are emergent phenomena. That is, when certain components are assembled, they give rise to properties that are not found in any of the components...Configurations, then, are emergent from, but irreducible to, the cluster of components that constitute them.' (ibid:48). In the context of Council X both the ICT Away Day and the Intranet Workshop are examples of causal configurations.

As a brief comparison with the discussion of definitions of emergent properties, above, and in Chapter 2, makes clear this is very similar to Archer's definition of a SEP (distributions of resources, roles, institutional structures, social systems). However, there are some significant differences. First, and as was made clear above, Archer maintains that a generative mechanism and an emergent property – in this case a SEP – are one and the same, whereas it is clear that under Fleetwood's rubric mechanisms (structures and relations), as causal components, *may* combine with other causal factors and components to form causal configurations. They are therefore, not one and the same. Second, Fleetwood makes no mention of internal and necessary versus contingent relations between the factors and components of a causal configuration, although he does clearly state that: '*it is the configuration as a totality, and not any of its individual components, that generates the tendency.*' (ibid: 48. Original emphasis). (it is worth adding that Fleetwood's 'tendency' is equivalent to Sayer's definition of a causal power, also discussed above and in Chapter 2).

Overall, therefore, it would seem that Fleetwood's approach allows the acceptance of *both* internal and necessary and contingent causal factors and components, which when combined produce emergence, although this is irreducible to the constituents (as noted in Chapter 2, this is a position that appears to be supported by Elder-Vass 2005). In so doing he appears to address exactly the questions concerning relations between entities, relations between causal powers and influences, and the conflation of mechanisms and emergent properties, raised above. Furthermore, his definitions of what a mechanism is and does creates the analytical space to place relations and structures, such as the groups that did not qualify as SEPs, as discussed above and in Chapter 5, and the two IS events noted above, on the same plane of causal significance (in a specific context) as fully fledged SEPs. This goes a long way to rectifying the tendency within the morphogenetic approach (because of its focus on the primacy of emergent properties/internal and necessary relations) to regard these as causally significant at the expense of the causal significance of entities that only enjoy contingent relations (despite acknowledging these can be important, as noted earlier in this chapter). Finally, it is worth noting that whether Fleetwood's approach also means that technologies/ICTs/IS can be treated as mechanisms in their own right, rather than as a property of a structure, remains unclear and therefore becomes a subject for further research. Ultimately, it would seem that Fleetwood's standpoint is both more "realist" and produces a more workable model than Archer's when applied to empirical research of the type presented in this book.

In conclusion, given the issues concerning mechanisms and relationships raised earlier in this chapter, and the questions posed above, it is unsurprising that my experience of the application of an exploratory methodology based on critical realism would lead me to concur fully with Ackroyd's comment that: '…specifying the context appropriately, and establishing the character of causal mechanisms *are key problems of realist research.*' (Ackroyd 2004:152, emphasis added). One of the major reasons for this, as already noted, is that neither contingency/emergence nor properties/mechanisms are directly observable. Of course, this is entirely consistent with the critical realist view of a stratified ontology: the empirical – the level of experiences; the actual – the level of events; and *the real – the level of structures and causal powers.*

The latter are not abstract constructs, they exist, hence Sayer's remark that: 'By "concrete" we mean something real, but not something that is reducible to the empirical: we mean more than factual.' (Sayer 1998:123). However, while critical realists would argue, as here, that by accepting this ontological standpoint a far fuller and deeper – "realist" – account of social phenomena can be constructed than by, for example, employing a positivist or post modernist approach, there is a downside. Hence, the evidence of this book strongly suggests that when Ackroyd concludes that: 'They [causal mechanisms] are usually only painstakingly reconstructed by iterative empirical research guided by theory.' in terms of working with the morphogenetic approach specifically he is really telling only half of the story. To this has to be added the equally painstaking work of constructing causal processes from 'chains of causal mechanisms', as Ackroyd refers to them, and the difficulties of identifying and untangling emergent from contingent unintended consequences. Furthermore, also to be added is the most significant issue to arise from the comparison of the applications of the morphogenetic approach discussed above: the level/strata/context and scope of the research to which the morphogenetic methodology is applied. Reintroducing, as it does, a discussion of the claims to originality of this book a brief discussion of this issue signals an obvious point at which to conclude this chapter.

In Chapter 1 the originality of this book was given as stemming from the combination of: i) the *application* of the morphogenetic approach to, ii) *all three* morphogenetic cycles (of IS development) within, iii) a predominantly *micro-level* case study of a public sector organisation. It was also important to recognise, as Carter and New (2004) made clear, that the use of Archer's approach has so far been limited and thus its potential has yet to be realised. The argument here is that this book goes some way to demonstrating that potential. There is no doubt, for example, that employing such an approach has allowed the '...location of the micro-level ethnographic descriptions of members' activities within the context of the complex interplay of macro-level structures which constrain members' activities...' noted in Chapter 1 Johnson and Dubberley (2000:165–166) state is central to the analysis of the relationship between structure and agency in an organisational context. On the other hand, however, the scope and complexity of the research necessary to capture the processes and generative mechanisms that were 'causally efficacious' (Kowalczyk 2004) at the micro-level strata *also* seems to be the source of the difficulties and issues that have emerged during the application of Archer's methodology.

There are, of course, measures which could have been adopted to try to counter these features of the research. Narrowing the scope and reducing the unit(s) of analysis are obvious ones. However, limiting the scope rather flies in the face of retroduction, because any causal processes subsequently identified would be artificially bounded. Consequently the analytical narrative produced would be incomplete and any conclusions drawn partial. Ultimately, therefore, it would seem that the underlying issue here is that as the granularity of the analysis of causal processes, mechanisms and powers increases so the complexity of the social systems that the morphogenetic approach is designed to explore becomes more and more apparent, making the construction of an ordered account of agency, structure and culture and their interactions and outcomes more and more difficult. In short, it is much less problematic to apply and maintain the morphogenetic methodology/analytical dualism at the level of social structures and institutional relationships, for example, than it is to an ethnographic study of the "real world" position-practice system of an organisation.

Nevertheless, and despite the issues reported in this chapter, it remains the case that the complexity of social structure, no longer 'remains hopelessly indefinite' once the morphogenetic approach has been employed to unravel the interplay between the two. Consequently, and as the material presented in the previous three chapters graphically demonstrates, what emerges from its use in the specific context of IS development in Council X is a detailed and nuanced analytical narrative of the history of 'where, when, who and how', as Archer aptly puts it, of the dualism and complexity of the information polity of one particular English local authority.

This is only one aspect of the outcome, however. This book also provides powerful support to a number of the propositions and theories of the relationship between technology and organisational change examined in Chapter 1. The relevance to Snellen's and Donk's (1998) non deterministic argument – that ICTs do not cause developments in public administration but act as attractors or stimulants for other aspirations – and De Sanctis and Poole's (1994) arguments concerning the powerful role that the 'spirit' of technology can play in organisational affairs were discussed at the end of the previous chapter. Directly related to the above is that the significance of technology, in this case ICTs specifically, as one of a range of *structural properties*, as both Archer (implicitly) and Orlikowski (explicitly), or artefactually real, as Fleetwood puts it, which can have a profound impact on the actions of agents has also been clearly illustrated.

This is important in that it demonstrates that there is no need to subscribe to the technologically determinist view of technology as a structure in it own right, with the subsequent tendency to significantly downplay agency, in order to argue for the importance of IS/ICT research to mainstream organisation and management studies. Furthermore, the major claim for conceptualising 'information age' public administration as an information polity in the early to mid 1990s was the argument that by the late 20th century, in the developed and the developing world alike, information flows, organisational relationships *and* ICT networks would *all* constitute relationships within government and the public sector (and apply to organisations in general, of course). As I made clear in Chapter 1, there is little doubt that this claim has been surpassed, as the discussion of recent and ongoing government initiatives in the UK aimed at organisational change – such as the *Transformational Government – Enabled by Technology* strategy – in which IS/ICT are deeply implicated, clearly illustrates. Consequently, the findings of this book are both timely and highly relevant, and, as such ought to make a significant contribution to both public administration and to IS research generally, and to the growing, but still small, body of work that seeks to apply critical realist philosophy, and the morphogenetic approach specifically, to organisation and management studies.

Source of quotations

[i] Interview: 27/7/96, Principal Policy Officer, Personnel, Policy and Review Unit, CE's. Coordinator PPG.

[ii] Interview: 19/6/96, Head of Committee Services.

[iii] Interview: 6/3/96, Chief Executive, Council X.

[iv] Interview: 15/8/95, Assistant Chief, Executive Council X.

[v] Interview: 27/7/96, Principal Policy Officer, Personnel, Policy and Review Unit, CE's.

[vi] Interview: 5/6/96, Contract Monitoring Officer.

[vii] Interview: 31/7/96, Head of Corporate Services Unit (CSU).

[viii] Interview: 31/7/96, Assistant Chief Education Officer, Chairperson ISSSG.

[ix] Interview: 5/6/96, Contract Monitoring Officer.

[x] Interview: 1/7/96, Assistant Director, Libraries, Member of ISSSG.

[xi] Interview: 6/3/96, Chief Executive, Council X.

[xii] Interview: 5/6/96, Contract Monitoring Officer, Member of ISSSG.

[xiii] Op Cit.

[xiv] Op Cit.

[xv] Interview: Interview: 1/7/96, Assistant Director, Libraries, Member of ISSSG.

[xvi] Interview: 19/9/96, Unit Manager, Financial Planning Unit, CE's.

[xvii] Interview: 5/6/96, Head of Chief Education Officer's Office.

[xviii] Interview: 31/7/96, Assistant Chief Education Officer, Chairperson ISSSG.

[xix] Interview: 3/5/96, EPIS Development Analyst.

[xx] Interview: 12/6/96, PCC Support Analyst, Engineers Department.

[xxi] Interview: 3/5/96, EPIS Development Analyst.

[xxii] Op Cit.

[xxiii] Interview: 27/7/96, Principal Policy Officer, Personnel, Policy and Review Unit, CE's. Coordinator PPG.

[xxiv] PPG Action Plan 1995, emphasis added.

^{xxv} Interview: 1/7/96, Assistant Director, Libraries, Member of ISSSG.

^{xxvi} Report of the Chairman of ISSSG to COMG, 26 April 1995.

^{xxvii} Report to COMG from ISSSG, 26/4/95. Emphasis added.

^{xxviii} Report to COMG by the chairman of ISSSG, 15th April 1996)

^{xxix} Interview: 5/6/96, Contract Monitoring Officer.

^{xxx} Interview: 31/7/96, Assistant Chief Education Officer, Chairperson ISSSG.

^{xxxi} Interview: 5/6/96, Contract Monitoring Officer.

^{xxxii} Op cit.

^{xxxiii} Op cit.

^{xxxiv} Report to COMG from the Chairman of ISSSG, 22nd May 1995)

^{xxxv} COMG papers, 22nd May 1995.

^{xxxvi} COMG papers 22nd May 1995.

^{xxxvii} Interview: 31/7/96, Assistant Chief Education Officer, Chairperson ISSSG.

^{xxxviii} Report to COMG by the Chairman of ISSSG, 15th April 1996.

^{xxxix} Consultants report from the ISSSG away day, November 1995.

^{xl} Interview: 1/7/96, Assistant Director, Libraries, Member of ISSSG.

^{xli} Interview: 31/7/96, Assistant Chief Education Officer, Chairperson ISSSG.

^{xlii} Report to COMG from the chairman of the ISSSG, 18th December 1995.

^{xliii} Report from the CWG to ISSSG, 20th March 1996.

^{xliv} Interview: 1/7/96, Assistant Director, Libraries, Member of ISSSG.

^{xlv} Report from the CWG to ISSSG, 20th March 1996.

^{xlvi} Report on the progress of the IMG, 8th January 1996.

^{xlvii} Agenda and accompanying briefing papers for the IOMG, 4th October 1996.

^{xlviii} PPG Meeting Papers, 15th April 1996.

^{xlix} PPG Meeting Papers, 15th April 1996. Emphasis in original

^l Report to COMG by the chairman of ISSSG, 15th April 1996

^{li} Annex 1 and 2, COMG papers, 15th April 1996

^{lii} PPG Development Plan, 1996, page 1

^{liii} PPG Development Plan, 1996, page 4

[liv] PPG Development Plan, 1996, page 12

[lv] PPG Development Plan, 1996, page 15

[lvi] Intranet Workshop papers, 9th October 1996. Appendix A

[lvii] Joint presentation to COMG by the PPG and the ISSSG, 11th November 1996, page 6

[lviii] Joint presentation to COMG by the PPG and the ISSSG, 11th November 1996, page 7

[lix] Joint presentation to COMG by the PPG and the ISSSG, 11th November 1996, pages 9–10

[lx] Interview: 31/7/96, Head of Corporate Services Unit (CSU)

[lxi] Interview: 3/5/96, EPIS Development Analyst

[lxii] Terms of reference for the IS&T Strategy Review, COMG papers, 22nd May 1995

[lxiii] The OMMP Final Report, December 1996. Page 2

[lxiv] All data presented in this section is taken from the PSTAG OSS Evaluation, Final report to Council X, November 1996

[lxv] Interview: 31/7/96, Head of Corporate Services Unit (CSU)

Glossary of Abbreviations

General

IS	Information Systems
ICT	Information and Communication Technology
IT	Information Technology
EC	European Commission
EU	European Union
PSTAG	Programme for the Study of Telematics and Governance
EGPA	European Group for Public Administration
COST A14/ GaDIA	Cooperation in Science and Technology A14 project: *Governance and Democracy in the Information Age*

Council X

ISSSG	Information Systems and Strategy Sub Group
PPG	Partnerships Project Group
CSU	Corporate Services Unit
COMG	Chief Officers' Management Group
CWG	Communications Working Group
OSS	One Stop Shop
FSS	First Stop Shop
LGR	Local Government Review
CCT	Compulsory Competitive Tendering
SSA	Standard Spending Assessment
EPIS	Electronic Public Information System
CIS	Community Information System
CE	Chief Executive
ITC	Information Technology Contractor
SLA	Service Level Agreement

IMP	Information Management Programme
IMG	Information Management Group
S&RC	Strategy and Resources Committee
SNWG	Security and Networks Working Group
IOMG	Informal Officers' and Members' Group
OMPP	Officers' and Members' ICT Pilot Project
PASG	Public Access Strategy Group

The Morphogenetic Approach

CR	Critical Realism
SEP	Structurally Emergent Property
CEP	Culturally Emergent Property
PEP	Peoples Emergent Property

References

Abrahamson, J.B., Arterton, F.C. and Orren, G.R. (1988) *The Electronic Commonwealth. The impact of new media technologies on democratic politics.* New York; Basic Books.

Ackroyd, S. and Fleetwood, S. (Eds) (2000) *Realist Perspectives of Business and Organization.* London: Routledge.

Ackroyd, S. (2004) Methodology for management and organisation studies – some implications of critical realism. In Fleetwood, S. and Ackroyd, S. (Eds) (2004) *Critical Realist Applications in Organisation and Management Studies.* London: Routledge.

Adler, P.A. and Adler, P. (1987) *Membership Roles in Field Research.* New York: Sage.

Agranoff, R. and Radin, B.A. (1991) The Comparative Case Study Approach in Public Administration. *Public Administration.* 1, pp. 203–231.

Alexander, A. (1982) *Local Government in Britain since Re-Organisation.* London: Allen and Unwin.

Alveson, M. & Skoldberg, K. (2000) *Reflexive Methodology. New Vistas for Qualitative Research.* London: Sage.

Archer, M.S. (1988) *Culture and Agency* Cambridge, UK: Cambridge University Press.

Archer, M.S. (1995) *Realist Social Theory. The Morphogenetic Approach.* Cambridge, UK: Cambridge University Press.

Archer, M.S. (1998a) Realism in the Social Sciences. In Archer, M. et al (Eds). *Critical Realism: essential readings.* London: Routledge.

Archer, M.S. (1998b) Realism and Morphogenesis. In Archer, M. et al (Eds). *Critical Realism: essential readings.* London: Routledge.

Archer, M.S. (1998c) Addressing the Cultural System. In Archer, M. et al (Eds). *Critical Realism: essential readings.* London: Routledge.

Archer, M, Sharp, R, Stones, R, and Woodiwiss, T. (1999). Critical Realism and Research Methodology. *Alethia*. 2, 1, pp. 12–16.

Archer, M.S. (2002) Realism and the Problem of Agency. *Journal of Critical Realism* (incorporating *Alethia*) 5, 1, pp. 11–20.

Armstrong, P. Glyn, A. and Harrison, J. (1991) *Capitalism since 1945*. Oxford: Basil Blackwell Ltd.

Arterton, F.C. (1987) *Teledemocracy. Can technology protect democracy?* New York: Sage.

Axford, B. & Huggins, R. (2001) *New Media and Politics*. London: Sage.

Bailey, M.T. (1994) Do Physicists use Case Studies? Thoughts of Public Administration Research. In White, J.D and Adams, G.B. (Eds) (1994) *Research in Public Administration*. Thousand Oaks, CA: Sage.

Bangemann, M. (1994) *Policies for a European Information Society. Recommendations to the European Council.* Brussels: European Commission.

Banham, J. (1993) Speech to the Conservative Party Local Government Conference, reported in *County News*, Association of County Councils, April.

Bannister, F. (2004) Citizen Centricity: A Model of IS Value in Public Administration. *Electronic Journal of Information Systems Evaluation*. 7, 1, pp. 1–16.

Barber, B. (1984) *Strong Democracy. Participatory politics for a new age*. Los Angeles: UCP.

Barley, S.R. (1986) Technology as an Occasion for Structuring: evidence from observation of CT scanners and the social order of radiology departments. *Administrative Science Quarterly*. 31, pp. 78–108.

Barley, S.R. (1990) The Alignment of Technology and Structure through Roles and Networks. *Administrative Science Quarterly*. 35, pp. 61–103.

Barley, S.R. and Tolbert, P.S. (1997) Institutionalization and Structuration: Studying the Links between Action and Institution. *Organization Studies*. 18, 1, pp. 93–117

Barnatt, C. (1995) *CyberBusiness: mindsets for a wired age*. Chichester, UK: Wiley.

Bartol, K.M. & Martin, D.C. (1998) *Management*. Boston, MA: Irwin McGrawHill.

Baskervill, R.L. & Wood-Harper, A.T. (1996) A Critical Perspective on Action Research as a Method for Information Systems Research. *Journal of Information Technology*, 11, pp. 235–246.

Bekkers, V., Koops, B-J. and Nouwt, S. (Eds) (1996) *Emerging Electronic Highways. New challenges for politics and law.* Amsterdam: Kluwer.

Bell, D. (1973) *The Coming of Post Industrial Society: a venture in social forecasting.* New York: Basic Books.

Bellamy, C. & Taylor, A.J. (1994) Exploiting IT in Public Administration - Towards the Information Polity? *Public Administration, 72*, pp. 1–12.

Bellamy, C. Horrocks, I. & Webb, J. (1995) Exchanging Information with the Public: From One Stop Shops to Community Information Systems. *Local Government Studies*, 21, 1, pp. 11–30.

Bellamy, C. & Horrocks, I. (1995) Community Information Systems: Strengthening Local Democracy? In Donk, W.B.H.J. van de, et al (Eds) *Orwell in Athens*. Amsterdam: IOS Press.

Bellamy, C. and Taylor, J.A. (1998) *Governing in the Information Age.* Buckingham: OUP,

Berg, P.O. (1989) Postmodern Management? From facts to fiction in theory and practice. *Scandinavian Journal of Management.* 5, 3, pp. 201–17.

Bhaskar, R. (1975) *A Realist Theory of Science.* London: Leeds Books.

Bhaskar, R. (1979) *The Possibility of Naturalism* (2nd ed). Brighton: Harvester.

Bhaskar, R. (1998) General Introduction (to critical realism). In Archer, M. et al (Eds). *Critical Realism: essential readings.* London: Routledge.

Bhaskar, R. and Lawson, T. (1998) Introduction: basic texts and developments.). In Archer, M. et al (Eds). *Critical Realism: essential readings.* London: Routledge.

Bijker, W.E. (1995) *Of Bicycles, Bakelites and Bulbs: Towards and Theory of Sociotechnical Change.* Cambridge, MA: The MIT Press.

Bijker, W.E. and Law, J. (Eds) (1992) *Shaping Technology/Building Society*. Cambridge, MA: The MIT Press.

Bloomfield, B.P. & Coombs, R. (1992) Information technology, Control and Power: The Centralisation and Decentralisation Debate Revisited. *Journal of Management Studies*. 29, 4, pp. 459–484.

Budge, I. (1996) *The New Challenge of Direct Democracy*. Cambridge: Polity Press.

Burns, D., Hambleton, R. & Hoggett, P. (1994) *The Politics of Decentralisation*. Basingstoke: Macmillan.

Burns, R.B. (2000) *Introduction to Research Methods*. London: Sage

Cabinet Office (2005) *Transformational Government – Enabled by Technology*. Norwich: HMSO.

Callon, M. (1987) *Society in the making: the study of technology as a tool for sociological analysis*. In Bijker, W.E. et al (Eds). Cambridge, MA: The MIT Press.

Calloway, L.J. & Ariaz, G. (1991) Developing and Using a Qualitative Methodology to Study Relationships among Designers and Tools. In Nissen, H-E, et al (Eds) *Information Systems Research: Contemporary Approaches and Emergent Traditions*. Amsterdam: Elsevier.

Carlson, S.A. (2004) Advancing Information Systems Evaluation (Research): A Critical Realist Approach. *Electronic Journal of Information Systems Evaluation*. 7, 1, pp. 16–24.

Carter, N. (2004) Performance Indicators: "backseat driving" or "hands off" control? In McKevitt, D. and Lawton, A. (Eds) *Public Sector Management: Theory, Critique and Practice*. London: Sage

Carter, B. and New, C. (Eds) (2004) *Making Realism Work: realist social theory and empirical research*. London: Routledge.

Castells, M. (1996) *The Rise of the Network Society*. Oxford: Blackwell Publishing.

Castells, M. (2000) *End of Millennium* (Second Edition). Oxford: Blackwell Publishing.

Castells, M. (2004) *The Power of Identity* (Second Edition). Oxford, Blackwell Publishing.

CCTA (1990) *Information Technology in Central Government: changes and trends.* London: HMSO.

CCTA (1994) *Information Superhighways: opportunities for public service applications.* London: HMSO.

CCTA (1995a) *Information Superhighways: an update on opportunities for public sector applications.* Norwich: CCTA.

CCTA (1995b) *Making the best use of the Internet.* Norwich: CCTA

Chadwick, A. and May, C. (2003) Interaction between States and Citizens in the Age of the Internet: "e-Government" in the United States, Britain, and the European Union. *Governance.* 16, 2, pp. 271–300.

Chandler, J.A. (1993) (Ed) *Local Government in Liberal Democracies.* London: Routledge.

Clark, P. (1972) *Action Research and Organisational Change.* London: Harper and Row.

Clarke, M. (1995) *District Councils and Community Governance: An Aspiration to Community Government.* London:Association of District Councils.

Clarke, M. and Stewart, J. (1992) *Shaping the Organisation and Management of Local Authorities: Challenges and Issues for the 1990s.* Luton: LGMB.

Clarke, M. and J.D. Stewart (1994) The Local Authority and the New Community Governance. *Local Government Studies,* 20, 2, pp. 163–176.

Clegg, S.R. and Hardy, C. (1999) *Studying Organization: theory and method.* London: Sage.

Collier, A. (1998) Stratified Explanation and Marx's Conception of History. In Archer, M. et al (Eds). *Critical Realism: essential readings.* London: Routledge.

Contu, A. and Willmott, H. (2005) You Spin Me Round: The Realist Turn in Organization and Management Studies. *Journal of Management Studies.* 42, 8, pp. 1645–1662.

Coombs, R., Knights, D. & Willmott, H.C. (1992) Culture, Control and Competition; Towards a Conceptual Framework for the Study of Information Technology in Organisations. *Organisation Studies*. 13, 1, pp. 51–72.

Craig, D. (2006) *Word of Mouth*. Radio 4, 11/9/06.

Crano, W.D. and Brewer, M.B. (1986) *Principles and Methods of Social Research* (Second Edition). Boston: Allyn and Bacon.

Culnan, M.J. (1986) The Intellectual Development of Management Information Systems, 1972–1982: A Co-citation Analysis. *Management Science*. 32, pp. 156–172.

Culnan, M.J. (1987) Mapping the Intellectual Structure of Management Information Systems, 1980–1984: Points of Work and Reference. *MIS Quarterly*. 11, pp. 289–302.

Danermark, B. et al (Eds) (2001) *Explaining society: an introduction to critical realism in the social sciences*. London: Routledge.

Danziger, J.N. et al (Eds) (1982) *Computers and Politics: High Technology in American Local Government*. New York: Columbia University Press.

Danziger , J.N. (1991) Management Information Systems and Interorganisational Relations within the American Governmental System. *Informatization and the Public Sector*. 1, pp. 169–187.

Davenport, T. et al. (1992) Information Politics. Sloan Management Review. Autumn/Fall, pp. 53–65.

Davenport, T. (1993) *Process Innovation. Reengineering Work through Information Technology*. Boston, MA: Harvard Business School.

Davenport, T. (1994) Saving ITs Soul: Human-Centred Information Management. *Harvard Business Review*, March-April.

Dawson, P. and Gunson, N. (2002) Technology and the politics and change at work: the case of Dalebake Bakeries. New Technology, Work and Employment. 17, 1, pp. 35–45.

Demos Quarterly (1994a) *Lean Democracy*. London: Demos

298

Demos Quarterly (1994b) *Liberation Technology*. London: Demos.

Denzin, N.K. (1983) Interpretive Interactionism, in Morgan, G. *Beyond Method: Strategies for Social Research*. Beverly Hills, CA: Sage.

De Sanctis, G. and Poole, M.S. (1994) Capturing the Compexity in Advanced Technology Use: Adaptive Structuration Theory. *Organization Science*. 5, 2, pp. 121–147.

Denzin, N. & Lincoln, Y. (1994) (Eds) *Handbook of Qualitative Research*. Thousand Oaks, CA: Sage.

Dobson, P.J. (2001) The Philosophy of Critical Realism – an opportunity for information systems research. *Information Systems Frontiers*. 3, 2, pp. 199–201.

Dobson, P.J. (2002) Critical realism and information systems research: why bother with philosophy? *Information Research*, 7, 2, pp. 13–24.

Dowding, K. (1995) Model of Metaphor? A Critical Review of the Policy Network Approach. *Political Studies*. XLIII, pp. 136–158.

Donk, W. van de, and Tops, P.W. (1992) Informatization and Democracy: Orwell or Athens? *Informatization and the Public Sector*. 2, pp. 169–196.

Donk, W. van de, Snellen, I.Th. M. & Tops, P.W. (Eds) (1995) *Orwell in Athens: a perspective on Informatization and Democracy*. Amsterdam: IOS Press.

Donk, W.van de, and Snellen, I.Th.M. (1998) Towards a Theory of Public Administration in an Information Age? In Snellen, I.Th.M. and Donk, W.vd. (Eds*) Public Administration in an Information Age: A Handbook*. Amsterdam: IOS Press.

Dutton, W.H., Blumler, J.G. and Kraemer, K.L. (Eds) (1987) *Wired cities: shaping the future of communications*. Los Angeles: Annenberg School of Communications

Dutton, W.H. et al. (1991) *State and local government innovations in electronic services: the case in Western and North-eastern United States*. A report to the Office of Technology, US Congress. Los Angeles: Annenberg School of Communications.

Dutton, W.H. (Ed) (1996) *Information and Communication technologies: visions and realities*. Oxford: Oxford University Press.

Edge, D. (1987) The Social Shaping of Technology. In Heap, N. et al (Eds) (1995) *Information Technology and Society: A Reader*. London: Sage.

Elder-Vass, D. (2005) Emergence and the Realist Account of Cause. *Journal of Critical Realism*. 4, 2, pp. 315–338.

Feenberg, A. (1999) *Questioning Technology*. London: Routledge.

Fielding, N. (1993) Ethnography. In Gilbert, N. (Ed) *Researching Social Life*. London: Sage.

Fleetwood, S. (2001) Causal Laws, Functional relations, and Tendencies. *Review of Political Economy*. 13, 2, pp.201–220.

Fleetwood, S. (2004) An ontology for organisation and management studies. In Fleetwood, S. and Ackroyd, S. (Eds) *Critical Realist Applications in Organisation and Management Studies*. London: Routledge.

Fleetwood, S. (2005) Ontology in Organization and Management Studies: A Critical Realist Perspective. *Organization*. 12, 2, pp.197–222.

Fleetwood, S. and Ackroyd, S. (Eds) (2004) *Critical Realist Applications in Organisation and Management Studies*. London: Routledge.

Fleetwood, S. and Hesketh, A. (2006) Prediction in Social Science. The Case of Research on the Human Resource Management – Organisational Performance Link. *Journal of Critical Realism*. 5, 2, pp.228–250.

Flynn, N. (1997) *Public Sector Management* (Third edition) Hemel Hempstead: Prentice Hall/Harvester Wheatsheaf.

Fontana, A. and Frey, J. (1994) Interviewing: the Art of Science. In Denzin, N.K. and Lincoln, Y.S. (Eds) *The Handbook of Qualitative Research*. Thousand Oaks, CA: Sage.

Foundation for IT in Local Government (FITLOG) (1993) *Future Perfect*.

Foundation for IT in Local Government (FITLOG) (1994) *In Touch: using technology to communicate with the public*. London, UK.

Foote-Whyte, W. (Ed) (1991). *Participatory Action Research*. Sage, Newbury Park, USA: Sage.

300

Frissen, P.H.A. et al (Eds) (1992) *European Public Administration and Informatization*. Amsterdam: IOS Press.

Frissen, P.H.A. (1998) Public Administration in Cyberspace: a postmodern perspective. In Snellen, I.Th.M. and Donk, W.vd. (Eds) *Public Administration in an Information Age: A Handbook*. Amsterdam: IOS Press.

Frissen, P.H.A. Snellen, I.Th.M. (Eds) (1990) *Informatization in Public Administration*. Amsterdam: IOS.

Galaskiewicz, J. & Wasserman, S. (1993) Social Network Analysis: Concepts, Models and Directions for the 1990s. *Sociological Methods & Research*. 22, 1, pp. 3–22.

Galliers, R.D. (1991) Choosing Appropriate Information Systems Research Approaches: a revised taxonomy. In Nissen, H-E, et al (Eds) *Information Systems Research: Contemporary Approaches and Emergent Traditions*. Amsterdam: Elsevier.

Galliers, R.D. (1992). Choosing information systems research approaches, in R.D. Galliers (Ed), *Information systems research: issues, methods, and practical guidelines*. Oxford: Blackwell Scientific Publications.

Galliers, R.D. (1993) Towards a Flexible Information Architecture: Information Systems Strategies and Business Process Redesign. *Journal of Information Systems*. 3, pp. 199–213.

Gamble, A. (1988) *The Free Economy and the Strong State*. Basingstoke: Macmillan Press.

Gash, D.C. & Orlikowski, W.J. (1991) Changing Frames: Towards an Understanding of Information Technology and Organisational Change. In Wall, J.L. & Jauch, L.R. (Eds) *Best Papers Proceedings*, Academy of Management, Fifty First Annual Meeting.

Gasman, L. (1994) *Telecompetition*. Washington: Cato Institute.

Gershon, P. (2004) *Releasing Resources to the Front Line. Independent Review of Public Sector Efficiency*. Norwich: HMSO/ The Treasury.

Giddens. A. (1984) *The Construction of Society*. London: Polity Press.

Glaser, B.G. and Strauss, A.L. (1967) *The Discovery of Grounded Theory*. Chicago: Aldine.

Goatcher, J.I. (2004) *The Philosophical Foundations of Participatory Democracy: Natural, Human, Critical*. Nottingham Trent University: PhD Theses.

Gray, C. (1994) *Government Beyond the Centre*. Basingstoke: Macmillan Press.

Grossman, L.K. (1995) *The Electronic Republic: Reshaping Democracy in the Information Age*. New York: Viking.

Guba, E.G. & Lincoln, Y.S. (1989) *Fourth Generation Evaluation*. Newbury Park: Sage.

Guthrie, K.K. & Dutton, W.H. (1992) The Politics of Citizen Access Technology: the Development of Public Information Utilities in Four Cities. *Policy Studies Journal*. 20, 4, pp. 574–597.

Hammer, M. & Champy, J. (1993) *Reengineering the Corporation*. New York: HarperCollins.

Hammersley, M. (1992) *What's Wrong with Ethnography?* London: Routledge.

Handy, C. (1991) *The Age of Unreason* (2nd Edition) London: Business Books.

Handy, C. (1996) *Understanding Organisations* (3rd Edition) London: Penguin.

Hansard Society (2003–2004) http://www.hansardsociety.org.uk/programmes/e-democracy

Harrison, D. and Easton, G. (2004) Temporally embedded case comparison in industrial marketing research. In Fleetwood, S. and Ackroyd, S. (Eds) *Critical Realist Applications in Organisation and Management Studies*. London: Routledge.

Hay,C. (1995) Structure and Agency. In Marsh, D. and Stoker, G. *Theory and Methods in Political Science*. Basingstoke: Macmillan.

Headstar (2002–03) E-government monthly bulletins. http://headstar.com/egb.

Hirscheim, R. & Klein, H.K. (1989) Four Paradigms of Information Systems Development. *Comm.ACM*. 32, 10, pp. 1199–1216.

Hirscheim, R., Klein, H.K. & Lyytinen, K. (1995) *Information Systems Development and Data Modelling: Conceptual and Philosophical Foundations*. Cambridge, UK: Cambridge University Press.

Hislop, D. (2006) *Taking Account of Structure: Re-evaluating practice based perspectives on knowledge via critical realism*. Paper presented at the Organisational Learning and Knowledge Conference, Warwick University, March.

Hoff, J. (1992) Evaluation of Information technology in Private and Public Sector Contexts. *Informatization and the Public Sector*. 1, 2, pp. 307–328.

Hoff, J. & Stormgaard, K. (1991) Information Technology between Citizen and Administration. *Informatization and the Public Sector*. 1, 1, pp. 213–235.

Hoff, J., Horrocks, I. and Tops, P. (Eds) (2000) *Democratic Governance and New Technology*. London: Routledge.

Hoff, J. (2000) Technology and social change: the path between Technological determinism, social constructivism and new institutionalism. In Hoff, J., Horrocks, I. and Tops, P. (Eds) (2000) *Democratic Governance and New Technology*. London: Routledge.

Holman, K. and Tizard, J. (1995) *Communities, governance and local democracy: Roles and Relationships*. Local Government Policy Making. 21, 5, pp. 27–34.

Horrocks, I.J. (1995) *The Impact of CIS on Processes and Management in Local Government*. Citizenship, Information Technology and Public Services Conference, Institute of Futures Studies, Stockholm, Sweden, November.

Horrocks, I. (1997) Community Information Systems and Process Reengineering: evidence from a case study. In Taylor, J.A. Et al (Eds) *Beyond BPR in Public Administration*. Amsterdam: IOS Press.

Horrocks, I. & Webb, J. (1994) Electronic Democracy: a policy issue for UK local government. *Local Government Policy Making*. 21, 3, pp. 22–30.

Horrocks, I. and Hambley, N. (1996) *How to win friends and influence people? The role of research in the informatization of "Council X"*. EGPA Annual Conference, September. Budapest.

Horrocks, I. and Hambley, N. (1997) *Council X Officers' and Members' Pilot Final Report*. PSTAG, Nottingham Trent University.

Horrocks, I. and Hambley, N. (1998) The Webbing of British Local Government. *Public Money and Management*, 18, 2, pp. 39–45.

Hughes, T.P. and Pinch, T.J. (Eds) (1987) *The Social Construction of Technological Systems: New Directions in the Sociology and History of Technology*. Cambridge, MA: The MIT Press.

Hughes, K. et al. (1994) *Organisational Structure and the Development of Information Systems Strategies*. London: Policy Studies Institute.

Huigen, J. (1993) Information and Communication Technology in the Context of Policy Networks. *Technology in Society*, 15, pp. 327–338.

Hayano, D. M. (1979). Auto ethnography. *Human Organization*, 38, pp. 99–104.

Iivari, J. (1991) A Paradigmatic Analysis of Contemporary Schools of IS Development. *European Journal of Information Systems*. 1, 4, pp. 249–272.

Iivari, J. And Hirscheim, R. (1996) Analysing Information Systems Development: A Comparison and Analysis of Eight IS Development Approaches. *Information Systems*, 21, 7, pp. 551–575.

Iivari, J., Hirschheim, R. and Klein, H.K. (1998) A Paradigmatic Analysis Contrasting Information Systems Development Approaches and Methodologies. *Information Systems Research*. 9, 2, pp. 164–193.

Jarvenpaa, S.L. (1989) Effects of Task Demands and Graphical Format on Information Processing Strategies. *Management Science*. 35, 3, pp. 285–303.

Jayachandra, Y. (1994) *Re-Engineering the Networked Enterprise*. New York, NY: McGraw-Hill

Johnson, P. & Duberley, J. (2000) *Understanding Management Research*. London: Sage.

Johnston, J. (1998) The Structure-Agency Debate and its Historiographical Utility. In Dobson, A. and Stanyer, J. (Eds) *Contemporary Political Studies 1998*. UK Political Studies Association.

Jones, M. (1998) Structuration Theory and IT. In Currie, W.L. and Galliers, B. (Eds) *Re-thinking Management Information Systems. An interdisciplinary Perspective.* Oxford: Oxford University Press.

Jordan, G. (1990) Sub-Governments, Policy Communities and Networks. *Journal of Theoretical Politics*. 2, 3, pp. 319–338.

Kennedy, C. and P. (2004) The moral management of nursing labour power: Conceptualising control and resistance. In Fleetwood, S. and Ackroyd, S. (Eds) (2004) *Critical Realist Applications in Organisation and Management Studies.* London: Routledge.

Kinder, T. (2002) Vote early, vote often? Teledemocracy in European Cities. *Public Administration*. 80, 3, pp. 557–582.

King, J.L. & Kraemer, K.L. (1986) Computing and Public Organisations. *Public Administration Review*. 46, pp. 488–496.

King, J.L & Kraemer, K.L. (1991) Information Technology in the Establishment and Maintenance of Civil Society. In Snellen. I.Th.M. and Donk, W.B.H.J. van de (1998) (Eds) *Public Administration in the Information Age*. Amsterdam: IOS

Knights, D. and Murray, F. (1994) *Managers Divided. Organisation Politics and Information Technology Management*. Chichester: John Wiley and Sons.

Kooiman, J. (1993) Governance and Governability: Using Complexity, Dynamics and Diversity. In Kooiman, J. (Ed) *Modern Governance*. London: Sage.

Kowalczyk, R. (2004) Tracing the effects of a hospital merger. In Fleetwood, S. and Ackroyd, S. (Eds) *Critical Realist Applications in Organisation and Management Studies*. London: Routledge.

Kubicek, H, Dutton, W.H. and Williams, R. Eds. (1997) *The Social Shaping of Information Superhighways. European and American Roads to the Information Society*. New York: Campus Verlag/St Martin's Press.

Lane, J-A. (1995) *The Public Sector: Concepts, Models and Approaches* (Second Edition). London: Sage.

Latour, B. (1987) *Science in Action*. Milton Keynes: Open University Press.

Latour, B. (1992) Where are the missing masses? The sociology of a few mundane artefacts. In Bijker, W.E. and Law, J. (Eds) (1992) *Shaping Technology/Building Society*. Cambridge, MA: The MIT Press.

Laudon, K. (1977) *Communications Technology and Democratic Participation*. New York: Praeger.

Ling, T. (2002) Delivering joined up government in the UK: dimensions, issues and problems. *Public Administration*. 80, 4, pp. 615–642.

Leach, S. Stewart, J. & Walsh, K. (1994) *The Changing Organisation and Management of Local Government*. Basingstoke: Macmillan.

Ledington, P. & Heales, J. (1993) The Social Context of Information Systems Development: an appreciative field perspective. In Avison, D. et al (Eds) *Human, Organisational, and Social Dimension of Information Systems Development*. Amsterdam: Elsevier.

LGMB (1993) *Fitness for Purpose - shaping new patterns of organisation and management*. Luton: Local Government management Board.

Lowndes, V. (1999) Management Change in Local Governance. In Stoker, G. (Ed) *The New Management of British Local Government*. Basingstoke: Macmillan Press.

Lyon, D. (1988) *The Information Society: issues and illusions*. Cambridge: Polity Press.

Lyons, M (2004) *Independent Review of Public Sector Relocation*. Norwich: HMSO/The Treasury.

Mackay, H. and Gillespie, G. (1992) Extending the Social Shaping of Technology Approach: Ideology and Appropriation. *Social Studies of Science*. 22, pp. 685–716.

MacKenzie, D. and Wajcman, J (Eds) (1985) *The Social Shaping of Technology*. Milton Keynes: Open University Press.

Mansell, R. (1993) *The New Telecommunications: a political economy of network evolution.* London: Sage.

Markus, M. and Robey, D. (1988) Information Technology and Organizational Change: Causal Structure in Theory and Research. *Management Science.* 34, pp. 583–598.

Margetts, H. (1998) Computerising the Tools of Government. In Snellen. I.Th.M. and Donk, W.B.H.J. van de (Eds) *Public Administration in the Information Age.* Amsterdam: IOS.

Margulies, N. and Raia, A.P. (1978) *Conceptual Foundations of Organisational Development.* New York: McGraw-Hill Book Company.

Martin, P.Y. & Turner, B.A. (1986) Grounded Theory and Organisational Research. The *Journal of Applied Behavioural Science.* 22, 2, pp. 141–157.

Maruyama, G. (1996) Application and Transformation of Action Research in Educational Research and Practice. *Systems Practice.* 9, 1, pp. 85–101.

Mason, J. (1996) *Qualitative Researching.* London: Sage.

McAnulla, S. (1998) The Utility of Structure, Agency and Discourse as Analytical Concepts. In Dobson, A. and Stanyer, J. (Eds) *Contemporary Political Studies 1998.* UK Political Studies Association.

McKevitt, D. and Lawton, A. (Eds) (1994) *Public Sector Management: Theory, Critique and Practice.* London: Sage

McLean, I. (1989) *Democracy and New Technology.* Cambridge: Polity Press.

Miles, M. & Huberman, A. (1984) *Qualitative Data Analysis.* London: Sage.

Mintzberg, H. (1979) *The Structuring of Organizations.* Englewood Cliffs, NJ: Prentice Hall.

Mintzberg, H. (1983) *Power in and Around Organizations.* Englewood Cliffs, NJ: Prentice Hall.

Morén, S. and Blom, B. (2003) 'Explaining Human Change: On Generative Mechanisms in Social Work Practice'. *Journal of Critical Realism.* 2, 1, pp.37–60.

Morgan, G. (1997) *Images of Organization.* Thousand Oaks: Sage.

Mosco, V. (1996) *The Political Economy of Communication*. Thousand Oaks: Sage.

Mumford, E. And Sackman, H. (Eds) (1975) *Human Choice and Computers*. Amsterdam: North Holland.

Mutch, A. (1999a) Critical Realism, Managers and Information. *British Journal of Management*. 10, pp. 323–333.

Mutch, A. (1999b) Information: a critical realist approach. In Wilson, T.D. and Allen, D.K. *Exploring the Context of Information Behaviour*. London: Taylor-Graham.

Mutch, A. (2002) Actors and networks or agents and structures: towards a realist definition of information systems. *Organisation*. 9, 3, pp. 477–496.

Mutch, A. (2005) Critical Realism, Agency and Discourse: Moving the Debate Forward. *Organization*. 12, 3, pp. 477–496.

Naisbitt, J. (1984) *Megatrends. Ten new directions transforming our lives*. London: Macdonald.

New, C. (2001) 'Realising the Potential: The ESRC Seminar Series on Social Realism and Empirical Research'. *Journal of Critical Realism* (incorporating *Alethia*) 4, 1, pp. 43–47.

Nora, S. and Minc, A. (1980) *The Computerization of Society. A report to the President of France*. Cambridge, MA: MIT Press.

Northgate (2005) Press release: 18th March. *Organisational re-engineering delivers efficiency and effectiveness.* www.northgate-is.com/press_centre/item.php?item_id=583

OECD (1998a) *Information Technology as an Instrument of Public Management Reform: A Study of Five OECD Countries*. Paris: OECD.

OECD (1998b) *The Use of the New Technologies in Policy and Democratic Governance*. Paris: OECD.

Orlikowski, W.J. (1992) The Duality of Technology: Rethinking the Concept of Technology in Organisations. *Organisation Science*. 3, 3, pp. 398–427.

Orlikowski, W.J. (1993) Case Tools as Organisational Change: investigating incremental and radical changes in systems development. *MIS Quarterly*, September.

Orlikowski, W.J. & Baroudi, J.J. (1991) Studying Information technology in Organisations: research Approaches and Assumptions. *Information Systems Research.* 2, 1, pp. 1–28.

Orlikowski, W.J. and Robey, D. (1991) Information Technology and the Structuring of Organisations. *Information Systems Research.* 2, 2, pp. 143–169.

In Orlikowski, W. Walsham, G. and Jones, M. (1995) *Information technology and changes in organisational work: images and reflections.* Preeedings of the IFIP 8.2 Working Conference, London: Chapman-Hall.

Osbourne, D. & Gaebler, T. (1992) *Reinventing Government. How the Entrepreneurial Spirit is Transforming the Public Sector.* Reading, MA: Addison Wesley.

Pawson, R. and Tilley, N. (1997) *Realistic Evaluation.* London: Sage.

Percy-Smith, J. (1995) *Digital Democracy; information and communication technologies in local politics.* London: Commission for Local Democracy.

Pettigrew, A.M. (1973) *The Politics of Organisational Decision Making.* London: Tavistock.

Pettigrew, A.M. (1980) The Politics of Organisational Change, in Anderson, A.B. (Ed) *The Human Side of Information Processing.* Amsterdam: North Holland.

Pettigrew, A.M. (1985) Contextualist Research: A Natural Way to Link Theory and Practice in *Doing Research that is Useful for Theory and Practice.* E.E.Lawler et al (Eds.). San Fransico, CA. Jossey-Bass.

Pettigrew, A.M. (1989) Issues of Time and Site Selection in Longitudinal Research on Change, in Cash, J.I. Jr, and Lawrence, P.R. (Eds) *The Information Systems Research Challenge: Qualitative Research Methods.* Boston, MA: Harvard Business School Press.

Pettigrew, A. (1990) "Longitudinal Field Research on Change: Theory and Practice," *Organizational Science.* 1, pp. 267–292.

Porpora, D.V. (1998) Four Concepts of Social Structure. In Archer, M. et al (Eds). *Critical Realism: essential readings.* London: Routledge.

Pratchett, L. (1994) Open Systems and Closed Networks: Policy Networks and the Emergence of Open Systems in Local Government. *Public Administration*. 72, Spring, pp. 73–93.

Pratchett, L. (1997) Reengeneering UK Local Government: Opportunities and Prospects. In Taylor, J.A., Snellen, I.Th.M. and Zuurmond.A. (Eds) *Beyond BPR in Public Administration*. Amsterdam: IOS Press.

Pratchett, L (1999) New technologies and the modernisation of local government: an analysis of biases and constraints. *Public Administration*. 77, 4, pp. 731–750.

Reason, P. (Ed). (1988) *Human Inquiry in Action: Developments in New Paradigm Research*. London: Sage.

Reason, P. (Ed) (1994) *Participation in Human Inquiry*. Thousand Oaks, CA: Sage.

Reed, M.I. (1997) In Praise of Duality and Dualism: rethinking Agency and Structure in Organizational Analysis. *Organization Studies*. 18, 1, pp. 21–42.

Reed, M.I. (2005a) Reflections on the 'Realist Turn' in Organization and Management Studies. *Journal of Management Studies*. 42, 8, pp. 1621–1644.

Reed, M.I. (2005a) Doing the loco-Motion: response to Contu and Willmott's Commentary on 'The Realist Turn in Organization and Management Studies'. *Journal of Management Studies*. 42, 8, pp. 1665–1673.

Rhodes, R.A.W. and Marsh, D. (1992) *Policy Network in British Government*. Oxford: Clarendon Press.

Rhodes, R.A.W. & Marsh, D. (1996) The Concept of Policy Networks in British Political Science: Its Development and Utility. *Talking Politics*, Spring.

Rhodes, R.A.W. (1996) The New Governance: Governing without Government. *Political Studies*, XLIV, pp. 652–667.

Ridley, N. (1988) *The Local Right*. London: Centre for Policy Studies.

Sackman, H, and Boehm, B. (1972) *Planning Community Information Utilities*. Montvale: AFIPS Press.

Sackman, H. N and Nie, N. (1973) *Information Utility and Social Choice*. Montvale: AFIPS Press.

Sayer, A. (1998) Abstraction: a realist interpretation. In Archer, M. et al (Eds). *Critical Realism: essential readings*. London: Routledge.

Sayer, A. (2004) Why critical realism? In Fleetwood, S. and Ackroyd, S. (Eds) *Critical Realist Applications in Organisation and Management Studies*. London: Routledge.

Scarbrough, H. (1995) Strategic change in financial services: the social construction of strategic IS. In Orlikowski, W. Walsham, G. and Jones, M. (1995) *Information technology and changes in organisational work: images and reflections*. Preceedings of the IFIP 8.2 Working Conference, London: Chapman-Hall.

Scarborough, H. & Corbett, J.M. (1992) *Technology and Organisation: Power, Meaning and Design*. London: Routledge.

Schein, E. H. (1991). *Organizational culture and leadership*. San Francisco: Jossey-Bass.

Scott Morton, M.S. (Ed.) (1991) *The Corporation of the 1990s: Information Technology and Organisational Transformation*. Oxford: Oxford University Press.

Scambler, G. (2001) 'Critical Realism, Sociology and Health Inequalities: Social Class as a Generative Mechanism and Its Media Enactment'. *Journal of Critical Realism* (incorporating *Alethia*). 4, 1, pp. 35–42.

Seale, C. (Ed) (1998) *Researching Society and Culture*. London: Sage.

Self, P. (1993) *Government by the Market. The Politics of Public Choice*. Basingstoke: Macmillan.

Sibeon, R. (1999) Agency, Structure and Social Chance as Cross Disciplinary Concepts. *Politics*. 19, 3, pp. 139–144.

Silverman, D. (2000) *Doing Qualitative Research*. London: Sage.

Skinningsrud, T. (2005) Realist social theorising and the emergence of state educational systems. *Journal of Critical Realism* . 4, 2, pp. 339–365.

Snellen. I.Th.M. and Donk, W.B.H.J. van de (Eds) (1998) *Public Administration in the Information Age*. Amsterdam: IOS.

311

Straus, A. and Corbin, J. (1990) *Basics of Qualitative Research: Grounded Theory, Procedures and Techniques.*, Newbury Park, CA: Sage

Stoker, G. (1991) *The Politics of Local Government* (Second Edition). Basingstoke: Macmillan Press.

Stoker, G. (1994) *The Role and Purpose of Local Government.* Commission for Local Democracy, Research Report No.4.

Stoker, G. (1999) (Ed) *The New Management of British Local Government.* Basingstoke: Macmillan Press.

Stones, R. (2001) Refusing the Realism-Structuration Divide. *European Journal of Social Theory.* 4, 2, pp. 177–197.

Stringer, E.T. (1996) *Action Research: A Handbook for Practitioners.* Thousand Oaks, CA: Sage

Symon, G. & Cassell, C. (1998) *Qualitative Methods and Analysis in Organisational Research: A Practical Guide.* London: Sage.

Taylor, J.A. (1995) Don't Obliterate Informate! Business Process reengineering for the Information Age. *New Technology, Work and Employment.* 9, 1, pp. 54–65.

Taylor, J. A. (1998) Informatization as X Ray: What is Public Administration for the Information Age? In Snellen, I.Th.M. and Donk, W.vd. (Eds) *Public Administration in an Information Age: A Handbook.* Amsterdam: IOS Press.

Taylor, J.A. & Williams, H. (1991) Public Administration and the Information Polity. *Public Administration.* 69, pp. 171–190.

Taylor, J.A. et al (Eds) (1997) *Beyond BPR in Public Administration.* Amsterdam: IOS.

Thompson, J.B. (1989) The Theory of Structuration. In Held, D. and Thompson, J.B. (Eds) *Social Theory and Modern Societies: Anthony Giddens and his critics.* Cambridge: Cambridge University Press.

Thursfield, D. and Hamblett, J. (2004) Human resource management and realism: a morphogenetic approach. In Fleetwood, S. and Ackroyd, S. (Eds) *Critical Realist Applications in Organisation and Management Studies.* London: Routledge.

Toffler, A. (1980) *The Third Wave.* New York: William Morrow.

Toffler, A. (1990) *Powershift.* New York: Bantam Books.

Toraskar, K.V. (1991) How Managerial Users Evaluate their Decision-Support?: a grounded theory approach. In Nissen, H-E, et al (Eds) *Information Systems Research: Contemporary Approaches and Emergent Traditions.* Amsterdam: Elsevier.

Trauth, E.M. & O'Connor, B. (1991) A Study of the Interaction Between Information Technology and Society: an illustration of combined qualitative research methods. In Nissen, H-E, et al (Eds) *Information Systems Research: Contemporary Approaches and Emergent Traditions.* Amsterdam: Elsevier.

Tsagarousianou, R., Tambini, D. and Bryan, C. (Eds) (1998) *Cyberdemocracy: technology, cities and civic networks.* London: Routledge.

Turner, B.A. (1983) The use of Grounded Theory for the Qualitative Analysis of Organisational Behaviour. *Journal of Management Studies,* 20, pp. 333–348.

US Congress Office of Technology Assessment (1990) *Critical Connections: Communications for the Future.* Washington DC: US Government Printing Office.

US Congress Office of Technology Assessment (1993) *Making Government Work: Electronic Delivery of Federal Services.* Washington DC: US Government Printing Office.

Walsham, G. (2000) *Making a world of difference: IT in a global context.* Chichester, UK: John Wiley and Sons.

Walsham, G. and Han, C.K. (1990) Structuration theory and information systems research. In DeGross, J.I. et al (Eds) *Proceedings of the Tenth Annual International Conference on Information Systems.* Copenhagen, Denmark.

Wamsley, G.L. (1996) A Public Philosophy and Ontological Disclosure as the Basis for Normatively Grounded Theorising in Public Administration. In Wamsley, G.L. and Wolf, J.F. *Refounding Democratic Public Administration. Modern Paradoxes, Postmodern Challenges.* Thousand Oaks, CA: Sage.

Ward, R. and Gibson, R. (1998) The First Internet Election? UK Political Parties and Campaigning in Cyberspace. *Political Communications: Why Labour Won the General Election of 1997.* London: Frank Cass.

White, J.D and Adams, G.B (1994) Making Sense with Diversity: the context of research, theory, and knowledge development in public administration. In White, J.D and Adams, G.B. (Eds) *Research in Public Administration.* Thousand Oaks, CA: Sage.

Willcocks, L. and Mason, D. (1987) *Computerising Work: People, Systems Design and Workplace Relations,* London: Paradign Publishing.

Willcocks, L. (1996) Does IT-enabled business process reengineering pay off? Recent findings on economics and impacts. In, Willcocks, L. (Ed). *Investing in Information Systems: Evaluation and Management.* London: Chapman and Hall.

Willcocks, L., Currie, W., and Mason, D. (1997) *Information Ssytems at Work: People, Politics and Technology.* Maidenhead: McGraw Hill.

Willmott, H. (1987) Studying Managerial Work: a critique and a proposal. *Journal of Management Studies.* 24, 3, pp. 27–36

Willmott, R. (2000) Structure, culture and agency: rejecting the current orthodoxy of organisation theory. In Ackroyd, S. and Fleetwood, S. (Eds) (2000) *Realist Perspectives of Business and Organization.* London: Routledge.

Wilson, D. & Game, C. (1998) *Local Government in the United Kingdom,* (2nd edition) London: Macmillan.

Winner, L. (1996) *The Whale and the Reactor.* Chicago: University of Chicago Press.

Winner, L. (Ed) (1992) *Democracy in a Technological Society.* Boston: Kluwer.

Winston, B. (1998) *Media, Technology and Society. A History: From the Telegraph to the Internet.* London: Routledge.

Worral, L. (1995) Managing Information in Complex Organisations: a local government perspective. Local Government Studies. 21, 1, pp. 115–129.

Wring, D. and Horrocks, I. (2001) Virtual Hype: new media and the transformation of political parties and party systems. In Axford, B. and Huggins, R. (Eds) *New Media and Politics*. London: Sage.

Yin, R.K. (1994) *Case Study Research Design and Methods* - Second Edition. Thousand Oaks: Sage.

Young, K. & Rao, N. (1997) *Local Government Since 1945*. Oxford: Blackwell.

Zuboff, S. (1988) *In the Age of the Smart Machine*. London: Heinemann.

Wissenschaftlicher Buchverlag bietet

kostenfreie

Publikation

von

wissenschaftlichen Arbeiten

Diplomarbeiten, Magisterarbeiten, Master und Bachelor Theses
sowie Dissertationen, Habilitationen und wissenschaftliche Monographien

Sie verfügen über eine wissenschaftliche Abschlußarbeit zu aktuellen oder zeitlosen
Fragestellungen, die hohen inhaltlichen und formalen Ansprüchen genügt,
und haben **Interesse an einer honorarvergüteten Publikation**?

Dann senden Sie bitte erste Informationen über Ihre Arbeit per Email
an info@vdm-verlag.de. Unser Außenlektorat meldet sich umgehend bei Ihnen.

VDM Verlag Dr. Müller Aktiengesellschaft & Co. KG
Dudweiler Landstraße 125a
D - 66123 Saarbrücken

www.vdm-verlag.de